RICHARD III: LOYALTY, LORDSHIP AND LAW

RICHARD III: LOYALTY, LORDSHIP AND LAW

edited by

P.W. HAMMOND

RICHARD III AND YORKIST HISTORY TRUST
LONDON

ISBN 0 948993 01 4

Printed in Great Britain

Produced by
Alan Sutton Publishing Limited
for
The Richard III and Yorkist History Trust
3 Campden Terrace, Linden Gardens
London W4 2EP

CONTENTS

ABBREVIATIONS

AJPA	American Journal of Physical Anthropology
BIHR	Bulletin of the Institute of Historical Research
CCR	Calendar of the Close Rolls
CFR	Calendar of the Fine Rolls
CIPM	Calendar of Inquisitions Post Mortem
CPR	Calendar of the Patent Rolls
EETS	Early English Text Society
EHR	English Historical Review
HMS	Historical Manuscripts Commission
J. Med. Hist.	Journal of Mediaeval History
NLS	National Library of Scotland
Rot. Parl.	Rotuli Parliamentorum
TRHS	Transactions of the Royal Historical Society
SJC	St John's College (Cambridge) Archives
WAM	Westminster Abbey Muniments

INTRODUCTION

The Symposium at which were given the papers published in the present volume, was designed to mark the quincentenary of Richard III's reign, and was originally planned to have as its theme the present view of Richard III and his times. Like most symposia this one developed a will and direction of its own, but nevertheless the papers that were given do in fact show what is the 'present view' of Richard III. They also illustrate, as a glance at the references will show, the wide range of theses, books, journal articles and symposium proceedings which have been published in the past few years, and which illuminate Richard of Gloucester as a man and a king, the people he had to deal with, and the long and short term effects of his actions. This explosion of publications on the late fifteenth century in the last thirty years has been to the great advantage of scholars of the period, who before the explosion were notoriously starved of sustenance. The growth of interest has been due to the work and influence of a number of scholars, notably the late K.B. McFarlane, and the late Professors Chrimes, Myers, and Ross.

The first two papers published here illustrate the interest that is being shown in individuals, how they lived, and how they exerted their political influence. Anne Crawford's paper demonstrates how the surviving household accounts of John Howard, first a rising member of the gentry and later duke of Norfolk, can be used to show this, and also how such a man organised his life. Much work has been done elsewhere on other aspects of social life in the fifteenth century, an unusual aspect is dealt with in Rowena Archer's fascinating essay 'Rich Old Ladies: The Problem of Late Medieval Dowagers'.[1] Most of the work on social life has been done on groups, rather than on individuals, as in the Introduction to Joel Rosenthal's *Nobles and the Noble Life 1295–1500*,[2] but one outstanding *tour de force*, showing how a fifteenth century country gentleman lived, is Colin Richmond's study of John Hopton.[3] Michael Jones' paper on the other hand, shows how much can be done by concentrating on the political life of one person, and questioning hitherto accepted judgements. In this potentially seminal paper he shows that Margaret Beaufort, far from being a constant opponent of the Yorkist Dynasty came to terms with them as far as she could. Studies of a number of individuals have in fact been done recently, for example by Michael Hicks, in his life of George Duke of Clarence, originally a thesis.[4] Several other theses have appeared in recent years which have concentrated on individuals, e.g. Henry Bourchier, Earl of Essex, a churchman George Neville, Archbishop of York, and indeed John Howard Duke of Norfolk.[5]

The opposite line is adopted by Keith Dockray in his useful study of Richard of Gloucester and the Yorkshire gentry. Much interest has recently been shown in this aspect of political events, (and indeed in Yorkshire gentry[6]), in the growth and use of the 'affinity' and the political use of patronage. A notable study of patronage is of course Rosemary Horrox' thesis *The Extent and Use of Crown Patronage under Richard III*.[7] Much work has been done on particular aspects of patronage, e.g., in Tony Pollard's *Tyranny of Richard III*,[8] a study of the 'planting' of Richard's northern supporters in positions of authority in the south after the Buckingham rebellion of 1483. That patronage was not limited to the elite but operated with and within the towns too has been shown by Rosemary Horrox and Lorraine Attreed, (the latter in the course of a magisterial survey of the relations of the Royal government with the towns), and Robert Dunning has demonstrated patronage at work in the medieval church.[9] Similarly many studies of families and their affinities have appeared in the last few years, to a large extent in theses, e.g. on the Parrs, the Stanleys and on the Staffords.[10] Studies of county groups, patronage and affinity from both sides as it were, and of the build up of estates by the use of patronage have also appeared.[11] In fact it could truly be said that the major thrust of work in the past few years has been towards further explanation and demonstration of the phenomena of affinity and patronage, far more work than can easily be noticed here.

With Anne Sutton's paper we come to Richard of Gloucester himself. Miss Sutton shows good reason to believe that he took seriously his moral duties as King, and that many of his actions were those expected of someone aspiring to the medieval ideal of a 'good Prince'. Richard of Gloucester as a human and political animal has been studied extensively of course, (although mainly as part of a general study of people and events), and it is perhaps true to say that the general view of his actions is rather more favourable than at times in the past, as a greater understanding of his problems and dilemmas has emerged as a result of recent studies. The thirty year old work by P.M. Kendall has been largely replaced as the standard biography by that of Charles Ross, the only new full biography,[12] and detailed studies of Richard's Coronation, and of one aspect of his government, in the full edition of his Signet Office docket book, have been published.[13] Another study, 'The Administration of Justice Whereunto We be Professed' by Miss Sutton herself shows that Richard demonstrated a great respect for law,[14] and this is an important consideration in our next paper. This is a detailed examination of a crucial point in Richard's life, the grounds on which he based his claim to the throne, the illegitimacy of his nephews. This important and valuable paper, contributed by Professor Helmholz, represents the first such study by an expert in medieval Canon Law. Professor Helmholz shows that in Canon Law Richard III made an arguable and far from negligible case. If Miss Sutton is correct in her conclusions concerning Richard's respect for law, and his view of his position as a Prince, this is perhaps what we might have expected.

Another crucial point is discussed in Hammond and White's paper. This deals with the rumours which circulated about the fate of Edward IV's sons, and with the bones found in the Tower in 1674, said to confirm one of the rumours. The rumours and the bones have been discussed many times before of course, for example by Kendall and Ross,[15] but the rumours have never been dealt with chronologically and as a whole, nor the bones discussed in detail in the light of modern forensic research.

The paper by Dr Macdougall breaks new ground in Ricardian studies at least and shows the startling similarities between the posthumous reputations of James III of Scots and Richard III, as well as giving a different, and Scottish, perspective to the English invasion of 1482, and to Scottish involvement in English affairs. The invasion is dealt with to some extent in recent work on Richard, e.g. Ross' life, as well as in greater detail in Dr Macdougall's biography of James III.[16]

Lastly, dealing with the final event of the reign, and of Richard's life, and in a sense with the military history of the late fifteenth century, Dr Richmond in his provocative paper talks of the sources for the Battle of Bosworth, and of how it could be described as an unnecessary battle. Bosworth itself has been dealt with recently by Dr Williams, the only full length study since Gairdner's of 1896,[17] but it is also discussed of course in the biographies of Richard III and Henry VII.[18] Much more work has appeared recently on medieval warfare in theory and practice, by Vale and Goodman and the chivalric ideal which was behind much of the military activity of the middle ages has been discussed by Maurice Keen, as well as by Vale.[19]

Enough has probably been said in this brief survey both to show how much work has been done in the field of late fifteenth century studies in the past few years (although inevitably much has had to be omitted), and that the essays in the present volume fit squarely within the fields in which work is being done. It only remains for me to thank Rosemary Horrox for her help in reading and commenting on these papers and my wife Carolyn for playing her usual indispensable part in my production of any book.

London, 1984   PWH

Notes

1. In A.J. Pollard (ed.), *Property and Politics: Essays in Later Medieval English History*, (Gloucester, 1984), pp. 15–35.
2. Rosenthal, (London, 1976).
3. Colin Richmond, *John Hopton, A Fifteenth Century Suffolk Gentleman*, (Cambridge, 1981).
4. M.A. Hicks, *False, Fleeting Perjur'd Clarence: George Duke of Clarence, 1449–78*, (Gloucester, 1980).
5. Linda S. Woodger, *Henry Bourchier, Earl of Essex, and his Family (1408–82)*, D.Phil thesis, Oxford 1974; Gillian I. Keir, *The Ecclesiastical Career of George Neville, 1432–76*, D.Phil thesis, Oxford 1970; Anne Crawford, *The Career of John Howard Duke of Norfolk, 1420–1485*, M.Phil thesis, London 1975.
6. E.g. A.J. Pollard, 'The Richmondshire Community of Gentry during the Wars of the Roses', in *Patronage, Pedigree and Power in Later Mediaeval England*, ed. Charles Ross, (Gloucester, 1979).
7. PhD thesis, Cambridge 1977. This is soon to be published as a book, *The Reign of Richard III*, (CUP).
8. A.J. Pollard, 'The Tyranny of Richard III', *J.Med.Hist.*, vol. 3 (1977), pp. 147–166. See also his article 'North, South and Richard III', *The Ricardian*, vol. 5 (1981), pp. 384–389.
9. Lorraine Attreed, *The English Royal Government and its Relations with the Boroughs of Norwich, Yorks, Exeter and Nottingham, 1377–1509*, PhD thesis, Harvard 1984; Rosemary Horrox, 'Urban Patronage and Patrons in the Fifteenth Century', and Robert Dunning, 'Patronage and Promotion in the Late Mediaeval Church', both in *Patronage, the Crown and the Provinces*, ed. Ralph A. Griffiths, (Gloucester, 1981). See also *The Church, Politics and Patronage*, ed. R.B. Dobson, (Gloucester, 1984).
10. Susan James, *The Parrs of Kendall, 1370–1571*, PhD thesis, Cambridge 1977; Joanna M. Williams, *The Stanley Family of Lathom and Knowsley, c.1450–1504. A Political Study*, MA thesis, Manchester 1979; Carole Rawcliffe, *The Staffords, Earls of Stafford and Dukes of Buckingham, 1394–1521*, (Cambridge, 1978).
11. Susan M. Wright, *The Derbyshire Gentry in the Fifteenth Century*, Derbyshire Record Society, vol. 8 (1983) and for example the studies by Michael Hicks on the Beauchamp and Neville estates in 'Descent, Partition and Extinction: the Warwick Inheritance', *BIHR*, vol. 54 (1981) pp. 116–128 and 'The Beauchamp Trust 1439–87' *BIHR*, vol. 54 (1981) pp. 135–149.
12. Paul Murray Kendall, *Richard the Third*, (London, 1955); Charles Ross, *Richard III*, (London, 1981).
13. Anne F. Sutton and P.W. Hammond, *The Coronation of Richard III*, (Gloucester, 1983); Rosemary Horrox and P.W. Hammond, *British Library Harleian Manuscript 433*, 4 vols (Upminster and London, 1979–83).
14. *The Ricardian*, vol. 4 part 53 (1976) pp. 4–15.
15. *Op. cit.* (note 12). See also Audrey Williamson, *The Mystery of the Princes: An investigation into a supposed murder*, (Gloucester, 1978).

16. Norman Macdougall, *James III*, (Edinburgh, 1982).
17. D.T. Williams, *The Battle of Bosworth 22 August 1485*, (Leicester, 1973); James
     Gairdner, 'The Battle of Bosworth, *Archaeologia*, vol. 55 (1896) pp. 159–178.
     Since the above was written there has been published Michael Bennett, *The
     Battle of Bosworth*, (Gloucester, 1985), a comprehensive account of the battle
     and the events that led up to it.
18. The best are in Ross, *Richard III*, and S.B. Chrimes, *Henry VII*, (London, 1972).
19. Malcolm Vale, *War and Chivalry*, (London, 1981); Anthony Goodman, *The
     Wars of the Roses: Military Activity and English Society 1452–97*, (London,
     1981); Maurice Keen, *Chivalry*, (London, 1984). See also Anne Curry, 'The
     First English Standing Army? – Military Organisation in Lancastrian Normandy,
     1420–1450', in Ross, *Patronage, Pedigree and Power*, pp. 193–214.

THE PRIVATE LIFE OF JOHN HOWARD: A STUDY OF A YORKIST LORD, HIS FAMILY AND HOUSEHOLD

Anne Crawford

To base a paper on the private life of any fifteenth century man, even a king, seems a very hazardous undertaking. Yet John Howard is one of the few men of his time who has left enough evidence behind for it to be possible. This evidence takes the form of several volumes of financial memoranda covering the years 1462–1471 and 1481–1483. They were edited in the nineteenth century for publication by the Roxburghe Club, those for the earlier years by T. H. Turner in a volume entitled *Manners and Household Expenses of the Thirteenth and Fifteenth Centuries* in 1841, and those of the later period by J. Payne Collier in *Household Books of John, Duke of Norfolk and Thomas, Earl of Surrey, 1481–1490* in 1844.[1] These financial memoranda cover almost every aspect of his busy life, from the purchase of laces for his wife's gown to the sale and purchase of ships. In the earlier volumes, too, some of the entries are in Howard's own handwriting. Taken together they give a detailed picture of the daily life of Howard, his family and his household. What they fail to do is to throw much light on the personal relationships of the people involved. For this aspect of their lives, the Howards have to be judged by their actions.

The basic outline of John Howard's career is familiar. He rose to prominence in the 1460s as a servant of Edward IV, was created a baron in 1470 and was one of Richard III's chief supporters. Richard granted him the dukedom of Norfolk, to which he was a co-heir through his mother, and he died at Bosworth, leading the van of the royal army. This paper, however, is not concerned with his royal service as a soldier, a councillor at Westminster, an envoy to France or an agent of the crown in East Anglia. It is an attempt to draw a much fuller picture of one of the most remarkable men of the fifteenth century, and to do that it is necessary to begin at the beginning, or even a little before. John Howard was born about 1425 and was thus an almost exact contemporary of Henry VI. He was the only son of Sir Robert Howard and his wife, Margaret, daughter of Thomas Mowbray, first duke of Norfolk. Howard's immediate family relationships are rather complicated, but it is necessary to understand them because family ties in the later Middle Ages are immensely important to the appreciation of any prominent layman. They determined his position in society, and are likely to help explain his political attachments and subsequent actions. Of no class is this more true than that of the substantial gentry into which Howard was born. Like many another family, the Howards owed their establishment to a successful lawyer, William Howard, who was knighted and made chief justice of the Common Pleas by Edward I at the end of the thirteenth century.[2] The family prospered during the fourteenth century, adding to its estates and marrying its heirs into the lower ranks of the peerage. The man who dominated Howard's youth was his grandfather, Sir John Howard. He was born about 1360 and married Margaret, daughter and eventual heiress of the fourth Lord Plaiz. With the addition of his wife's lands, Sir John became one of the richest men in East Anglia and active in the political field. He had one son by this marriage, who died young, leaving only an infant daughter, Elizabeth. On the death of Margaret Plaiz, Sir John married a second, though much lesser, heiress. She was Alice Tendring, who brought him a small estate centred on Stoke-by-Nayland in Suffolk, and Sir John moved there to live. By Alice he had two more sons, Robert and Henry. Henry is unimportant, but Robert entered the household of one of the local peers, John Mowbray, duke of Norfolk, a natural step for a boy of his class. What is more unusual is that Robert made a spectacular marriage to Margaret, the duke's sister. She was a direct descendant of Thomas of Brotherton, younger son of Edward I, and also of Edward's brother, Edmund of Lancaster, but at the time of her marriage the Mowbray fortunes were at a low ebb. Her father, the first duke, had died in exile, banished by Richard II after the famous duel with Henry Bolingbroke in 1399, and he was deprived of his dukedom. His son John did not in fact get the title back until 1426, by which time Margaret had married Robert Howard. There were three children of this marriage, John Howard himself, and two girls, Margaret, who married Thomas Daniel, for many years one of Henry VI's court party and thus in simple terms a Lancastrian in the civil war, and Catherine, who married Edward Nevill, Lord Abergavenny, brother of her aunt, Catherine, duchess of Norfolk.

John Howard's father died in 1436 and in the following year so did his grandfather. Although young John was his grandfather's male heir, the bulk of old Sir John's lands went to Elizabeth, the only child of his eldest son, and John inherited only his grandmother's estates round Stoke-by-Nayland. The young heiress, Elizabeth was quickly snapped up as a wife by John de Vere, 12th earl of Oxford. Several sources suggest that Elizabeth's inheritance of the Howard lands began a feud between John Howard and the de Veres which only ended with his death at the hands of John de Vere at Bosworth. With two branches of a family on opposite sides in a civil war and a possible

HOWARD PEDIGREE

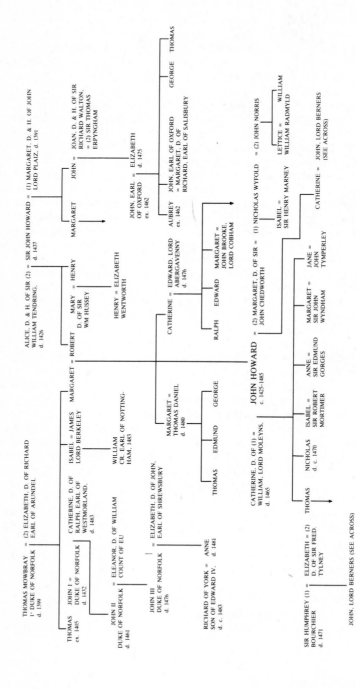

grievance between them it is not difficult to see how the idea arose, but there is plenty of evidence in the household books to show that this was not the case.[3] Soon after he inherited his estate, John Howard himself married. His bride was Catherine Moleyns, and she was the daughter of William, Lord Moleyns. The date of the marriage is unknown, but Thomas, their elder son and probably their eldest child, was born in 1443.[4] His brother, Nicholas, was a year or two younger, and then there were four girls, Isabel, Anne, Margaret and Jane.

This then is the family that lived at Tendring Hall, Stoke-by-Nayland, in the early 1460s when the surviving household books begin. Before turning to family affairs, however, it is necessary to deal very briefly with Howard's financial position. We know that he inherited quite a small estate from his grandmother, but when the household books begin he held twenty-two manors, including seven granted him by the king in 1462. In 1475 he was granted eleven more.[5] Most of these manors were farmed out and Howard received rents of between £10 and £60 p. a. for each. The estate round Stoke-by-Nayland he retained in his own hands and this provided for most of the needs of his household in the way of grain, meat, fish and wool. Howard took a great deal of care and interest in the running of his estate, though he had both bailiff and steward. In 1467, for instance, he noted in his own handwriting that he owned over a thousand sheep, and there is a whole series of memoranda entered by him about his ponds, stocked with bream, tench and carp.[6] He was a careful and efficient administrator, a man who went through his personal accounts every week, checking and annotating and was very unlikely, therefore, to let estate accounts escape his vigilance. As a member of the landed classes, Howard was not remarkable in his attitude to his estates, only in the degree of his involvement in their daily management. At this date, it was not possible to increase one's income from land substantially by improving its administration. To get richer one had to marry, purchase, or be granted more land. By a combination of the last two methods, Howard built up his estates from the original nucleus of his grandmother's inheritance until his income from land, prior to his elevation to the dukedom, was in the region of £500 p.a. in the 1460s and about £700 p.a. in the 1470s. His income from public and private offices at that period was about £150 p.a.[7] These two sources alone made him one of the wealthy men of his day, when only about ten peers had incomes of more than £1000 p.a., but it takes no account of his business interests and it is in these that his significance lies.

Ship-owning in the Middle Ages was largely a matter for the Crown and the mercantile classes, though a few gentlemen and peers were an exception in every period. William Canynges of Bristol is generally supposed to have been the largest ship-owner of the Yorkist period. According to William Worcestre, of seventeen sea-going ships registered at the port of Bristol, Cannynges owned ten. The 'Kingmaker', Richard Nevill, earl of Warwick, had a fleet of eight ships, built up while he was Captain of Calais, largely for political and military purposes, but also providing a profitable mercantile sideline. It is not possible to assess how many ships Howard owned at any one time, or indeed the total number. The first volume of his accounts is dominated by payments for a ship he was having built at Dunwich.[8] She was a carvel, that is, she was built in the Mediterranean style with her planks edge to edge instead of overlapping in the northern European clinker fashion. She incorporated one or two innovations fresh to England; she had three masts, main, mizzen and foremast, and square sails beneath her bowsprit. She was probably bigger than most east coast ships of her time, for she made voyages to Spain and Prussia and was used to convoy a state visitor home to Burgundy. She was named the *Edward*, in honour of the king. None of Howard's other ships are as fully documented; from the accounts and other sources they can be named as the *Mary Howard*, sold to the Crown in 1481 for 500 marks, the *Trygo Howard*, the *Paker Howard*, the *George*, the *Margaret*, the *Thomas Howard*, the *Michael of Barnstaple* and the *Katherine*, a total of ten, with the strong possibility that the *Christopher* and the *Margery of Sandwich* were also owned by him. Now, what use did Howard make of his ships? Canynges built ships for his own trading business with Iceland. The king, slowly building up a royal fleet, which had hitherto not existed, wanted ships capable of fighting and troop-carrying, but also in peacetime for shipping wool, the profits of which were a useful addition to the Crown's income. The obvious answer is that Howard also wanted ships to import and export goods, in fact to run a mercantile business. A study of the customs accounts for London and the east coast ports show that this was not so.[9] He shipped very few goods himself. His ships were used to transport goods for other merchants and to waft, or convoy, smaller ships up and down the Channel, protecting them from both pirates and enemy shipping.[10] In addition, most royal fleets ordered to sea during the Yorkist period contained one or more of Howard's ships. There were several occasions when he either commanded a fleet or was responsible for fitting it out. In the latter cases, detailed records occur in the accounts of the manner used to supply the ships with meat, bread, ale and other essentials. As a commander, on either land or sea, Howard was therefore aware of the importance of an efficient commissariat, an attribute as essential to an armed force as good leadership, but more often overlooked.

It is against this background of wealth and competence that his home life is to be viewed. Home was his grandmother's house, Tendring Hall, in the village of Stoke-by-Nayland, about fifteen miles from Ipswich. The house we know little about. It had been in the Tendring family since 1285, and after he married Alice Tendring, the elder Sir John Howard had made his home there. It seems likely that the wealthy Sir John either rebuilt the Hall or substantially improved it, for there is no evidence to show that his even wealthier grandson undertook any large scale building works save for a chapel which he added in the early 1480s. There are no real clues to its size or layout in the accounts. Howard's family was not particularly large by medieval standards. He had six children by Catherine Moleyns, and when the household books begin in 1462 they were all living at home, the eldest, Thomas, being about nineteen. The upbringing of Thomas and his brother, Nicholas, seems to have differed from the norm for boys of their class. Neither boy seems to have been sent to serve in the household of one of their aristocratic connections. Thomas, who left behind a curious autobiographical epitaph, makes no mention of it, but says he spent 'a sufficient season at the grammar school', probably the one at Ipswich.[11] This indication of his father's belief in the importance of book-learning is underlined by the fact that he supported several local boys at Cambridge.[12] In the accounts for 1464 is a reference to his sons' schoolmaster. Although the boys accompanied their father on his trips to London in the early 1460s, they did not go with him on any of his military expeditions against the Lancastrians in the north. This is again unusual, for boys in their mid and late teens often formed part of a fighting force, even if they were kept to the rear in an actual engagement: the careers of Richard III and his brothers illustrate how young a man could become a seasoned campaigner. In 1466 Howard escorted to Calais the commissioners who were to treat for the marriage of Margaret of York to Charles of Burgundy. Thomas, presented with a 'gestraunt' of mail and two swords by his father, went with him. The Howards stayed in Calais while the commissioners went on to Burgundy and occupied their time buying cloth. One of the entries in the accounts relating to this cloth is in Thomas' hand, prefaced by the words 'my fader bowt'.[13] In September 1467 entries referring to Master Thomas at Windsor indicate that this is when he embarked on his long career as a royal servant.[14] Nicholas remained at home until 1468 when he went on Lord Scales' expedition to Brittany. He was fitted out with a new harness, complete with ostrich feather, and entrusted with £20 to pay the expenses of the men under his command.[15] When the expedition returned he came back to Suffolk and in the following November the accounts note that he was bought five pairs of shoes, perhaps an indication that he was about to leave home again, but that is the last that is ever heard of Howard's second son and the date and circumstances of his death are unknown. Nor is there any clue as to Howard's relationship with his sons, save that their upbringing seems to have been rather sheltered and they probably spent more time in their father's company than would have been true for most boys of their class.

In contrast to their brothers, the Howard girls received at least part of their upbringing in the households of suitable ladies. When the accounts begin, all four girls were at home and there are numerous entries of gowns and shoes purchased for them and their waiting woman, Margaret Notbem. In 1465 the third daughter, Margaret, joined the household of Jane, wife of Sir William Norris of Berkshire, escorted thither by her father. Lady Norris was the daughter of Howard's cousin Elizabeth, countess of Oxford. In the following year his youngest daughter, Jane, went to live with the countess herself. Probably the two elder girls, Isabel and Anne, had spent a year or two in other households.[16]

Howard's marriage to Catherine Moleyns seems to have been successful by medieval standards. She presented him with a nursery full of children and they seem to have been fond enough of each other for her to travel with him if he was to be away from home for more than a few days. In his shorter absences she managed the houshold and estates, presenting her accounts for her husband's approval on his return. In September 1465 Lady Howard fell ill. There is no indication of the nature of her illness, but the accounts give a vivid picture of the attempts made to cure her. First, a messenger was sent to Lord Berners' place to fetch a physician named Friar Robert Wotton, and considerable sums were expended on medicines. Then physicians from London were summoned and medicine purchased there rather than locally. As she grew worse, the emphasis changes from medicines to purchases that would make her more comfortable and soothe her, sugar candy, honeysuckle water, special wine. She lingered until November, dying on the 'morrow after Soulmass day' (3 November).[17]

Fifteen months after Catherine's death, Howard was showering a new wife with gifts. She was Margaret, daughter of Sir John Chedworth, recently widowed for the second time. Her first husband had been Nicholas Wyfold, a grocer who had been Mayor of London in 1450 and died in 1456, leaving her a wealthy widow with a young daughter called Isabel. She then married a man of her own class, John Norris of Bray, esquire, as his third wife. She had step-sons as old as herself, including Sir William Norris, mentioned above. There were younger Norris children and she bore two more, Lettice and another William. John Norris died nearly a year after Catherine Howard, leaving most of his lands to his widow, provided she did not remarry. Within four months of his death and before she had proved his will, she married John Howard.[18] Since Howard could have married widows both wealthier and better connected, and since the Norris family were well-known to him, it seems likely that Margaret and John were already acquainted. Given the widow's somewhat unseemly haste, it also seems likely that some degree of personal preference was involved.

Among the Paston correspondence are two stray Howard accounts, one the funeral account for the first Lady Howard, the other a list of wedding gifts her widower gave the second Lady Howard. It is a very long list. Among the items of jewellery were two 'rings of gold set with good diamonds the which the Queen gave my master', and a 'collar of gold with thirty-four roses and suns set on a course of black silk with a hanger of gold garnished with a sapphire', and added in Howard's own hand 'a pot of silver to put in green ginger that the king gave.'[19] Margaret brought with her to Suffolk her own three children and her youngest Norris step-daughter. She soon bore Howard another daughter whom they named Catherine. Perhaps partly because he had two grown sons and partly because he had a new wife still capable of child-bearing, Howard does not seem to have been over-anxious to see his heir Thomas married and producing sons. Howard himself had become a father in his late teens, and there was talk of a match for Thomas with Margery Paston as early as 1454, but nothing came of it.[20] However the death of Nicholas in 1469 and Thomas' severe wounds at Barnet brought the

Howard line perilously close to extinction. Thomas was nearly thirty before he married, far older than the majority of his contemporaries. In 1472 he took to wife Elizabeth, daughter and heiress of Sir Frederick Tylney of Ashwellthorpe in Norfolk. Elizabeth his wife was also the widow of Humphrey Bourchier, Lord Berners' son and heir, with a son of her own to inherit her lands and his grandfather's title. Thomas held her lands for his lifetime only and as Lord Howard's heir could almost certainly have done better for himself if he had had a mind to. The couple lived at Ashwellthorpe and set about producing sons; the eldest, Thomas, later the third duke, was born in 1473, Edward in 1477 and Edmund, father of Queen Catherine Howard, in 1479. Their daughter Elizabeth was the mother of Queen Anne Boleyn. The question of Elizabeth Tylney's inheritance was settled by the Howards in sensible fashion. They married her son, the young Lord Berners, to John Howard's youngest daughter, Catherine. He entered Howard's household at the time of his mother's remarriage and the two young children were brought up together.

In a worldly sense, the marriage of Catherine was the best match made by any of Howard's children. His four elder girls all married into the ranks of the gentry. The matches were made in the 1460s when Howard was wealthy and coming into prominence at court, but before he became a peer. Two of his sons-in-law were members of his household. Edmund Gorges of Wraxall was already betrothed to Howard's second daughter, Anne, when his father died in 1466 and Howard secured the wardship of Edmund and his younger brother, John.[21] Both boys were already part of the household in 1465, at the time of Lady Howard's death. So, too, was John Wyndham of Felbrigg, aged fourteen, who a few years later married the third daughter, Margaret.[22] It is known that Howard settled the manor of Colby on the latter couple at their marriage and it seems reasonable to suppose that his other daughters were similarly endowed,[23] Isabel, when she married Robert Mortimer of Essex, and Jane, when she married John Timperley of Hintlesham in Suffolk. Both these came from similar gentry stock, their families undistinguished save in local affairs and of no great wealth. Although both spent quite a lot of time with Howard, there is no evidence that they were actually resident in the household like Gorges and Wyndham, and their role was more that of a retainer. They both accompanied Howard on his expeditions to Scotland in 1481 and both were with him in London at the time when he was raised to the dukedom by Richard III. For none of his daughters' husbands did Howard use his influence at court to obtain offices, grants or annuities. Timperley, whose father had been an M.P. on several occasions, was himself first elected to Parliament in 1467 in the Mowbray interest, but since his father was a member of the duke of Norfolk's council, this probably owed nothing to Howard. The sole piece of patronage which may be attributed to him is the appointment of Edmund Gorges, together with his own son, Thomas, as esquires of the body. There were other family members in Howard's household besides his sons-in-law. He gave shelter to his three nephews,

Thomas, Edmund and George Daniel, sons of his sister Margaret and the attainted Lancastrian, Thomas Daniel. His own squire, Thomas Moleyns, was presumably a relative of his first wife, though he cannot be positively identified.

The size of the household can be assessed most satisfactorily for November 1465 when the accounts list the people for whom Howard purchased mourning clothes on the death of his wife. Apart from members of the family, and one or two others, like Master John Cranwyse, vicar of Stoke-by-Nayland, who were clearly not resident at Tendring Hall, one hundred and ten people are named. Of these, one hundred and three were men. The seven women are all mentioned elsewhere in the accounts and held senior positions in the household. A household numbering over a hundred was considerably larger than that expected of a knight. £100 p.a. was the sum considered reasonable for a man of that rank to spend on the upkeep of his household. Howard was spending about £200–£300 p.a. on wages alone and probably nearer £500 in total. He was therefore living in the style considered appropriate for a baron years before his elevation to the peerage.[24]

It is hard to analyse the composition of the household. Virtually no personal details are added to the names in the accounts. There was no need: the men keeping the accounts and Howard for whom they were prepared, knew everyone involved. The household officers can be identified for they are often given their titles. When the accounts open, the steward was John Braham of Boxted (a neighbouring village to Stoke-by-Nayland), gentleman, and he was succeeded by John Bliant. Bliant was almost certainly also of gentle birth and probably related to Simon Bliant of Ryngefield, Suffolk, gentleman, for the name is an unusual one. When Howard became duke of Norfolk, Bliant was advanced to the position of comptroller of the household. Howard's squire has already been mentioned, and his sons' squire was Thomas Thorpe, who was the brother of a prominent Norwich merchant, Robert Thorpe, who rented one of Howard's manors. No single person seems to have been responsible for keeping the acccounts. John Skinner, Thomas Dalamar, and the brothers Giles and Thomas Seynclow, all made entries at the same period. Skinner was unusual in not having been a local man. He came from Reigate in Surrey, the son of an M. P. who had sat for the town in the Mowbray interest, and he himself had trained as a lawyer. He entered the household some time before 1481 and was the only member of the household outside Howard's own family who held public office, representing Reigate in Richard III's parliament and serving as under-sheriff of Surrey and Sussex in 1483. Thomas Dalamar may have come to Suffolk with Margaret Chedworth, since the Dalamars were a Berkshire family and he does not appear in the accounts prior to her marriage to Howard. The Seynclow brothers on the other hand, were the sons of an attainted Lancastrian whose manor of Merton Hall in Norfolk was granted to Howard in 1462. Disinherited, the brothers joined Howard's household and served him for the rest of his life. John Davy, whose father rented another of Howard's manors was a senior member of the household throughout the period covered by both sets of accounts. Two knights, Sir John Dew and Sir John Comberton seem to have joined the household for a specific period of military service with Howard in the north, but he had no one of a similar rank in a permanent position, even, apparently, after he became duke.

Howard's Mowbray cousins had a ducal council containing not only Howard himself, but prominent local gentry such as Sir Gilbert Debenham, Sir Robert Wingfield, Sir John Heveningham, Sir William Brandon and Sir Robert Chamberlain, as well as the lawyer, James Hobart. Howard himself, therefore, was for most of his life a retainer of the duke of Norfolk. His fellow council members cannot have been delighted at his own elevation to the dukedom in place of the king's younger son, and he does not seem to have had a similar retinue himself. There was only one man of rank who could possibly be classed a retainer of the new duke, and it should not come as any great surprise to learn that he was a family connection of Howard's. He was John Brooke, Lord Cobham, formerly a ward of Lord Abergavenny, and married to Abergavenny's daughter, Howard's niece, Margaret. On the Scottish expedition, Cobham was Howard's second in command, and there are several other references to him in the accounts, attending Howard on his visits to London. Howard sent for him to come to London in June 1483 and again when Buckingham's rebellion broke out. Cobham's home was in Kent, so it was only a short journey. Sir John Lyones of Hadley indented to serve Howard for a year in January 1482 for the sum of five marks. He received money in October and November of that year, but seems not to have renewed his indenture for he is not included in the list of men Howard promised to the crown in February 1484.[25]

The payment of wages to members of the household occurs throughout the accounts, but not in such a way as to enable an accurate assessment of annual expenditure on wages to be made. It was not the medieval way to line the household up once a week, once a month or even once a year for them all to be paid. Instead payments of odd sums were made at various times, sometimes just to one person, sometimes to several. As far as can be judged, the lesser members of the household received 3s. 4d. per month, their seniors twice that, making the annual wage for a senior man six marks (£4) a year. In addition to cash wages, each man would receive a gift of a new gown and a pair of shoes each year, or possibly the cash equivalent. One exception to this rule was made in 1467 when Howard obtained the services of an 'archer de maison', or an archer of the elite type that the earl of Warwick once described to Louis XI as worth two ordinary archers, even English ones.[26] To persuade this man, Daniel, to enter his service, Howard contracted to pay him no less than £10 p.a., with two gowns and a house in the village for his wife. As an extra inducement he was given on the spot two doublets, a gown, boots, two spears, a bow and arrows and a shooting glove, all noted in Howard's own hand. When next he visited London he bought a bow for his own use at two shillings, while two for Daniel cost more than ten shillings.[27]

Having considered the people who formed Howard's household, it is time
to look at how they lived. To house well over a hundred people, Tendring
Hall must have been large, but there are few clues to the accomodation
provided for most of them. What little information exists relates to the
family's living quarters. There is an entry in the accounts referring to the glass
put into the window of young Lady Berners' chamber in May 1482. It took the
local glazier nine days to complete the work, suggesting that both the
chamber and the window were sizable. As early as 1465, the glazier, Robert
Lawson, had supplied nine feet of glass for a new closet, or private room,
quite possibly for Howard's own use. Glass windows at this date were still a
luxury but not an exclusive one. Howard also had two new chimney pieces
shipped from London, but there is no indication of whether they were for
public rooms or the family's private use. Wall hangings were the popular
method of reducing draughts and discomfort before the introduction of
panelling, and the finest came from Arras in France. Since Howard was
wealthy and his ships travelled regularly to France, it is not surprising that
several pieces of arras feature in the list of wedding presents he gave Margaret
Chedworth. Unfortunately few of the references make any mention of the
subject matter of the tapestries, whether religious, pastoral or mythological,
which might give a clue to Howard's taste. Some bought in the summer of
1483 were embroidered with lions, the Norfolk badge, and one, bought a few
months later showed the story of 'patient Griselda'. Clearly intended for a
lady's room, it might well have been destined for Lady Berners' chamber.[28]

Apart from the hangings, beds and cushions listed among the presents to
Margaret, no furniture is mentioned in the accounts as having been purchased
for Tendring Hall, or for Howard's London house in Stepney. The list of
personal equipment which Howard took with him on the expedition to
Scotland gives an indication of the things he regarded as indispensable for his
comfort, even on board ship, or necessary for his prestige as Admiral. The list
includes carpets, curtains, sheets, towels, napkins, tablecloths, quilts and
pillows of down, and featherbeds. Nearly all the basins and bowls he took
were silver, but in some ways the most interesting item is a 'case with four
goblets'. Although they may have been silver, the fact that they required a
case suggests that they were glass. The fine crystal manufactured in Italy at
this date was still rare in England and consequently very expensive. That
Howard owned four glasses which he was prepared to risk on board ship
illustrates very well not only his wealth but his taste.[29]

Similarly he took with him a small library of books. Twelve in number, they
were unlikely to be all he owned. The titles of those he selected for a
campaign are illuminating. None were devotional. Howard may have built a
chapel for his house, employed children to sing in it and bought music for
them, but his books do not reveal him as deeply devout. They were mainly
light romances or tales of heroic doings, including one on Baldwin, Count of
Flanders and two on the Trojan War. Two were treatises on dice and chess
and one was the ever-popular *La Belle Dame Sans Merci*. All were written in

French, and as Edward IV's leading envoy to France, Howard must have spoken the language fluently. They form the sort of collection that a soldier of cultivated but unscholarly mind might have taken with him on a campaign for relaxation. Whether they were printed or manuscript copies is impossible to tell. At least five of them had been printed by 1481, either in England or abroad, and as an indication that Howard's taste accurately reflected that of his age, most of the others were printed in the following decades. Two of them, *Les Dites des Sages* and one on Troy, Caxton chose to print in English.[30]

Purchases of cloth occur throughout the accounts, but the only clothes described in detail are those he took to Scotland. They were rich, but certainly not sober, as befitted one of advancing years – he was about fifty-five, an old man for his time. He took two long gowns, one in black satin lined with purple velvet, the other russet trimmed with leopard skin; two crimson satin doublets and one of popingay colour (usually a sort of turquoise), a short mantle of blue velvet, a short gown of tawny velvet, and, presumably to impress the Scots, a jacket of cloth of gold. All these materials would have been purchased in London, but cloth for the household, worsted or Kendal cloth, in the Howard colours of red and blue, was generally purchased locally. Minor things, like seven pairs of hose, two pairs of slippers and three other pairs of shoes are all listed.[31]

The provision of food for any household the size of that at Tendring Hall was a major task. Howard went some way towards dealing with it by retaining in his own hands the estates in and around Stoke-by-Nayland. These could provide the bulk of the produce the household needed, and the long series of entries in the accounts, most of them in Howard's own handwriting, and relating to the care with which his ponds were broken and restocked, testify to the importance he attached to good husbandry. The home estates could not supply all the meat required by the household and Woolpit Fair seems to have supplied most of the extra stock. Each autumn and spring saw the main purchases of livestock, but throughout the rest of the year there was a constant trade with local butchers, particularly for pigs, geese and pigeons rather than beef and mutton. As with meat, much of the corn came from the estates. In addition to what was grown on the demesne, Howard came to various arrangements with his tenants; for instance his farmer of the manor of Merton Hall in Norfolk, besides his cash rent, was also liable for a corn rent of sixty quarters of barley, and in another case he purchased from Sir Pers, his chaplain, who held the living of Polsted, all his tithe corn for the sum of £10 a year. At Stoke the household obviously made its own bread, but in London it also made use of a local baker, John Melton, to such an extent that in September 1483 he received payment of £20. The same pattern is true for beer, the third staple of medieval diet. A delivery of 221 lbs of hops at Stoke indicates that it was indeed beer that was drunk, at least by some of the household, and not ale.[32] With his shipping interests, Howard had no difficulty in ensuring a supply of good quality wine. On one occasion a ship belonging to Richard Felaw, his Ipswich agent, came in with a cargo of wine and Howard arranged for a pipe of white wine and a pipe and two tierces of red French wine to be sent to his manor of Winch, near Lynn in Norfolk, and a similar amount to Stoke. In September 1483 he was licenced to import a hundred tuns of wine free of duty and any amount surplus to his own requirements he was free to sell if he wished.[33]

Although the estate provided staple food, any luxuries had to be purchased. Many of these were spices and dried fruits sent from London to Suffolk; dates and raisins and ginger bought from William Clerke of Gracechurch Street, pepper, cloves, lemons, mace, almonds, rice, cinnamon, currants, figs, sugar, capsicums and olive oil all show what a range of goods from overseas were available to the fifteenth century Englishman who could afford them. Sometimes the purchases were so exotic that whoever was keeping the accounts had no name for them and in one case noted that ten shillings had been paid for a 'sort of fruit', and the cost alone indicates its rarity. An earlier entry is for something described as '16 pongarnettes', which are probably pomegranates. Howard also seems to have been partial to fish he could not stock in his ponds at home; he often bought Colchester oysters, in 1466 he bought 'forty great eels' and for his wedding breakfast four pike.[34]

Having detailed the lavish spending that Howard made on his own comfort, his appearance and his stomach, it is only fitting to note here that he was a generous man to others less fortunate. Whenever he travelled, he would open his purse to any in need. His workmen and ships' crews were often given a little extra on top of their wages for drink and any messenger or one who did him service was sure to receive a reward. Henry Elyse, a gentleman who had turned hermit, was a favourite recipient of alms, not just small sums but as much as 6s. 8d. at a time. The Colchester friars were other favourites, though all churchmen whom he met might expect something, but the most interesting cases are those to whom he gave on the spur of the moment, often borrowing from one of his men in order to do so because he had no cash on him. 'My lord paid to Robert Clarke for alms he laid out at Colchester's town end, 2d., and to the lazars, 6d.'; 'memorandum that my lord borrowed 3s. 4d. from Braham at Colchester to give to a man that was in debate with Thorpe's man' (what was the subject of the debate that so caught his attention ?); 'for burying a poor woman, 8d.'; 'to a poor man that had his house burnt, 2s.'; 'to the young man of the stable that is sick, 4d.'[35] Nor was his charity entirely random. He supported several local boys at Cambridge, either totally or with contributions from their families. Although not a scholar himself, Howard seems to have been genuinely interested in learning and had he lived to see it, he would surely have been proud of his son-in-law, Lord Berners, later noted for his translation of Froissart.[36]

Whether or not Howard played an instrument himself, he enjoyed music in all forms. He employed young choristers to sing in his chapel and sought out copies of anthems and pricked song books for them. His chapel had an organ installed as soon as it was built. By 1465 the household had its own harper, a musician named Thomas. Nor was Howard averse to talent spotting, for in October 1482 'my lord made covenant with William Wastell of London, harper, that he shall have the son of John Colet of Colchester for a year to teach him to sing and harp, for which teaching my lord shall give him 13s. 4d. and a gown and he took him in earnest 6s. 8d. and at the end of the year he shall have the remnant and the gown'.[37] By 1482 Howard may have had his own troupe of minstrels, since an item in the accounts gives the cost of mending a lute for them, but it may have been on behalf of a visiting troupe, such as the Duchess of Norfolk's minstrels, who visited Tendr..g Hall in 1481. They received 3s. 4d. for the performance, but the martial music of the Duke of Gloucester's trumpeters stirred him enough to give them 5s. Musicians were not the only performers who found it worth their while to visit Stoke-by-Nayland, and on a number of occasions strolling players were welcomed. At Christmas 1481 it was a group from Coggeshall and a few days later one from Hadleigh. There seems to have been an abundance of plays at this particular festive season, for a few days after the village players came the Earl of Essex's troupe. Gloucester had a similar band who played at Stoke the following Christmas.[38] In between such visits, the household amused itself with the antics of its own two fools, Tom and Richard, the latter known as the fool of the kitchen. They also seem to be indicative of Howard's increasingly affluent lifestyle, for neither appear in the first set of accounts. Even when players came at Christmas, the household provided its own Twelfth Night disguisings. In 1482 Howard paid a large bill to Gerard of Sudbury for stuff that was required for costumes and which included more than four dozen sheets of gold and silver paper, two dozen sheets of gold foil, twelve quires of ordinary paper, nearly three pounds of something called 'arsowde' and a pound of glue, a pack of thread and the unlikely item of a pound of gunpowder.[39]

For the rest of the year, leisure time was whiled away with cards and chess as well as books and music. A bag of chessmen was part of the indispensible equipment Howard took with him to Scotland and on another occasion he paid a limner 20d. for painting two chessboards. Card games were a relatively new pastime in England, but had become an extremely popular form of gambling. While campaigning in Wales in 1463, long winter evenings meant considerable sums of money changed hands. On one such night, the Duke of Norfolk's steward had to lend Howard four marks to pay his debts and 13s. 4d. to pay the duke's, receiving his money back in instalments over the next ten days, presumably when Howard's luck changed. The older game of tables or backgammon remained popular, but Howard seemed no luckier there than at cards, since he once lost the large sum of 28s. 4d. at it.[40] The accounts may, perhaps, cast an unfair light on both his luck and skill, since they probably only record his losses. His other pastimes were rather more strenuous. Hunting and archery he indulged in whenever possible. Hunting usually meant a few days away from home, either at Castle Rising when his brother-in-law, Thomas Daniel still held it or with the Earl of Oxford at Lavenham or

Wivenhoe.[41] There are fewer references to hawking, but payments for a hawk's bag and bells indicate that he did own birds. Archery was another temptation to wager. In Wales he lost 7d. at it, but in London in 1466 he was prepared to bet 10s. on a contest between himself and Sir Harry Waffers and he gave his opponent's wife the money to hold until the match was over. In London he was able to play tennis and once lost 3s. 4d. at it to Sir Robert Chamberlain. 'Pykynge' or bowls was yet another chance to wager on a test of skill and one bet of 4d. was lost to Lord Stafford.[42] By and large Howard played these sports away from home, in London or on campaign; hunting and music, reading and chess were the more domestic pleasures to be had at Tendring Hall.

Finally what of the man himself? What clues are there to Howard's own personality? He seems to have been a fond husband and father. We know he was a shrewd and successful businessman, an efficient administrator, who oversaw things personally. That these qualities were appreciated by his contemporaries is clear. A list of local offices he held in the early 1460s includes stewardships of the East Anglian lands of, among others, the duchess of York, the duke of Suffolk, two widowed duchesses of Norfolk, the priors of Lewes and Canterbury, Lady Scrope and the Provost of King's College Cambridge.[43] Edward IV first appointed him to a minor household office in 1462 and he advanced him rapidly to the post of Treasurer of the Household, one of the three great Household offices, and rarely held by any but peers. Edward had succeeded to an insolvent and badly administered household, but the insecurity of his early years as king meant that household reforms were not an important consideration. It seems reasonable to suppose that the appointment of a noted businessman in 1468 meant that the king intended him to improve the financial footing of the household. It was also an important step in Howard's career. In 1470 his loyal service to the Yorkist crown was recognised when Edward created him a baron. Only eight men were raised from the gentry to the peerage in Edward's reign, five of them immediately he became king. Howard was the last. For another aspect of his career, we have to turn to a Tudor historian. Polydore Vergil, who would have met men who knew Howard well, describes him as being 'a man very politic and skilfull in wars'.[44] There is no particular reason not to accept Vergil's statement and indeed there are two occasions when Howard was in independent command which suggest it was accurate. The first was the Scottish naval campaign of 1481, when his fleet surprised the Scots, burned some ships, and captured others at Leith, Kinghorn and Pettenween, and burned the town of Blackness, and then retired to blockade the Firth of Forth. The second was his effective defence of London with the minimum of men during Buckingham's rebellion, which left the king free to concentrate his forces against the rebels in the west.[45]

That he was as resourceful in peace as he was in war is reflected in Edward's increasing reliance on him as an envoy to France in the 1470s. This was aided by his residence in Calais as deputy-lieutenant from 1471 to about 1474. At the end of the 1475 campaign in France he was one of the two hostages left behind with the French to ensure the swift withdrawal of the English army. Howard and his fellow hostage, Sir John Cheyne, were taken to Paris and entertained in the household of Louis XI. By the end of the reign, he was Edward's leading envoy to France. Why was he so successful ? There is no evidence of any diplomatic cunning in his character, indeed, rather the reverse. His usefulness seems to have resided in a bluff openess of manner and a strong determination to achieve his aims, qualities which are apparent in his business dealings and which proved equally productive of results at foreign courts. Philippe de Commines, the shrewd French chronicler, who spent a lot of time negotiating with Howard prior to the Treaty of Picquigny in 1475, commented that the English did not conduct their treaties with the cunning of the French – not for nothing was Louis known as the Spider King – but proceeded with more ingenuousness and straightforwardness, and yet, he adds, a man must be cautious and not affront them, for it was dangerous to meddle with them.[46] This may well have been an accurate generalisation about fifteenth century Englishmen, but it also tallies with all that is known of Howard's character. Since he and Commines had been in each other's company, and Howard was the most frequent ambassador to France, it is difficult not to believe that Commines was generalising from the particular.

There was an eye-witness on at least one occasion when Howard lost his temper in a most undiplomatic fashion, admittedly long before he became an envoy. In the parliamentary election of 1455 he was nominated by the duke of Norfolk to be one of the knights of the shire for Norfolk. The Norfolk gentry took exception to Howard because at that date he owned no land in the county. It was a perfectly reasonable objection and the duke accepted it, agreeing that there should be a free election, provided, of course, that no adherent of the duke of Suffolk should be elected. This did not please Howard. According to John Jenney in a letter to John Paston, Howard was 'as wode as a wilde bullok'.[47] He need not have worried; the duke's known wishes carried the day and Howard was one of those elected.

Finally, the last facet of Howard's character that needs to be explored is his loyalty. This was given first to the Mowbray dukes of Norfolk, his maternal family. He served his cousin John, who died in 1461, indeed his first contact with Edward IV was with Norfolk's troops on the way to Towton, and then his son John, the last Mowbray duke, who died in 1475. He led their forces in the field, deputisd for them as Earl Marshall, and was a member of their ducal council. Rather more informally he kept the last duke, who was much impoverished, supplied with ready cash. Even in 1475, when he led his own force to France, it was the Norfolk badge his men wore: the white lion, differenced for Howard with an azure crescent.[48] It was through his connection with Norfolk that he was given his first household appointment as a king's carver, but it was his own talents that raised him thereafter – his talents, and his loyal service to the house of York. He remained loyal through the Readeption, and he was the first in East Anglia to proclaim Edward's return.

He was never associated with any faction at court and that he was regarded as a man of integrity by almost all is clear from the fact that when the widowed queen, Elizabeth Woodville, was required to surrender her younger son, the duke of York, from sanctuary it was to the Archbishop of Canterbury and Howard that she agreed to hand him over. The question of Howard and the Mowbray inheritance has been discussed elsewhere, suffice to say that having been granted the dukedom by Richard III, Howard remained loyal to him also.[49] He does not seem to have spent much time at Richard's court, but he was always there when Richard needed him, first during Buckingham's rebellion and then at Bosworth. The famous verse pinned to his tent before the battle 'Jockey of Norfolk, be not so bold, For Dickon thy master is bought and sold' gives an indication of the atmosphere of treachery which surrounded the king. If Howard had wished to throw in his lot with Henry Tudor at the last minute, there is no doubt that he could have come to very comfortable terms with the new king. Whether Henry would ever have trusted him is another matter. That Howard's attitude was respected, and indeed highly thought of in the following decades is clear from comments made by the Tudor historian, Edward Hall. Hall had no reason to write as he did except to express a widely held view, since he was describing a man who died an enemy of the Tudors and whose descendants were no longer so powerful that all may be explained by sycophancy. I shall let Hall's words stand as Howard's epitaph, for he now has no other on his grave at Thetford Priory:

'He regarded more his oath, his honour and his promise made to King Richard like a gentleman and a faithful subject to his Prince, and absented not himself from his master, but as he faithfully lived under him, so he manfully died with him, to his greater honour and laud.'[50]

And thus passed one of the truly great men of the fifteenth century.

Notes

1. *Manners and Household Expenses of England in the Thirteenth and Fifteenth Centuries* (Household Expenses of Sir John Howard, 1462–1471), ed. T.H. Turner, (Roxburghe Club 1841); *Household Books of John, Duke of Norfolk and Thomas, Earl of Surrey, 1481–1490*, ed. J. Payne Collier, (Roxburghe Club 1844).
2. For a fuller picture of the earlier Howard family, see G. Brennan and E.P. Statham, *The House of Howard*, vol. 1, (London 1907).
3. Turner, *op. cit.*, pp. 176, 300, 338–9, 385, 509.
4. See his autobiographical epitaph printed in J. Weever, *Ancient Funeral Monuments* (1631), p. 839.

5. *CPR, 1461–1467*, p. 10; *CPR, 1467–1477*, pp. 538, 545, 547.
6. Turner, pp. 555, 560–4.
7. *Ibid.*, p. 546.
8. For example, *ibid.*, pp. 200, 202, 210, 309, 319.
9. P.R.O. Particular Customs Accounts, E122/52/49, E122/194/21, E122/194/19, 20.
10. Arundel Castle manuscript G1/3.
11. Weever, *op. cit.*, p. 839.
12. Turner, pp. 214, 338, 379.
13. *Ibid.*, pp. 356, 366.
14. *Ibid.*, pp. 428, 430.
15. *Ibid.*, pp. 567–8.
16. *Ibid.*, pp. 286, 292, 398, 508.
17. *Ibid.*, pp. 303–4.
18. Prerogative Court of Canterbury, 19 Godyn.
19. *The Paston Letters*, ed. J. Gairdner (1904), vol. 4, pp. 211–3, 262–4.
20. *Ibid.*, vol. 2, p. 331.
21. Turner, pp. 327, 369; *CPR, 1461–67*, p. 527.
22. Gairdner, *op. cit.*, vol. 4, pp. 211–3.
23. H.A. Wyndham, *A Family History, 1410–1688: The Wyndhams of Norfolk and Somerset* (London 1939), vol. i, p. 23.
24. A.R. Myers, *The Household of Edward IV* (Manchester, 1959), p. 110.
25. Payne Collier, pp. 9, 244; 150, 301, 320, 481.
26. P.M. Kendall, *The Yorkist Age* (London 1962), p. 199; Turner, pp. 587ff.
27. *Ibid.*, pp. 423, 429.
28. Payne Collier, pp. 188, 285, 421, 467; Turner, p. 511.
29. Payne Collier, p. 275.
30. *Ibid.*, p. xxvii.
31. *Ibid.*, pp. 219, 275, 293.
32. Turner, pp. 107, 172, 560–3; Payne Collier, pp. 208, 440.
33. Turner, p. 274; Payne Collier, p. 465. A tierce was one third of a pipe, a pipe was half a tun, and a tun contained 252 gallons.
34. *Ibid.*, pp. 42, 338, 352; Turner, pp. 330, 386, 388.
35. *Ibid.*, p. 202ff; Payne Collier, pp. 169, 367; 175, 364, 432.
36. *Ibid.*, pp. 214, 338, 379.
37. *Ibid.*, pp. 145, 149, 158, 161, 163, 465; 300.
38. *Ibid.*, pp. 116, 145; 146, 149, 336.
39. *Ibid.*, p. 339.
40. *Ibid.*, pp. 158, 275; Turner, p. 234.
41. *Ibid.*, pp. 277, 300; Payne Collier, p. 104.
42. Turner, pp. 368, 250, 252.
43. *Ibid.*, p. 456.
44. *Polydore Vergil's English History*, ed. H. Ellis, Camden Society (1844), p. 187.
45. Payne Collier, pp. 74–9, 468–479; J. Lesley, *History of Scotland from the Death of King James I in the year 1436 to the year 1561*, (Bannatyne Club 1830), pp. 44–5.

46. Philippe de Commynes, *Mémoires*, ed. J. Calmette et G. Durville (Paris, 1924), vol. 2, p. 60.
47. Gairdner, *op. cit.*, vol. 3, p. 38–9.
48. F.P. Barnard, *Edward IV's French Expedition of 1475* (London 1925), pp. 24–5, 78–9.
49. See my article, 'The Mowbray Inheritance', in *The Ricardian*, vol. 5 (1981), 334–340.
50. Edward Hall, *Union of the Two Noble and Illustre Famelies of Lancastre and York* (1809), p. 419.

Appendix 1: John Howard's Household

Family Members: (a) Sons–in-law
        John, Lord Berners
        John Wyndham of Felbrigg, Norfolk
        Edmund Gorges of Wraxall, Somerset

      (b) Nephews
        Thomas Daniel
        Edmund Daniel
        George Daniel

Gentlemen: John Gorges, brother of Edmund
      Thomas Moleyns, esquire to Howard, related to Lady Howard
      Thomas Thorpe, esquire to Howard sons
      John Braham, steward
      John Bliant, steward, later comptroller
      Giles Seynclow
      Thomas Seynclow
      John Skinner
      Thomas Dalamar
      John Davy
      John Penley, receiver
      Robert Cumberton

Retainers: John Brooke, Lord Cobham, nephew by marriage
      John Timperley of Hintlesham, Suffolk, son-in-law
      Robert Mortimer, son-in-law
      Sir John Dew ⎫
      Sir John Cumberton ⎬ for military service only

RICHARD III AND LADY MARGARET BEAUFORT: A RE-ASSESSMENT

Michael Jones

Margaret Beaufort, countess of Richmond and mother of Henry VII, was by any standards a remarkable woman. Her concern for religious matters and education, which led to foundations at Christ's and St John's College Cambridge and patronage of theologians and mathematicians, was noted and praised by Erasmus.[1] Yet the conspicuous piety which came to dominate her later life should not obscure her pragmatism or political astuteness. These qualities were clearly in evidence during the reign of Henry VII, when Lady Margaret was prominent in settling disputes involving not only her own tenants and retainers but also independent parties.[2] In the vivid words of her confessor John Fisher, 'If any faccyons or bendes were made secretly amongst her hede officers, she with great polycye did boulte it oute'. Fisher had been greatly impressed by Margaret's religious devotion, but also by her exceptional determination. She had a 'holding memory' which might pass over 'tryfelous thynges that were lytell to be regarded' but for those 'of weight and substance wherein she might profit, she would not let for any pain or labour to take upon hand'.[3] Such characteristics were never more evident than during the brief period of Richard III's reign, when the countess plotted and conspired to achieve her son's return to England and his winning of the throne. Henry VII was to reward his mother generously, restoring her lands and granting her a new mass of properties. Yet how far was the Tudor portrait of Margaret as an inveterate opponent of the Yorkist dynasty essentially an accurate one? The aim of this paper is to reconstruct the countess's background and to ask some new questions about her role in the events of 1483–5.

Margaret was born on 31 May 1443, the only daughter of John duke of Somerset and his wife Margaret Beauchamp of Bletsoe.[4] The death of her father less than a year later left her a wealthy heiress and rights to her wardship and marriage were rapidly acquired by the duke of Suffolk. The

Commons were later angrily to accuse Suffolk of enriching himself through this wardship and also of strengthening his family's dynastic position by arranging Margaret's marriage to his own son, John de la Pole.[5] The marriage was annulled in March 1453 and Margaret herself neither understood or recognized it.[6] Her wardship was transferred to the Tudor earls of Pembroke and Richmond, and her marriage to Edmund earl of Richmond, again of considerable dynastic significance, produced her only son on 28 January 1457.[7] The birth had a deep emotional impact on Margaret, both because of her very young age and also the death of her husband only a few months earlier. The event was movingly referred to in the dating of one of her letters to Henry, many years afterwards: 'thys day of Saint Annes, that y did bryng into this world my good and gracyous Prince, Kynge and only beloved son'.[8] It was also reflected in the provisions made for the reburial of Edmund in her first will of 2 June 1472. Edmund's remains were to be translated from the House of the Grey Friars in Carmarthen to her own foundation at Bourne in Lincolnshire, and on her death Margaret would be laid to rest beside him.[9] However, the will was subsequently cancelled and this stipulation was never in fact carried out. It is important to emphasise this strength of affection for an only child. Margaret was to take a vow of celibacy much later in her life.[10] Yet at no earlier occasion did she conceive another child, and giving birth to Henry at such an early age may have been the reason for it.[11]

Within a few months of the birth of her son, Margaret had married again. Her match with Sir Henry Stafford, a younger son of the duke of Buckingham, had taken place by April 1457,[12] and from the evidence of their surviving household accounts the couple appear to have enjoyed a close and affectionate relationship. Although Stafford had fought for the Lancastrians at Towton he had quickly made his peace with the new regime, and had secured a general pardon for both himself and Margaret by late 1461.[13] However, custody of Henry Tudor was granted to William Lord Herbert, who by 12 February 1462 had purchased the wardship and marriage of Tudor for the sum of £1,000.[14] Henry was brought up at Raglan castle under the supervision of Lady Herbert, and from the evidence of her husband's will an eventual marriage to their daughter Maud was intended.[15] Henry Tudor's status at this stage was rather unclear. He had been deprived of the honour of Richmond in August 1462.[16] Yet he remained earl of Richmond by right title (neither he nor his father had been attainted) and was referred to as such by Herbert, Stafford and Margaret herself. In the longer term Edward IV may well have planned some sort of territorial restitution for Henry. It is most unlikely that he would have intended the wardship of a deprived heir for his loyal supporter Lord Herbert otherwise. Similarly Herbert, intensely ambitious, would hardly have planned a prospectless match for one of his own daughters.[17]

Margaret and her husband resided principally at Bourne (Lincs.) and after 1467 at the palace of Woking in Surrey.[18] The countess retained a keen interest in her son, visiting him at Raglan and sending him frequent messages.[19] Henry's custodian continued to rise in royal favour, being created earl of Pembroke by Edward IV in 1468. However disaster was to overtake the Herbert family. In July 1469 Pembroke was captured and executed after the battle of Edgecote. His brothers Richard and Thomas were also killed, leaving the earl's fourteen-year-old son as heir to his estates. The countess of Pembroke's position was highly vulnerable, and she prudently transferred Henry Tudor to the residence of her brother Lord Ferrers at Weobley in Herefordshire.[20] Margaret and her husband Stafford had been following events closely, sending messengers to London at the end of July to find out the latest news of the earl of Pembroke.[21] The new situation offered them a chance to renegotiate the wardship of Henry. Given the unsettled condition of the marches eight trusted household men were despatched to Weobley to meet with the countess of Pembroke.[22] Servants were hurriedly sent off to search the chancery records in London. By October 1469 a meeting of the legal councils of both sides had been arranged to find an 'accommodation' over the terms of the wardship.[23] Henry's welfare at Weobley was not forgotten. Payments were made by Margeret to servants waiting on him and money was deliverd for his 'disportes', to 'bie him bowe and shaftes'.[24] Some sort of interim compromise may have been reached over the matter, but legal proceedings were to continue into the following year. Certainly there is no evidence in the Stafford household accounts that custody of Henry was regained by the couple before the Readeption.[25]

If Margaret's concern for the fortunes of her son was significant, so too were her good relations with Edward IV. Edward had treated the countess remarkably well. Although he had regranted the honour of Richmond, Margaret's own dower rights were safeguarded, as were her rights to the substantial Beaufort estates she had inherited from her father. Both these interests were protected from parliamentary acts of resumption. [26] Stafford and Margaret enjoyed fairly close access to the king. In December 1468 husband and wife took advantage of the proximity of Edward to invite him to their hunting lodge at Brookwood. A banquet was served with wild fowl, oysters, eel, tench and pike; Margaret wore fine new velvet for the occasion.[27]

Lady Margeret's position under Edward's first period of rule had been remarkably favourable, but the confused politics at the time of the Readeption government offered even greater gains. There is no reason to doubt Polydore Vergil's account of how Jasper Tudor, on his return from exile, released his nephew from the custody of Herbert's widow and took him to London. The records of the Stafford household books show Jasper, restored to his title of earl of Pembroke, and 'lord Richemond' present in the capital on 28 October 1470. The presence of the king's chamberlain Sir Richard Tunstall at the banquet arranged by Stafford supports Polydore's story of a meeting between Henry VI, Jasper and Henry Tudor.[28] This was the first lengthy reunion between Margaret and her son since the early years of his childhood. On 30 October she and Henry rode from London to Woking, where they stayed for over a week. Henry then accompanied Margaret and Stafford to Maidenhead and Henley before parting from them on 12 November.[29]

Henry's freedom may have been secured but there remained the matter of the restoration of his rights to the honour of Richmond. At the beginning of October Lady Margaret had paid a number of visits to Clarence, who held the estates, at his house in London. She and her husband were in regular contact with the duke over the next few months. While the new Lancastrian regime was being consolidated these discussions seem to have led to a compromise agreement over the Richmond lands.[30] The politics of this period reveal Margaret as active and opportunist. She maintained close contacts with her cousin, Edmund duke of Somerset, one of the chief members of the Lancastrian party. The countess visited him on his return from exile in October 1470; they met again at Woking after Somerset's embassy to the Burgundians at the beginning of March 1471.[31] With Edward marching on London, Somerset tried to recruit Stafford for the Lancastrian cause. The duke and his retinue rode over to Woking on 26 March and a flurry of discussions took place during the next few days.[32] However, Stafford did not commit himself, and as Somerset moved west to join the forces of Queen Margaret, he and his wife rode to London to welcome the arrival of Edward IV in the city. Henry Stafford fought for Edward at Barnet; Lady Margaret remained in London until the return of the king's army after Tewkesbury.[33]

The defeat of the Lancastrians on 4 May 1471 left Pembroke and his nephew, in south Wales at the time of the battle, little choice but to flee abroad. According to Bernard André, such a course of action was urged on Pembroke by Margaret Beaufort, in a conversation between the two some time after Tewkesbury.[34] Doubts have been raised about the authenticity of this episode and the clear evidence of Margaret's whereabouts at this time shows it to be entirely imaginary.[35] The decision was almost certainly taken on the initiative of Jasper himself, who had been attainted in 1461 and had little hope of a restoration of lands or influence under Edward IV. The countess of Richmond, prophesying the dire consequences of her son falling into Edward's hands, is given an additional role in André's narrative. Later in the reign, she secretly warns Henry against accepting Edward's offer of a marriage to one of his daughters if he were to return to England.[36] This reference is important as it reinforces the image of Margaret as a determined opponent of the Yorkists. However, its authenticity is again highly questionable and the evidence that does survive suggests a totally different picture.

The period following Edward's restoration saw Margaret strengthening her contacts with the Yorkist regime. Her husband, Sir Henry Stafford, had died on 4 October 1471.[37] His will, drawn up two days earlier, contained gifts to his stepson Henry earl of Richmond (now exiled in Brittany) and to his receiver-general Reginald Bray. He was particularly generous towards his wife, the sole executor, who was to receive his Berkshire manors and all the lands settled on the couple by the duke of Buckingham in 1460. These stipulations were to be the cause of considerable legal difficulties; the will was contested and not proved until 4 May 1482.[38] Margaret herself had remarried within a year of Stafford's death and her new choice of husband was particularly significant. Thomas Lord Stanley was a wealthy magnate with substantial estates in Lancashire and Cheshire. More important he enjoyed the close favour of Edward IV as one of the king's inner councillors and steward of his household. The marriage took place early in June 1472[39] and was marked by an important marriage settlement. Its provisions included Stanley conveying land worth 500 marks a year (including his lordship of Hawarden in Flintshire) in trust for the use of the countess during her life and Margaret assigning to her husband for life the majority of her own estates (valued at 800 marks a year).[40] It was a careful agreement, of mutual benefit, that represented a powerful alliance of interests and it was with Stanley's assistance that some of the properties contested in Stafford's will were finally recovered.[41] It also symbolised Margaret's acceptance of the Yorkist dynasty and the need to have influence in the court and council of Edward IV.

It was during the next few years that Margaret was to give an indication of the religious enthusiasm that was to become so marked in her later life. In March 1477 the papal *nuntio* in England granted her an indulgence for her contributions to the wars against the Turks. The next year Margaret and her husband were granted the right of participation in the spiritual benefits of the order of the Carthusians.[42] But her main concern was the position of her exiled son.

In her first will of 2 June 1472, Margaret had made special arrangements for Henry. Her substantial west country estates, which had been conveyed to trustees, were to revert to him alone on her death.[43] This enfeoffment was accepted by her husband, Lord Stanley, and remained separate from the assignment of properties made in their own marriage settlement. Significantly, these proceedings were aided by the approval and active co-operation of Edward IV himself, who had given the countess licence to grant the lands on 22 May 1472, and confirmed her right of title to one of her Devon manors, Sampford Peverell.[44]

On the death of the duchess of Somerset another important disposal of property was made. In an indenture of 3 June 1482, sealed in the presence of the king, Margaret and Stanley confirmed the putting into effect of the marriage settlement and the conveyance of the west country estates. Then a highly significant clause outlined the agreement over apportioning the lands of Margaret's mother. If Henry returned to England, to be admitted to 'the grace and favour of the kynges highnesse', he was to receive the larger share of these lands. His part of the inheritance was to be worth around 600 marks a year. However, if Henry did not return the properties were to be divided equally between the countess and her husband.[45] Edward IV, at the special request of both parties, witnessed the arrangements, and added his own seal to the indenture in confirmation of it. The detail of the document, and the circumstances in which it was signed and sealed, offers clear evidence that

Margaret and Edward IV were working together to secure Henry's return from exile and his reinstatement at the Yorkist court. The provision made for Henry's failure to return indicates the uncertainty felt over his likely reaction to the agreement.

In the light of this important, if inconclusive, indenture, Bernard André's account of Margaret opposing Edward's plan to marry Henry to one of his own daughters seems very unlikely. It is probable that she would have been an active supporter of such a scheme. The chronicler Edward Hall described a chance meeting between the countess and the duke of Buckingham soon after Richard III's accession. Margaret is said to have asked Buckingham to intercede with his master for the return of her son to the English court. She then expressed her wish for a marriage between Henry and one of Edward IV's daughters, adding that if this could be achieved she would ask for no dowry.[46]

Margaret was an astute political observer. With the fortunes of the Yorkist dynasty seemingly secure after 1471, she had worked hard to achieve the best possible settlement for her son. Her prominent role in the coronation ceremony of Richard III comes as no surprise.[47] Richard himself was prepared to advance the interests of the countess and her husband. On 5 July 1483, on the eve of his coronation, he gave his full support to Margaret over the complex ransom dispute with the Orléans family that she had inherited from her mother.[48] If only Richard had enjoyed an untroubled accession, it is likely that she would have tried to continue negotiating conditions for a return of her son to England and royal favour. But as the events of the Readeption had shown, Margaret was also an opportunist. With a serious rebellion flaring up within weeks of Richard's departure from the capital, political conditions were once again highly uncertain.

According to Polydore Vergil, Margaret began plotting with her son after the death of the princes became known and Henry had emerged as a claimant to the throne.[49] However, there is an interesting possibility that the countess was involved in an earlier conspiracy with the Woodvilles to restore Edward V, and that this was to be supported by Henry Tudor. According to the annalist John Stow, there was a widespread plot in London at the end of July 1483, involving former members of Edward IV's household and Woodville supporters, in which it was planned:

> that they should have sent writings into the parts of Britaine to the earls of Richmond and Pembroke, and other lords, and how they were purposed to have set fire to divers parts of London, which fire, whilest men had been staunching, they woulde have stolen out of the Tower, the prince Edward and his brother the Duke of Yorke.[50]

Margaret may have been involved at this early stage of the rebellion. The charges brought against her in the act of attainder refer to frequent communication with Henry in Brittany, and the raising of money for him in

London.[51] Interestingly, her close kinsman, her half-brother John Welles, who resided at the Beaufort stronghold of Maxey in Northamptonshire, was in rebellion against Richard early in August 1483.[52] He subsequently fled to Brittany with Thomas marquis of Dorset and Sir Edward Woodville.

Once it was generally believed that the princes were dead, Margaret took a major role in the conspiracy. According to Polydore Vergil, communication between her and Buckingham was carried out by her steward Reginald Bray. This was very plausible because Bray, as receiver-general of Sir Henry Stafford, had paid frequent visits to the Buckingham household. But his part in the proceedings was not serious enough to prevent him from being granted a general pardon in January 1484.[53] The most interesting element of the plot was the Woodville marriage; originally intended as a means of reconciliation between Henry and the Yorkists, it was now to forward his own ambitions for the throne. The physician Lewis Caerlyon, despatched by Margaret to visit Elizabeth Woodville in sanctuary, was to be employed regularly by Henry after his accession.[54] The countess was also able to send a substantial sum of money to her son to assist his invasion preparations.[55]

The projected rebellion was to fail disastrously. Torrential downpours flooded the Severn and ended any plans Buckingham may have had of joining his supporters in the west country.[56] Instead he turned northward along the Welsh marches, but if he hoped to gain support from the Stanley family, and surviving evidence indicates that he did, he was to receive nothing.[57] Abandoned by his Welsh tenantry, he was finally betrayed by a servant and taken in captivity to Shrewsbury.[58] The Stanleys' refusal to join the revolt was of crucial importance, and was regarded with considerable gratitude by Richard himself.[59] The remainder of the conspirators were forced to flee abroad and Henry had to return to Brittany.

Despite the fact that Thomas Lord Stanley had not committed himself to the rebellion, many contemporaries felt he was implicated to some extent in the treasonable activities of his wife. In the words of Polydore Vergil, 'yt went very hard that Thomas Stanley also was not accowyntyd amongst the number of the kinges enemies, by reason of the practyses of Margaret his wife, mother unto erle Henry, who was commonly caulyd the head of that conspiracy'.[60] Yet Stanley had been examined by the king's council, and his declaration of innocence was not implausible in that he and his wife kept separate households. However, once Richard had decided to favour Thomas with a considerable degree of patronage, in consideration of good services both present and future, he was left with the problem of how to deal with Margaret. His difficulty was how to punish the countess severely without alienating her husband. Two particular factors worked against passing the sentence of attainder on her which would have been the normal course of action in the circumstances. The first was the marriage settlement of 1472, which guaranteed Stanley a substantial yearly income from his wife's estates. The second was the more general consequence of extinguishing all Margaret's legal rights. This would be an affront to Stanley both personally and materially. In particular, it would jeopardise his interest in the large Orléans ransom being claimed by his wife in the *Parlement* of Paris.

Richard's solution was workmanlike. In the parliament of 1484 Margaret was spared attainder, 'remembrying the good and feithfull service that Thomas Lord Stanley hath doon . . . and for his sake'.[61] Yet she was to forfeit her right to all titles and estates. The income in trust that she enjoyed from her husband was declared void, and the enfeoffment of her west country estates, intended for the use of her son, was dissolved. The properties were regranted to Stanley. Her right of inheritance to the lands of her mother was also cancelled, and lands that might have been conserved for Henry were dispersed among others.[63] The main body of her estates, which had been assigned to her husband for life, was to revert to the king on Stanley's death.[63] Finally, Thomas was charged to keep his wife confined in some secret place, without her own servants.

Richard's treatment of Margaret has been described as remarkably lenient.[64] However, if he wished to keep the loyalty of Lord Stanley it was the only reasonable course open to him. It was the fact that Stanley could not be relied on, rather than Richard's failure to imprison Margaret, that was to help cause his downfall. By late 1484 it seems likely that both Margaret and her husband were in secret communication with Henry, and the countess was able to send him substantial sums of money.[65] The Stanleys' ambivalent attitude after Henry Tudor's landing in 1485 was one of the main reasons why Richard lost the throne.

The forfeiture of property that Margaret had suffered under Richard was rapidly reversed by the first parliament of Henry VII's reign. Margaret's marriage settlement with Lord Stanley was confirmed, and in a statute vesting the honour of Richmond in the king, a special clause safeguarded her own rights.[66] In August 1486 she was granted the wardship of the duke of Buckingham's sons and an annual income of £1,000 to be drawn from their estates.[67] It is possible that the king intended this as a reward to his mother for her part in the rebellion of 1483. It is also likely that Henry remembered with gratitude Margaret's endeavours to secure a landed inheritance for him. On 22 March 1487 he made over to her for life a large body of estates, including the whole of the honour of Richmond.[68] This was an arrangement which combined generosity with prudence, since the king was, of course, Margaret's sole heir. Mother and son were to enjoy a relationship of mutual trust typified by Henry's licence that Margaret could recruit and retain servants on the crown's behalf.[69]

Considering Lady Margaret's part in the events of Richard's reign against the wider background presented in this communication, two major points emerge. The first is her extraordinary concern for the interests of her son. The second is her political pragmatism. It was her willingness to work with the Yorkists to achieve favourable conditions for her son's return from exile that provides the real counterpoint to her role in the rebellion of 1483. Tudor commentators like Bernard André and Polydore Vergil were anxious to underplay this. As the dynastic position of Henry after Tewkesbury, and as sole Lancastrian claimant after 1475, was significant they preferred to give a partisan role to Margaret. Yet Henry himself did not regard his Beaufort lineage, through his mother, as sufficient to advance his claim to the throne. It was the proposed Woodville marriage and the political turbulence of Richard's reign that really strengthened his position. If Margaret's considerable efforts to support her son's bid for the throne were typical of her remarkable determination, so too were her earlier attempts to secure his return to favour at the Yorkist court.

I am grateful to Professor Ralph Griffiths and Dr. Rosemary Horrox for their comments on an earlier draft of this paper.

Notes

1. Margaret's religious devotion and her daily routine of worship are movingly described by Bishop Fisher in his 'mornynge remembraunce': *The English Works of John Fisher*, ed. J. Mayor, EETS, vol. 27 (1876), pp. 293–6. Her educational patronage has recently been surveyed in an important article: M. Underwood, 'The Lady Margaret and her Cambridge connections', *The Sixteenth Century Journal*, vol. 13 (1982), pp. 67–81.
2. M. Condon, 'Ruling Elites in the reign of Henry VII', in *Patronage, Pedigree and Power in Later Medieval England*, ed. C.D. Ross (Gloucester, 1979), p. 114.
3. *The Works of John Fisher*, pp. 291, 296.
4. C.H. Cooper, *The Lady Margaret* (Cambridge, 1874), p. 2, suggested the alternative date of 31 May 1441. However the case for the later date is supported by the negotiations between John duke of Somerset, king and council, before his expedition to France in 1443. The wardship of an expected child was to be retained by Somerset's wife if he himself perished: *Proceedings and Ordinances of the Privy Council of England*, ed. N.H. Nicolas (7 vols, Record Commission, 1834–7), vol. 5, pp. 252, 255–6. Indeed the likely date for John's marriage to Margaret Beauchamp of Bletsoe is July 1442: *Calendar of Papal Registers*, vol. 9, p. 368.
5. R.A. Griffiths, *The Reign of King Henry VI* (1981), pp. 535, 679. The actual marriage seems to have taken place early in February 1450 (*ibid.*, p. 705).
6. *Ibid.*, p. 841. Fisher gives a remarkable description of Margaret's confused memory of the incident, a choice between two suitors, John de la Pole and Edmund Tudor, decided in favour of Edmund (*Works*, pp. 292–3). In Margaret's earliest will of 1472 Edmund was clearly referred to as her first husband: St. John's College Cambridge (henceforth SJC) Archives, D56/195.
7. Griffiths, *Henry VI*, pp. 802–3. Edmund Tudor had died on 1 November 1456. For the dynastic context see *ibid.*, p. 698.

8. Cited in Cooper, *The Lady Margaret*, p. 67.

9. SJC Archives, D56/195. Edmund's remains were transferred at the Reformation to St David's Cathedral.

10. Margaret's vow of celibacy made to Fisher on the death of her third husband in 1504 was the renewal of an earlier vow made during Stanley's lifetime: *Works*, p. 294.

11. The statement from a nineteenth century source (cited by Cooper, *The Lady Margaret*, p. 18) that the marriage of Stanley and Margaret was only allowed by Edward IV on the condition it was never to be consummated is not supported by any contemporary evidence. However, the terms of their marriage settlement make no provision for any future children. Margaret's lack of offspring from her marriages with Stafford and Stanley was commented on by Polydore Vergil: *Three Books of Polydore Vergil's English History*, ed. H. Ellis, Camden Society, vol. 29 (1844), p. 135.

12. Griffiths, *Henry VI*, p. 841.

13. C.L. Scofield, *The Life and Reign of Edward IV* (2 vols, 1923), vol. 1, p. 203.

14. *CPR, 1461–7*, p. 117.

15. D.H. Thomas 'The Herberts of Raglan as supporters of the House of York in the second half of the fifteenth century' (unpublished University of Wales MA thesis, 1968), pp. 55–8, 71–2, 289.

16. *CPR, 1461–67*, p. 197.

17. For Herbert's exploitation of wardship and marriage to further his family's position see M.A. Hicks, *False, Fleeting, Perjur'd Clarence* (Gloucester, 1980), pp. 38–9.

18. The transfer of the household from Bourne to Woking after the death of Eleanor duchess of Somerset is recorded in Westminster Abbey Muniments (henceforth WAM), 12181, ff. 52–4.

19. For a visit paid to Henry in September 1467 see WAM, 12185 (12), ff. 39–42v. The itinerary is printed in E.M. Routh, *Lady Margaret* (1924), p. 27. References to communication between Lady Margaret and her son occur in WAM, 5472, ff. 8v, 41v.

20. The countess of Pembroke and Henry Tudor had moved to Weobley by early August 1469: WAM, 5472, f. 41v.

21. *Ibid.*

22. *Ibid.*, f. 42v.

23. *Ibid.*, ff. 44, 46v; Hicks, *Clarence*, pp. 56–7.

24. WAM, 5472, ff. 43, 44v, 47.

25. An extract from the receiver–general's account of Reginald Bray indicates that the terms of wardship were being discussed in October 1469 (WAM, 5472, f. 47; Hicks, *Clarence*, p. 57). However the matter of custody had not been settled. Lady Margaret was still paying lawyers' fees in London for the 'lord of Richemond's matter' in January 1470 (WAM, 5472, f. 57v). There is no evidence of a reunion between Henry and Margaret before the end of October 1470 (WAM, 12190, ff. 39 et seq.); on the contrary, documentary evidence clearly supports Polydore Vergil's statement that Henry was still in the countess of

Pembroke's custody when Jasper Tudor was restored to his earldom, see n. 28 below.

26. Scofield, *Edward IV*, vol. 1, p. 203.
27. WAM,, 5472, ff. 22, 22v.
28. WAM, 12183, f. 19v.; *Polydore Vergil*, pp. 134–5; Hicks, *Clarence*, p. 97. A petition to Henry VII by the Lancastrian Sir Richard Corbet refers to Henry's release from Herbert custody, in that 'after the death of the Lord Herbert after the field of Banbury, hee was one of them that brought your grace out of the danger of your enemyes, and conveyed your grace unto your town of Hereford, and there delivered you in safety to your great uncle now Duke of Bedford': H. Owen and J.B. Blakeway, *A History of Shrewsbury* (2 vols, 1825), vol. 1, p. 248.
29. WAM, 12183, ff. 19–23; 12190, ff. 39–41v. Henry was to rejoin his uncle Jasper Tudor, and both travelled to south Wales towards the end of November 1470 (Scofield, *Edward IV*, vol. 1, p. 544).
30. WAM, 12183, ff. 14v–15, 25, 27v, 32v. Clarence was regranted the honour, but only for life, on 24 February 1471 (Hicks, *Clarence*, pp. 97–99).
31. WAM, 12183, f. 18; 12189, f. 58; 12190, f. 71v.
32. WAM, 12183, f. 39v; 12190, ff. 77v–79v.
33. WAM, 12183, ff. 50 et seq.; 12190, ff. 79v–80, ff. 83v–90v.
34. *Memorials of King Henry VII*, ed. J. Gairdner (Rolls Series, 1858), pp. 15–16.
35. S.B. Chrimes, *Henry VII* (1972), p. 17, n.2; WAM, 12190, ff. 83v, 90v et seq.
36. *Memorials of Henry VII*, p. 23.
37. Public Record Office, C140/36/6.
38. PRO, PCC/PROB 11/7/5. The long delay before the will was proved has led to uncertainty over the dating of Stafford's death, especially as W. Dugdale, *The Baronage of England* (2 vols, 1675), vol. 1, p. 167, mistakenly gave the date of the will as 2 October 1481, instead of 2 Oct. 1471. 400 marks worth of land had been settled on the couple by the terms of the duke of Buckingham's will, 10 July 1460: C. Rawcliffe, *The Staffords, Earls of Stafford and Dukes of Buckingham 1394–1521* (Cambridge, 1978), p. 21, n.45.
39. The marriage had taken place between the drawing up of Lady Margaret's will on 2 June 1472 and the arrangements for the marriage settlement of 12 June (SJC Archives, D56/195, 200).
40. The transfer of property (partially referred to in SJC Archives, D56/157, 189, 200) was protected against parliamentary resumption in 1473: *Rotuli Parliamentorum*, ed. J. Strachey (7 vols, 1783–1832), vol. 6, p. 77.
41. WAM, 28195; PRO, CP25 (I)/294/77.
42. SJC Archives, D56/6, 185. Margaret's wish to support a crusade against the Turks was recalled by Fisher: *Works*, p. 308.
43. SJC Archives, D56/195.
44. *CPR, 1467–76*, pp. 339, 343. Edward IV's licence allowed the properties to be granted out to the trustees on 26 May 1472 (SJC Archives, D56/205).
45. SJC Archives, D56/158. According to the *inquisition post mortem* Margaret duchess of Somerset did not die until 8 August 1482 (PRO, C140/82/7) but this date is inaccurate. The duchess of Somerset's death had been announced in the

Parlement suit between her and the Orléans family on 3 June 1482 (Archives Nationales, X^la4823, f. 212). Lady Margaret had received writs of sequestration by 16 September (SJC Archives, D56/202).

46. E. Hall, *Chronicle containing the history of England during the reign of Henry IV to the end of the reign of Henry VIII*, ed. H. Ellis (1809), pp. 388–389. This account is very important. According to Hall Margaret proposed the Woodville marriage to aid the chances of Richard accepting the return of Henry Tudor. The arrangement of the marriage would be entirely in the king's hands, 'without any thing to be taken or demaunded for the same espousals but only the kynges favour'. But according to *Polydore Vergil*, p. 195, Margaret only decided on the Woodville marriage after the death of the princes made her son a claimant to the throne.

47. *The Coronation of Richard III. The Extant Documents*, ed. Anne F. Sutton and P.W. Hammond (Gloucester, 1983), pp. 167, 169, 278–81.

48. Margaret had taken over the claim from her mother in January 1483 (Archives Nationales, X^la1490, f. 225). On 5 July, in the royal palace of Westminster, Richard had given Margaret and Stanley the full support of his own chief justice Sir William Hussey: WAM, 12320.

49. *Polydore Vergil*, p. 195.

50. J. Stow, *The Annales or General Chronicle of England* (1615), p. 460. Dr. Rosemary Horrox has kindly drawn my attention to this reference.

51. *RP*, VI, p. 250.

52. *British Library Harleian MS. 433*, ed. Rosemary Horrox and P.W. Hammond (Upminster/London, 4 vols, 1979–83), p. 7. For his flight from England see *Polydore Vergil*, p. 200.

53. *CPR, 1476–85*, p. 411. For Bray's earlier links, as Stafford's receiver-general, with the Buckingham household, see Hicks, *Clarence*, p. 57.

54. C.H. Talbot and E.A. Hammond, *The Medical Practitioners in Medieval England* (London, 1965), p. 203. After the failure of his invasion attempt Henry solemnly proclaimed his intention to marry Elizabeth Woodville once he had been made king of England: B.A. Pocquet du Haut-Jussé, *François II duc de Bretagne et l'Angleterre (1458–88)* (Paris, 1929), p. 252.

55. *Polydore Vergil*, 197. For Henry's invasion preparations see Haut-Jussé, *op. cit.*, pp. 249–51.

56. The floods are described in *Adam's Chronicle of Bristol* (Bristol, 1910), p. 74.

57. *Plumpton Correspondence*, ed. T. Stapleton, Camden Society (1839), pp. 44–5; Owen and Blakeway, *History of Shrewsbury*, vol. 1, p. 241.

58. Owen and Blakeway, *op. cit.*, p. 240.

59. Buckingham's lordship of Kimbolton was granted to Thomas Lords Stanley on 2 November 1483 (the date of Buckingham's execution). For a full list of the lands granted to Stanley over the next year see B. Coward, *The Stanleys, Lords Stanley and Earls of Derby, 1385–1672, the origins, wealth and power of a land owning family* (Manchester, 1983), p. 12.

60. *Polydore Vergil*, p. 204.

61. *Rot. Parl.*, vol. 6, p. 250.

62. *CPR, 1476–85*, pp. 472, 479, 532; *Harleian 433*, vol. 1, pp. 203, 271.

63. Large parts of the estates were immediately granted out in reversion: *CPR, 1476–85*, pp. 389, 423–8, 501: *Harleian 433*, vol. 1, p. 173, p. 186.
64. For early criticisms of Richard's leniency towards Margaret see *The History of King Richard III*, ed. A.N. Kincaid (Gloucester, 1979), cv, on the views of Cornwallis and Buck. For a more recent comment on the same theme see S.B. Chrimes, *Henry VII*, p. 28.
65. *Polydore Vergil*, pp. 215–16.
66. *Rot. Parl.*, vol. 6, pp. 272, 284.
67. SJC Archives, D15/54.
68. Cooper, *Lady Margaret*, pp. 35–6.
69. M. Underwood, *op. cit.* (note 1), p. 67.

RICHARD III AND THE YORKSHIRE GENTRY c. 1471–1485*

Keith Dockray

The Tudor chronicler Edward Hall believed that Richard III 'more loved, more esteemed and regarded the Northernmen than any subjects within his realm'; moreover, he concluded, northerners in turn 'entirely loved and highly favoured him'. The more nearly contemporary second Croyland continuator, likewise, was of the firm opinion that Richard gave his greatest confidence to, and placed the greatest reliance on, men from the north of England. Recently, historians too have been more and more inclined to emphasise the importance of Richard's northern background and connections. Charles Ross, for instance, strongly committed himself to the view that:

> Richard III is unique among medieval English kings in the extent of his connections with the north of England. By 1483 he had come to know the region and its people more thoroughly than any of his predecessors. He is also exceptional in the degree to which his power base was very largely north-country.

A.J. Pollard has vigorously argued that Richard's reputation for tyranny, already to be found in the powerful anti-northern sentiments permeating the Croyland Chronicle, largely derived from the 'colonization' of southern England by northerners following Buckingham's rebellion in October 1483. Jeremy Potter has assured us, in splendidly colourful language, that:

> To the southerner England north of the Humber was, like Scotland, a barbarous region inhabited by savage brutes, the Ostrogoths of Britain, who represented an ever-present threat to the lives and livelihoods of the prosperous and civilised south.

Desmond Seward has even gone so far as to describe Richard III's northern household knights and squires as a veritable 'mafia' of alien toughies who, not surprisingly, soon came to be both feared and hated in southern England.[1]

In a very real sense, it seems to me, Richard III's roots *did* lie in the north rather than the south of England, and in Yorkshire in particular; and, after he became King, it is probably true to say that his greatest support stemmed from the nobility and gentry of that county. Richard first took up residence in Yorkshire, it seems, late in 1465 when, at the age of some thirteen years, he was placed in the custody of Warwick the Kingmaker. For the next three years or so he remained in Warwick's household, and it was presumably during this time that he acquired the fondness for Yorkshire and its inhabitants which he was to retain for the rest of his life.

Initially, Yorkshire must have seemed a strange, even frightening, environment, and certainly not one in which a member of the Yorkist house could feel immediately at home. Not that the county had any real unity in the fifteenth century: rather it was a land of contrasts, most notably between the extensive areas of bleak upland in the north and west on the one hand, and lowland areas of the Vale of York and East Riding on the other. The community of Richmondshire, revolving around the Neville lords of Middleham and so comprehensively analysed by A.J. Pollard[2], probably had relatively little in common with the wild, economically backward and chronically lawless Craven area (until recently dominated by the Clifford family from their formidable castle at Skipton); similarly, the inhabitants of Cleveland can have felt at best a distant affinity with their fellow Yorkshiremen in Holderness or the lordship of Wakefield. Neverthless, all had more in common with each other than with the men of the midlands and the south; many lived in the shadow of one or other of the great castles and fortified houses which littered the landscape; and, as Charles Ross emphasised, northern society in general was 'tightly clannish, independent and resentful of outside control'.[3]

In the 1450s two great aristocratic families – the Percies and the Nevilles – had dominated much of Yorkshire, and their rivalry had been of crucial importance in explaining the onset of the Wars of the Roses. In 1461, however, the power of the Percies had been temporarily eclipsed, and, when young Richard of Gloucester entered Richard Neville Earl of Warwick's household in 1465, he gained as his mentor a man who had now become by far the most powerful aristocrat north of Trent. Most of Gloucester's time was probably spent either at Sheriff Hutton (Warwick's castle situated a few miles to the north of the city of York) or at Middleham (in Wensleydale, in the heart of the North Riding). There he must first have made the acquaintance of many of the lesser noblemen, knights and squires who were to serve him in the 1470s and early 1480s, men like John Lord Scrope of Bolton, Sir John Conyers of Hornby and Thomas Metcalfe of Nappa (all seated in Richmondshire).

Warwick the Kingmaker, however, became increasingly discontented with his lot in the later 1460s, and, in 1469, he moved into open rebellion against Edward IV (although, by that time, Gloucester had left his household).

Edward IV seems to have had precious little backing in Yorkshire: not only was there powerful pro-Neville sentiment in the county (which Warwick could clearly draw upon), but also there remained a considerable fund of sympathy for the Lancastrian cause as well. Percy sentiment remained strong, too, particularly in the East Riding, and this may help explain the King's decision to restore Henry Percy to the Earldom of Northumberland in March 1470. Nevertheless, following Warwick's unholy alliance with Margaret of Anjou in the summer of 1470, Edward was temporarily deprived of his throne and the hapless Henry VI restored (at least in name) to his regal dignity. Returning to England in March 1471, Edward, probably against his better judgment, put ashore at Ravenspur in Holderness. If he expected a rush of men to join him, unlikely as that is, he was sadly disappointed: instead, the local countryside showed itself notably unenthusiastic, even hostile, and the King may well have owed his survival at this time to the Earl of Northumberland's success in preventing his gentry and tenants following their natural inclinations and forcibly opposing him. Even in south Yorkshire, there seems to have been a distinct lack of support for Edward, despite the fact that the lordship of Wakefield had long been in Yorkist hands. Seemingly, only the arrival of news of the King's victory at Tewkesbury prevented a pro-Lancastrian rebellion taking off in the north early in May 1471. Clearly, however, with both Henry VI and his son Prince Edward now dead, the cause of Lancaster no longer seemed viable; also dead, of course, were Warwick the Kingmaker and his brother John Marquis Montagu, and Edward IV must needs address himself to filling the power-vacuum which now prevailed in Yorkshire.[4]

Richard of Gloucester, notably loyal to his brother throughout the crisis of 1469–1471, could reasonably expect generous treatment and major responsibility (even though he was still only eighteen years of age): he was, moreover, well fitted to assume Warwick's mantle in northern England, and it was clearly essential that Yorkist rule now be made a reality in Yorkshire in particular. Despite the opposition of his brother George Duke of Clarence, Gloucester both married Warwick's daughter Anne Neville and returned to the north as virtual heir to the Kingmaker's power and influence (most especially in Yorkshire). Only Henry Percy Earl of Northumberland had anything like comparable stature in Yorkshire, and even then only in the East Riding: moreover, it is clear that, even before he was appointed King's Lieutenant in the North in 1482, it was Gloucester who had *final* authority overall.[5]

Desmond Seward has recently suggested that:

> No great Northern lord can have liked having a Royal Duke, and an unusually formidable one, on his doorstep . . . Even minor gentry must have been unsettled by so brutal a transference of loyalties as that which took place after the Yorkist triumph [in 1471] . . . It is logical to suspect that conservative Northern magnates were only too anxious to be rid of this meddlesome

interloper, but because of the fear he inspired they hid their resentment under a mask of friendship and cooperation. The fact that he trusted them until the very last indicates a serious inability to judge his fellow men.

Seward is nothing if not ingenious, but his strictures on Richard as 'a self-made imitation Northerner (who) must have had irritating Southern ways' can safely be relegated to the realm of anti-Ricardian fantasy.[6] The bulk of the evidence not only points to the fact that Richard of Gloucester became Warwick the Kingmaker's political heir in the north but that he *did* come to enjoy genuine popularity and inspire deep loyalty from its people, especially the many Yorkshire knights, squires and gentlemen who entered his service during the 1470s. As A.J. Pollard, in writing of the Middleham connection, has concluded:

> . . . there is no reason to doubt that his attachment to the lordship [or Middleham] was genuine or that he revealed . . . an almost charismatic quality of leadership. [Richard of Gloucester] was able through his council to bring a degree of harmony and unity to Yorkshire society which had been noticeably lacking in the preceding decades.[7]

Certainly, in my view, Richard's success in winning, and retaining, gentry support in Yorkshire was indeed impressive.

Not surprisingly, Richard of Gloucester's connection included some men who might be dubbed traditional Yorkist supporters, men whose prime loyalty was probably to the house of York rather than Richard of Gloucester personally, whose fathers or grandfathers (or they themselves) had served Richard of York in the 1440s and 1450s, passed into the service of Edward IV after 1461, and, in 1483, were willing to support his brother as their King as well. Two West Riding families are particularly worthy of mention: the Fitzwilliams of Wadworth and the Savilles of Thornhill.

The Fitzwilliams of Wadworth, near Doncaster, had had close connections with the house of York ever since the family's foundation at the beginning of the fifteenth century. Edmund Fitzwilliam, its founder, became steward of the Yorkshire estates of Edmund of Langley Duke of York in 1401, and constable of Conisborough castle in 1410, retaining both offices until his death in 1430.[8] Both his son Edmund Fitzwilliam (died 1465) and grandson Sir Richard Fitzwilliam (died 1479) served Richard of York and Edward IV: in November 1460, for instance, Richard of York granted for life 'to his servant Richard Fitzwilliam Esquire, for his good service to himself and his son Edward Earl of March, a yearly rent of 20 marks', a grant confirmed by Edward IV in July 1461; also in July 1461, Edmund Fitzwilliam was appointed constable of Tickhill castle for life, an office which he held jointly with his son Richard from March 1463, and which Richard continued to hold after his father's death; the constableship of Conisborough castle was likewise held by both men, jointly from March 1465 (by which time Richard was being described as 'King's servant' and his father as 'Esquire of the King's Household'); while Sir Richard Fitzwilliam served, too, as sheriff of Yorkshire in 1465/6 and sheriff of Lincolnshire in 1468/9.[9] In the 1470s Sir Richard's son Thomas Fitzwilliam (1448–1497/8) continued the tradition of service and loyalty to the Yorkists established by his predecessors: in March 1473 he was made joint-constable of Tickhill with his father, retaining the office after Sir Richard's death, and as the 'King's servant', became parker of the King's park of Conisborough in 1481; also, as well as serving on various commissions, he, in company with many other Yorkshire gentlemen, served Richard of Gloucester in Scotland in 1482 (where he received his knighthood).[10]

The Savilles of Thornhill near Sandal castle had an equally impressive record, and, along with numerous branch families, clearly represented a powerful force in the politics of the West Riding by the later fifteenth century (not least on account of their considerable wealth).[11] As early as 1399 we find Edmund Duke of York granting offices to Sir John Saville; Sir Thomas Saville (1390–1449) likewise served the house of York, as did his son, another Sir John Saville (1415–1482), who was both steward of the lordship of Wakefield and constable of Sandal castle for many years.[12] His grandson, yet another Sir John Saville (died 1505), developed a connection with Richard of Gloucester in the early 1480s (and was probably knighted by him in Scotland in 1482), attended Richard IIIs coronation in 1483, and became one of the Yorkshire knights transplanted to southern England following Buckingham's rebellion (where he was, in fact, appointed captain of the Isle of Wight).[13]

A second, and clearly much more numerous, group of Yorkshire gentry who served Richard III (both as Duke of Gloucester and as King) were former retainers of Richard Neville Earl of Warwick: particularly notable here, as A.J. Pollard has so effectively demonstrated, was the so-called Middleham connection. Of 36 men receiving fees charged upon the lordship of Middleham in 1473/4, no fewer than 22 seem to have been in Warwick's service in 1465/6; many of them, or their fathers, had indeed been retained by Warwick's father Richard Neville Earl of Salisbury in the 1450s.[14] Two Richmondshire families perhaps merit most attention: the Conyers of Hornby and the Metcalfes of Nappa.

The Conyers of Hornby were one of the wealthiest of all non-baronial families in Yorkshire in the later fifteenth century, richer than some lesser baronial houses indeed:[15] Sir William Conyers (1468–1524) was himself raised to the peerage in fact during the reign of Henry VII.[16] The core of their estates lay in Richmondshire, not many miles from Middleham castle, and the family's record of service and loyalty to the Nevilles in the 1450s and 1460s was impressive indeed. Christopher Conyers, head of the family until his death in 1459 or thereabouts, forged an increasingly close link with Salisbury and Warwick in the 1450s.[17] Sir John Conyers (died 1490), his son and heir, soon became even more deeply involved in Neville politics: as a retainer of Salisbury in the 1450s, he fought for the Yorkists at Blore Heath and

Ludford, and was attainted for his troubles by the Coventry Parliament in November 1459.[18] In the 1460s he became a retainer and loyal adherent of Warwick the Kingmaker and, like his father before him, occupied the office of steward of Middleham.[19] As long as Warwick served Edward IV, so did Conyers: for instance, he was sheriff of Yorkshire in 1467/8.[20] When the breach between Warwick and Edward IV began to open up, however, his main loyalty soon became abundantly clear. In all probability he was 'Robin of Redesdale', leader of a pro-Neville rebellion in the north in the summer of 1469: his son and heir, another John Conyers, lost his life at the ensuing battle of Edgecote. Sir John, for his part, was once more active in stimulating rebellion in Yorkshire on Warwick's behalf in 1470.[21] Infuriatingly, there is no record of his behaviour during the short-lived Readeption of Henry VI, but it certainly did not take him long to throw his weight behind Richard of Gloucester as the new lord of Middleham post-1471: A.J. Pollard has plausibly suggested, indeed, that it may well have been he who played the major role in ensuring a smooth transition of power in Richmondshire from Warwick to Gloucester.[22] Certainly, in 1473, he was on the payroll of Richard of Gloucester at an enhanced fee of £20 per annum, still steward of Richmondshire as well as constable of Middleham castle, and probably a member of Richard's ducal council as well.[23] Sheriff of Yorkshire in 1474/5, and on a range of government commissions thereafter,[24] he seems to have given full backing to Gloucester's seizure of the throne in 1483, attending his coronation and being raised to the prestigious Order of the Garter, as well as receiving a splendidly generous annuity of 200 marks (not to mention the manors of Aldbrough, Catterick and other North Yorkshire estates), as Knight of the Body, 'in remuneration of his labours and expenses on the King's business in England and Scotland'.[25] Several other members of the Conyers family likewise passed from Warwick's service to that of Gloucester in the 1470s: Sir Richard Conyers of South Cowton, Sir John's younger brother, certainly did so; so did William Conyers of Marske, another brother; while a number of other members of what was clearly a large clan similarly found their way on to Gloucester's payroll both as Duke and King.[26]

The Metcalfes of Nappa, a family of hitherto only modest fortunes, clearly owed their rise in the second half of the fifteenth century to their connections first with Warwick and afterwards with Gloucester (and, by the end of the century, they had firmly established themselves as the third most important family in Wensleydale, trailing only the Scrope Lords of Castle Bolton and the Conyers of Hornby). No fewer than nine members of the family seem to have been retained by Warwick in the 1460s, mainly as reeves, parkers and foresters on Neville estates.[27] Thomas Metcalfe Esquire (died c. 1504), probably one of them, certainly entered Gloucester's service in 1471 at a fee of £6.13.4, and he may also have been a member of his ducal council, as well as holding offices within the lordship of Middleham.[28] Following Gloucester's seizure of the throne (in which he, along with other members of his family, seems to have materially aided the Protector), he enjoyed spectacular advancement when he was appointed Chancellor of the Duchy of Lancaster for life (with a substantial salary).[29] Thomas's brother Miles Metcalfe (died 1486), a trained lawyer, was retained as Warwick's Attorney-General in 1465 (at a fee of £6.13.4); he passed into Gloucester's employ in the 1470s (including becoming a member of his council and serving as the Duke's Deputy Steward in the North Parts of the Duchy of Lancaster); and no doubt thanks in part to Gloucester's influence in the city, he was elected Recorder of York in 1477.[30] Then, during Gloucester's Protectorate in 1483, he was appointed Second Justice in the County Palatine of Lancaster and confirmed as Deputy Chief Steward of the Duchy of Lancaster (North); he continued to perform these tasks after Gloucester became king.[31] Other members of the Metcalfe family developed connections with Gloucester as well. Brian Metcalfe, another brother of Thomas and Miles, was retained successively by Warwick and Gloucester, and received an annuity of ten marks per annum (as the 'King's servant)' in December 1484.[32] Even more worthy of note is Thomas Metcalfe's son and heir James Metcalfe Esquire (died 1539) who in July 1483 was granted the office of Coroner of the Marshalsea of the King's Household, as well as receiving rewards in North Yorkshire for his good service in England and Scotland.[33]

Not all former retainers of Warwick who passed into Gloucester's service in the 1470s were Middleham men by origin however, as is nicely illustrated by the West Riding family of Middleton. John Middleton of Stockeld, near Wetherby, both received a bequest in the will of Richard Neville Earl of Salisbury and acted as one of his executors; in 1465/6 he was Treasurer of Warwick's household at Middleham, and in the 1470s he seems to have retained this office under Gloucester.[34] John's brother Richard Middleton, probably a Neville retainer in the 1460s, is certainly known to have been a member of Gloucester's household in the 1470s and a Squire of the Body to Richard III after he became King. Another brother Thomas Middleton, a lawyer, enjoyed similar connections.[35]

A third, albeit relatively small, group of Yorkshire gentry who served Richard III were men whose prime loyalty was probably to the Percy Earls of Northumberland. Sir Hugh Hastings (1440–88), of Fenwick in the West Riding, for instance, seems to have been a notable disturber of the peace in the 1460s (perhaps as a result of his pro-Percy sympathies).[36] In the 1470s, however, he developed a connection with Richard of Gloucester, sat as M.P. for Yorkshire 1472–5, served as sheriff of his county 1479/80, and was in Gloucester's retinue during the Scottish campaign of 1482.[37] In the autumn of 1483, moreover, he seems to have aided Richard III in suppressing Buckingham's rebellion, served on government commissions thereafter, and received, by way of reward, both appointment as Knight of the Body and confiscated Stafford estates in Norfolk worth in excess of £78 per annum.[38] Sir William Gascoigne (c. 1450–87), of Gawthorpe near Harewood, another West Riding knight, married a daughter of the third Percy Earl of Northumberland and in the 1470s was the fourth Earl's deputy as steward, constable, and master forester of Knaresborough. Nevertheless, he seems to have been in Richard of Gloucester's retinue in Scotland in 1482, was a Knight of Richard III's Body, as well as receiving an annuity of £20 from him, and served on various government commissions both before and during his reign.[39] Mention should also be made in this context of the Constables of Flamborough, a wealthy and influential East Riding family, possessed of lands worth more than £300 per annum in 1488. Both Sir Robert Constable (1423–88) and his son Sir Marmaduke (c. 1455–1518) can be shown to have had strong Percy connections, yet the latter at least was to play a prominent role in the service of Richard III, notably in Kent and the Midlands.[40]

Finally, in this section, consideration needs to be given to a fourth group of Yorkshire gentry, men who had no known connections with York, Neville or Percy, yet who became retainers of Gloucester in the 1470s (no doubt attracted, as Charles Ross has suggested, either by the patronage the Duke had at his command or by geographical proximity to his centres of power).[41] Most of these were in fact lesser gentry of no particular significance before they came to Richard of Gloucester's attention. The Markenfields of Markenfield near Ripon were certainly an ancient Yorkshire family, and their hall, built originally in the early fourteenth century, has been described as one of the best surviving examples in Yorkshire of a fortified residence.[42] Yet Thomas Markenfield (died 1497) had no public career before 1471 when he was retained by Gloucester at a fee of £10 per annum. Even in the 1470s, although seemingly a member of Richard's council, he figures but sparsely in the records.[43] Nevertheless, by December 1484, when he was granted a generous annuity of 100 marks from the revenues of Middleham (as the 'King's servant'), he had become a Knight of the Body and begun a term of office as sheriff of Yorkshire; soon afterwards the King granted him lands in Somerset as well, and placed him on the commission of the peace for that county.[44] John Everingham (died 1502), of Birkin in the West Riding, was a very minor figure indeed until he entered Richard of Gloucester's service, perhaps first drawing attention to himself during the 1482 expedition against Scotland: yet, by March 11 1484 he too had become a Knight of the Body and appeared on the commission of the peace for Norfolk; shortly afterwards he was also furnished with an annuity of 100 marks.[45] John Dawney (died 1497) of Cowick in the West Riding, emerged from a similarly deep obscurity to become, under Richard III, Treasurer of both the Prince of Wales' Household and the King's Household in the North Parts, receiving an annuity of £40 payable from the issues of Pontefract. No doubt he was, in fact, a member of the newly created Council of the North, institutionalised under the headship of the Earl of Lincoln following the death of Richard's only son in the spring of 1484.[46]

Recent research has conclusively demonstrated that Richard of Gloucester has indeed built up an impressive and notably loyal affinity among the Yorkshire gentry by the time of his brother's death in April 1483, and the strength of his northern connection had been amply demonstrated during the

Scottish campaign of 1482.[47] Dominic Mancini came very near the truth of the matter when he remarked that, in the last years of Edward IV, Richard of Gloucester:

> . . . kept himself within his own lands (in the North) and set out to acquire the loyalty of his people through favours and justice. The good reputation of his private life and public activities powerfully attracted the esteem of strangers. Such was his renown in warfare, that whenever a difficult and dangerous policy had to be undertaken, it would be entrusted to his discretion and his general-ship. By these arts Richard acquired the favours of the people . . .[48]

Not surprisingly therefore, when Richard went south in 1483, and, after a few insecure weeks as Protector, made his bid for the throne, it was to the north in general (and Yorkshire in particular) that he especially looked for support. Northern knights and gentry were certainly present in very consider-able numbers at the King's coronation on July 6, including Yorkshire knights – like Sir John Conyers, Sir John Saville and Sir James Strangeways – who were in the very top bracket of Yorkshire gentry society.[49]

Initially, although his personal preference was clearly for northerners (hence the number who rapidly appeared in the royal household as Knights and Squires of the Body),[50] Richard III probably had no intention of inaugurating a full-scale colonisation of southern England from the north. Buckingham's rebellion in the autumn of 1483 (involving as it did men from most of the southern counties) changed all that, for in the wake of it, the King now seems to have concluded that the only way of making his rule effective in areas which had risen against him was by advancing his loyal northerners to all manner of lucrative and key positions in southern administration in defence (as well as distributing a great deal of confiscated land among them). The Croyland continuator's lament on this is, of course, only too well known, yet it is still worth quoting once more. Commenting on the large number of men who were attainted and had their lands confiscated by parliament in January 1484 as a consequence of the rebellion (103 altogether), he declared:

> What immense estates and patrimonies were collected into this king's treasury in consequence of this measure! All of which he distributed among his northern adherents, whom he planted in every spot throughout his dominions, to the disgrace and lasting and loudly expressed sorrow of all the people in the south, who daily longed more and more for the hoped-for return of their ancient rulers, rather than the present tyranny of these people.[51]

A.J. Pollard has demonstrated in some detail how this veritable colonisa-tion of south-eastern, central-southern and south-western counties was carried out.[52] Moreover, Pollard has particularly (and rightly) stressed the advancement in these shires of Yorkshire knights and squires, many of whom had never held office south of Trent before. Indeed, even before parliament met, the process had begun: in Kent, for instance, William Mauleverer, a member of the minor Yorkshire gentry family hailing from Allerton Mauleverer in the West Riding, was appointed echeator in November 1483, while at about the same time Edward Redman of Harewood became sheriff of Somerset and Dorset.[53] During the next few months Yorkshiremen (and other northerners) began to appear as sheriffs, constables of castles, justices of the peace, commissioners of array, stewards of confiscated estates, and so on, right across southern England from Kent to Cornwall.

In south-eastern England, the advancement of Sir Ralph Bigod, Sir Marmaduke Constable, Sir Ralph Ashton and Sir Robert Percy is perhaps particularly worthy of note. Sir Ralph Bigod (1458–1515), of Settrington in the East Riding, developed a connection with Richard of Gloucester towards the end of the 1470s, served as sheriff of Yorkshire in 1481/2, and campaigned under the Duke's banner in Scotland in 1482.[54] Then, in December 1483, he was appointed to the commission of the peace in Kent, and was a commissioner of array there in May 1484, while at the same time retaining office in the East Riding and receiving advancement in the royal household. By March 1484 he had become a Knight of the Body and Master of the Ordinance, and may also have served as carver to Queen Anne. Rewards coming his way certainly included an annuity of £40.[55] Sir Marmaduke Constable of Flamborough, recently castigated by Desmond Seward as both a 'Northern Gauleiter' and a key figure in Richard IIIs northern 'mafia',[56] was despatched to Kent in the immediate aftermath of Buckingham's rebellion, seemingly with a brief to restore law and order there and contain the practice of livery and maintenance. Perhaps it was as a result of his success in Kent that the King, in the spring of 1484, transferred him to the Midlands to perform similar service (notably as steward and constable of Tutbury in Staffordshire). A continuing personal connection with Richard III is suggested by his status as a Knight of the Body and his probable membership of the King's Council,[57] and he certainly received considerable reward in the way of both annuities and estates (including the manor of Market Bosworth in Leicestershire).[58] Sir Ralph Ashton (died c.1489), of Fritton-in-Redesdale, who served as both sheriff and justice of the peace in Yorkshire in the 1470s, campaigned in Scotland in 1482, and attended Richard IIIs coronation,[59] was appointed Vice-Constable of England on October 24 1483 (with a brief 'to proceed against certain persons guilty of lese majesté', i.e. to try treason cases in the aftermath of Buckingham's rebellion).[60] Apparently known as the Black Knight on account of his black armour, he seems to have earned himself an unenviable reputation for severity; legend had it, indeed, that he indulged in such sadistic practices as rolling prisoners downhill in barrels filled with spikes, while a jingle of the time ran:

Sweet Jesu for thy mercy's sake
And for thy bitter Passion,
Save us from the axe of the Tower
And from Sir Ralph of Assheton.[61]

In Kent, he was included on the same commissions as Sir Marmaduke Constable, as well as being appointed (in May 1484) lieutenant to the aged Earl of Arundel as constable of Dover Castle and Warden of the Cinque Ports; he also continued to serve on commissions in the North Riding.[62] As Knight of the Body, in March 1484, he was granted 'a tun of wine yearly during his life', while in May of the same year he received ('for his good service against the rebels') a series of confiscated manors in Kent to the value of some £116.[63] Finally, Sir Robert Percy (who seems to have lost his life at Bosworth), of Scotton near Knaresborough in the West Riding, became Controller of the King's Household, served as sheriff of Essex and Hertford, and was granted the stewardship of the king's manor of Kennington in Surrey.[64]

In central-southern England, Sir Christopher Warde (died 1521), of Givendale near Ripon, another Knight of the Body, was employed on government business in Surrey, Sussex and Southampton, and received an annuity of £24.[65] William Mirfield (died 1520), of Howley in the West Riding, was appointed (as King's Esquire) keeper of the royal castle of Portchester and governor of the town of Portsmouth, in Hampshire, and provided with lands and tenements in the county of Southampton.[66] Even more significant was the advancement of Sir John Saville of Thornhill, particularly his appointment, in February 1484, as lieutenant or captain of the Isle of Wight (with a massive fee of £200 per annum, no doubt reflecting the strategic importance of the office).[67] Clearly, by February 1485, Richard III was anticipating a landing by Henry Tudor since Saville and Mirfield were then bound in the sum of 5000 marks, as a guarantee of their good behaviour and commitment to serve him 'in time of war as of peace' and maintain the integrity of the Isle of Wight.[68]

The south-western counties seem to have been particularly disturbed in the autumn of 1483, and there was to be further trouble there in the summer of 1484. Again Yorkshiremen were prominent among the northern transplants. Edward Redman (c.1455–1510), from far off Harewood in the West Riding, was a lawyer, and it was perhaps in this capacity that he first attracted the attention of Richard III. An Esquire of the Body by December 1484, he served on commissions to arrest and imprison rebels in Devon and Cornwall in November 1483, and as a justice of oyer and terminer in Devon in July 1484; he was appointed to the commission of the peace in Wiltshire in December 1483, and was a commissioner of array there in May 1484; he held office as sheriff of Somerset and Dorset in 1483/4, and was a commissioner of array in the latter county in December 1484; also in December 1484, he received lands in Somerset and Wiltshire worth some £84 per annum.[69] Sir Thomas Markenfield too was active on commissions in the south-west, this time in Somerset.[70]

There were Yorkshire gentry prominent in Richard III's service outside the southern counties as well, notably in the midlands. Sir Thomas Wortley (died 1514), of Wortley in the West Riding, for instance, had been in the government's service in the 1470s, particularly in a military capacity: he had both served in France during the great expedition there in 1475 and campaigned in Scotland with Gloucester in 1482 (where he had received his knighthood).[71] Present at Richard III's coronation in July 1483 and a Knight of the Body by December 1483, he was employed for most of the time in the midlands, notably as sheriff of Staffordshire in 1483/4 (during which time, in December 1483, he received orders to take oaths of allegiance from the inhabitants and forbid the wearing of liveries), as a commissioner of array in Staffordshire and Derbyshire, and as a justice of the peace in Derbyshire.[72] Several stewardships also came his way: in March 1484 for instance, he was granted the office of steward of the lordship of Scarsdale and the town of Chesterfield, in Derbyshire; and in the same month he was made constable of the castle of Stafford, and steward of all lordships and lands formerly belonging to Henry Duke of Buckingham in Staffordshire, with fees of £100 per annum.[73] When the danger from Henry Tudor Earl of Richmond seemed to be becoming ever more threatening, the King appointed him (in May 1485) lieutenant of Hammes castle for seven years.[74] Sir Marmaduke Constable, too, was active in the midlands, in Leicestershire, Derbyshire and Staffordshire, from March 1484,[55] as was Sir Robert Harrington (another knight with strong Yorkshire connections).[76]

Clearly, Richard III did introduce Yorkshire knights, squires and gentry into the administration of midland and southern shires on a very considerable scale, as well as employing them extensively in his own household. Many who were not so used, moreover, continued to be employed in their native county, often with enhanced rewards: Sir Thomas Fitzwilliam of Wadworth, for instance, and Sir John Conyers of Hornby.[77] Richard III's preference for northerners is not difficult to understand, of course, given his background and the mistrust he must have felt towards southern gentry in the wake of Buckingham's rebellion. Not that he was solely dependent on northern support, or unique in deploying men from the north in administrative and military tasks south of Trent: Henry Bolingbroke in 1399, for instance, drew heavily on the northern estates of the Duchy of Lancaster and enjoyed powerful backing from great northern lords such as the Earls of Westmorland and Northumberland,[58] while Henry Vs expeditionary forces to France benefited greatly from the presence of many northern men.[79] Nevertheless, what Richard III was doing was unprecedented in the fifteenth century: neither Edward IV before him, nor Henry VII after 1485, whatever the provocation (and both experienced considerable opposition in the north in the early years of their reigns), ever went so far as to introduce southern gentry into the administration of Yorkshire as a deliberate and sustained act of policy.[80] Richard III did not of course replace in their entirety the 'natural rulers' of the southern shires, but he certainly went further than was prudent (whatever the extent of southern disaffection in the autumn of 1483). To appoint Yorkshiremen to offices in Lancashire or Durham was not unusual, nor to provide Nottinghamshire men with administrative positions in Derbyshire: county boundaries were never regarded with that degree of rigidity. However, to place Yorkshiremen, often with no previous experience of local government outside the north, in key administrative posts in southern England was novel to say the least. And the wisdom of such action must be seriously questioned even if, as Rosemary Horrox has suggested, Richard may not have intended it to be permanent.[81] Richard III's northerners were intruders into southern society, and were much resented as such, as the Croyland continuator rightly perceived. Indeed, it could well be that the King's preference for such men, both in his household and in his administration, together with the very generous rewards which he often gave them, meant more to the knights and squires of the southern shires than any shock or dismay they may have felt when they heard rumours that Richard had murdered his nephews in the Tower of London.[82]

Bosworth provides the final proof both of Richard III's continuing reliance on northerners in August 1485 and the depth of southern resentment against him, at any rate if we can accept the testimony of the Ballad of Bosworth Field. As Colin Richmond has recently pointed out, doubts still persist as to the Ballad's admissibility as a source;[83] if we can rely upon it, however, the extent of Richard's dependence on his northern connection right to the end is striking indeed. Not a single man from counties south of Thames and the Bristol Channel is mentioned by name as fighting for the king at Bosworth, but northerners are very well represented (despite the speed with which many of them needed to travel in order to make it to the battlefield at all), including prominent Yorkshire knights such as Sir Marmaduke Constable, Sir Ralph Ashton, Sir Henry Percy, Sir John Melton, Sir Robert Ryder, Sir Brian Stapleton and Sir Robert Harrington.[84] No doubt self-interest brought many of them to Leicestershire (just as it ensured that almost all passed into Henry VII's service in the years following Richard's unlucky defeat in the battle), but genuine loyalty to, and even affection towards, the King must have had a place in at least some of their hearts as well.[85]

Notes

*   This paper is based, in part, on an unpublished survey of Yorkshire Knights and Squires in the service of Richard III, originally delivered to a Research Seminar at the University of Bristol in 1969.

1.   *Edward Hall's Chronicle*, ed. H. Ellis (1809), pp. 426, 442–3; *Ingulph's Chronicle of the Abbey of Croyland*, trans. H.T. Riley (1854), p. 499; Charles Ross, *Richard III* (London 1981), p. 44; A.J. Pollard, 'The Tyranny of Richard III', *Journal of Medieval History*, vol. 3 (1977), pp. 147–64; Jeremy Potter, *Good*

King Richard? (London 1983), p. 46; Desmond Seward, *Richard III: England's Black Legend* (London 1983), p. 117.

2. A.J. Pollard, 'The Richmondshire Community of Gentry during the Wars of the Roses', *Patronage, Pedigree and Power in Later Medieval England*, ed. Charles Ross (London 1979), pp. 37–59, and *The Middleham Connection: Richard III and Richmondshire 1471–1485* (Middleham 1983).

3. Ross, *Richard III*, p. 8

4. K.R. Dockray, 'The Yorkshire Rebellions of 1469', *The Ricardian*, vol. 6 no. 83 (December 1983), pp. 246–57; Charles Ross, *Edward IV* (London 1974), especially chapter 7.

5. *CPR 1467–77*, pp. 260, 266, 338, 408, 483, 549, *1476–85*, pp. 90, 123, 205, and other references; Indenture between Richard Duke of Gloucester and the Earl of Northumberland 1474, *England under the Yorkists*, ed. I.D. Thornley (London 1920), pp. 146–8; Ross, *Edward IV*, pp. 199–202; Pollard, *Middleham Connection*, pp. 1–4; M.A. Hicks, 'The Warwick Inheritance – Springboard to the Throne', *The Ricardian*, vol. 6 no. 81 (June 1983), pp. 177–80.

6. Seward, *op. cit.*, pp. 74–5.

7. Pollard, *Middleham Connection*, p. 20.

8. *CPR 1413–16*, p. 377.

9. *CPR 1461–7*, p. 46; R. Somerville, *History of the Duchy of Lancaster*, 1 (London 1953), p. 529; *CPR 1461–7*, p. 479; *CFR 1461–71*, pp. 191 221. Edmund Fitzwilliam also served as a commissioner of array and J.P. in the West Riding, as did his son: *CPR 1461–7*, p. 577, *1467–77*, pp. 199, 349, 638, *1476–85*, p. 580. In January 1470, as King's knight and late sheriff of Lincoln, Richard Fitzwilliam was pardoned by Edward IV for having 'lost a great part of the profits of his office through the insurrection of divers lieges of the King in the said county of Lincoln' and 'because of his great expense in attending on the King's person with 100 persons, of all offences committed by him and all debts, views of accounts, fines and sums of money due to the King': *CPR 1467–77*, p. 185.

10. Somerville, *op. cit.*, p. 529; *CPR 1476–85*, pp. 269, 112, 214, 580; W.A. Shaw, *The Knights of England*, vol. 2 (1906), p. 20. The fact that the Fitzwilliam family was high in Yorkist favour is perhaps shown too by Thomas Fitzwilliam's marriage to Lucy Neville, daughter of Warwick the Kingmaker's brother John, whom Edward IV created Earl of Northumberland in 1464.

11. Branches of the family in existence by the end of the fifteenth century included the Savilles of Copley, Hullenedge, New Hall (Elland), Lupset and Wakefield. At his death in 1505 Sir John Saville held estates in Yorkshire valued at some £172.13.4, and, judging by the contents of his will, he must have been worth a good deal more than the inquisition post mortem suggests: *Calendar of Inquisitions Post Mortem, Henry VII*, vol. 2 (1898), no. 803.

12. *CPR 1405–8*, p. 15, for appointment of Sir John Saville as Master Forester of Sowerbyshire by Edmund of Langley. Sir Thomas Saville also held this office, and was an Esquire of Edward Duke of York by May 1414, as well as appearing on various commissions in Yorkshire. Sir John Saville (died 1482) was Master Forester of Sowerbyshire by the 1450s, and seemingly was steward of Wakefield

from 1442 until his death. Richard of York's influence can probably be detected as well behind Sir John's election as M.P. for Yorkshire in 1450/1, and his appointment as sheriff of Yorkshire in November 1454; he continued active in the 1460s and 1470s, as sheriff of Yorkshire again in 1461 and M.P. in 1467/8, as well as appearing on a variety of commissions: A Gooder, *The Parliamentary Representation of the County of York 1283–1832*, Yorkshire Archaeological Society Record Series (1935), vol. 1, no. 151; *CFR 1452–61*, p. 101, *1461–71*, p. 10; *CPR 1452–61*, pp. 220, 651, *1461–7*, pp. 66, 466, 577, *1467–77*, pp. 199, 261, 310, 349, 408, 638, *1476–85*, p. 193.

13. Shaw, *op. cit.*, vol. 2, p. 20; Anne F. Sutton and P.W. Hammond, *The Coronation of Richard III*, (Gloucester 1983) p. 391–2; *British Library Harleian Manuscript 433*, ed. Rosemary Horrox and P.W. Hammond, vol. 1 (Upminster 1979), p. 113.

14. Pollard, *Middleham Connection*, and 'The Northern Retainers of Richard Nevill Earl of Salisbury', *Northern History*, vol. 11 (1976), Appendix, pp. 67–8; G.M. Coles, 'The Lordship of Middleham, Especially in Yorkist and Early Tudor Times' (unpublished Liverpool M.A. thesis, 1961), Appendix B.

15. Some indication of the extent of the family's landed wealth is provided by inquisitions post mortem held following the death of Sir John Conyers in 1490, in Yorkshire, Middlesex, Northumberland, Lincolnshire and Nottinghamshire. Sir John's greatest holdings were in Yorkshire and Lincolnshire but unfortunately the Yorkshire return is partially illegible. Even so, despite excluding valuations for such important manors as Hornby, West and East Brompton (in Yorkshire), and Kirkby in Ashfield (in Nottinghamshire), the total value comes to over £112: *CIPM, Henry VII*, vol. 1, nos. 637 (Middlesex), 638 (Northumberland), 639 (Lincolnshire), 675 (Yorkshire), 111, no. 1172 (Nottinghamshire). The true figure must have been at least double this.

16. Conyers had certainly become a baron by February 1505: *CPR 1494–1509*, p. 420.

17. Pollard, 'Northern Retainers of Salisbury', pp. 54, 68, for evidence of Conyers as a retainer of Salisbury in the 1450s, and also steward of Middleham and other lordships in Richmondshire.

18. *Ibid.*, p. 67; *Rotuli Parliamentorum*, vol. 5 (1439–1468), pp. 348a, 348b, 349a. The fact that he was primarily a Neville man in the 1450s is shown by his involvement, as a Neville partisan, in the Percy/Neville feuding of 1453: *Proceedings and Ordinances of the Privy Council of England*, ed. N.H. Nicolas (1834–7), vol. 6, pp. 149–50.

19. PRO, SC6/1085/20. Conyers' fee was £13.6.8 per annum.

20. *CFR 1461–71*, pp. 210, 222. As Neville partisans, both he and his son John (died 1469) figure on a number of government commissions: *CPR 1461–7*, pp. 30, 66, 102, 233, 450, 530, 576, *1467–77*, p. 637; *Rotuli Scotiae*, ed. D. Macpherson et al (1814–19), vol. 2, p. 420b.

21. Dockray, *loc. cit.*, pp. 253–5.

22. Pollard, 'Richmondshire Gentry', p. 53, *Middleham Connection*, p. 5.

23. PRO, DL29/648/10485.

24. *CFR 1471–85*, pp. 84, 102; *CPR 1467–77*, pp. 349, 353, 408, 637, *1476–85*, pp. 49, 213, 579; T. Rymer, *Foedera, Conventiones, Literae . . . et Acta Publica* (1704–35), vol. 5, iii, pp. 18, 29, 33, 105.
25. Sutton and Hammond, *op. cit.*, p. 325; W. Dugdale, *The Baronage of England* (1675), vol. 2, p. 291; *Harleian MS 433*, vol. 1, pp. 253, 92; *CPR 1476–85*, p. 450.
26. PRO, SC6/1085/20, DL29/648/10485; *CPR 1476–85*, p. 439; Coles, *op. cit.*, pp. 117, 132–3, 308, 310, Appendix B; Pollard, 'Richmondshire Gentry', pp. 53–4, 56.
27. Pollard, *Middleham Connection*, pp. 5–6.
28. Coles, *op. cit.*, pp. 308, 310, Appendix B.
29. *Harleian MS 433*, vol. 2 (Upminster 1980), pp. 27, 68–9; Somerville, *op. cit.*, p. 258. Metcalfe certainly received substantial rewards from the King, including the manor of Wimington in Northamptonshire (valued at £66.13.4) and, jointly with the King's Secretary John Kendal, an annuity of 500 marks per annum: *Harleian MS 433*, vol. 1, pp. 158–9, 11, p. 117. He also figures on commissions in the North Riding, and is numbered among envoys to treat with the Scots in April 1485: *CPR 1476–85*, pp. 401, 492, 579; *Calendar of Documents relating to Scotland*, ed. J. Bain (1888), vol. 4, p. 310. For James Metcalfe's help to Gloucester in 1483, see *CPR 1476–85*, p. 456.
30. PRO, SC6/1085/20; Coles, *op. cit.*, pp. 308, 309, 310; Somerville, *op. cit.*, p. 426; *York Civic Records*, vol. 1, ed. A. Raine, Yorkshire Archaeological Society Record Series (1939), p. 19. Metcalfe sat as one of the M.P.s for York in the 1478 parliament, as well as appearing on a range of commissions 1472–83: *York Records: Extracts from the Municipal Records of the City of York*, ed. R. Davies (1843), pp. 65–6; *CPR 1467–77*, pp. 572, 637, *1476–85*, pp. 51, 112, 343, 345, 579. As Recorder of York, he figures frequently in the York records, and was again elected M.P. for the city in December 1482: Davies, *op. cit.*, pp. 59–61; *York Civic Records*, vol. 1, pp. 27, 32, 46, 67.
31. Somerville, *op. cit.*, p. 473; *Harleian MS 433*, vol. 1, pp. 60, 71. On the occasion of Richard III's first visit to York as King, he agreed to contribute £100 towards a present, as well as continuing active in the service of York and on government commissions: *York Civic Records*, vol. 1, pp. 79–80, 87, 102, 110, 116; Davies, *op. cit.*, pp. 168, 189, 206–7; *Harleian MS 433*, vol. 2, p. 147; *CPR 1476–85*, pp. 394, 401, 425, 492, 579.
32. PRO, SC6/1085/20, DL29/648/10485; *CPR 1476–85*, p. 517.
33. *Ibid.*, pp. 363, 456.
34. *Testamenta Eboracensia*, vol. 2, Surtees Society, vol. 30 (1855), p. 246; Coles, *op. cit.*, pp. 289, 290. Perhaps he was also the Sir John Middleton who attended Richard III's coronation (although this is more likely to have been Sir John Middleton of Belsay, Northumberland): Sutton and Hammond, *op. cit.*, p. 373.
35. *Testamenta Eboracensia*, vol. 3, Surtees Society, vol. 45 (1864), p. 344; *Harleian MS 433*, vol. 1, p. 92, 11, p. 93; PRO, SC6/1085/20; Coles, *op. cit.*, p. 104.
36. *CCR 1461–8*, pp. 379–80, 451; *CPR 1467–77*, p. 131; John Leland, *Collectanea* (1774), vol. 4, p. 186.

37. Gooder, *op. cit.*, no. 156; *CFR 1471–85*, pp. 178, 207; Shaw, *op. cit.*, vol. 2, p. 17. Hastings also appeared on various commissions 1471–83: *CPR 1467–77*, pp. 349, 378, 408, 638, *1476–85*, p. 580.

38. *Ibid.*, pp. 394, 397, 425, 442, 490, 543, 567; *Harleian MS 433*, vol. 1, p. 184, 11, pp. 116, 159; Rymer, *Foedera*, vol. 5, iii, p. 153.

39. Somerville, *op. cit.*, pp. 524–5; Shaw, *op. cit.*, vol. 2, p. 17; DL29/482/7778 (for which reference I thank Dr. Rosemary Horrox); *Harleian MS 433*, 1, p. 200; *CPR 1467–77*, pp. 199, 638, *1476–85*, pp. 214, 345, 399, 492, 580.

40. K.R. Dockray, 'Sir Marmaduke Constable of Flamborough', *The Ricardian*, vol. 5, no. 71 (December 1980), pp. 262–7.

41. Ross, *Richard III*, p. 52.

42. N. Pevsner, *The Buildings of England: Yorkshire, the West Riding*, p. 359.

43. PRO, DL29/648/10485; Coles, *op. cit.*, p. 308; *CPR 1476–85*, pp. 214, 345.

44. *Ibid.*, pp. 470, 572; *CFR 1471–85*, p. 301; PRO, E404/78/3/13; *Harleian MS 433*, vol. 1, pp. 235, 134–5, 137, 111, p. 140.

45. Shaw, *op. cit.*, 11, p. 18; *Harleian MS 433*, vol. 2, p. 115, 1, p. 174; *CPR 1476–85*, pp. 397, 567.

46. *Harleian MS 433*, vol. 1, pp. xxviii, 276, 11, pp. 153, 212–3, 111, pp. 115–6 (where he is described as 'our beloved servant John Dawney, Esquire, Treasurer of our household at Sandal'); *CPR 1476–85*, pp. 393, 399, 492, 579, 580 (for evidence of Dawney's appearance on commissions in Yorkshire under Richard III).

47. Yorkshire gentry were certainly prominent among those men created bannerets and knights by Gloucester in Scotland in 1482, including William Gascoigne, Edmund Hastings, James Danby, Hugh Hastings, William Redman, Brian Stapleton, William Eure, Christopher Warde, John Everingham, John Aske, Thomas Gower, John Saville, Ralph Bigod, John Constable of Holderness, Thomas Fitzwilliam, Thomas Wortley and Richard Conyers of Cowton: Shaw, *op. cit.*, vol. 2, pp. 17–8, 20.

48. *Dominic Mancini's Usurpation of Richard III*, trans. C.A.J. Armstrong (Oxford 1969), pp. 63, 65.

49. Sutton and Hammond, *op. cit.*, pp. 325, 391–2, 401–2. Others said to have been there included Sir Thomas Wortley, Sir Ralph Ashton, Sir Henry Percy and Sir John Constable.

50. As Charles Ross has pointed out, of 32 men described as Knights of the Body in Patent Rolls of the reign, no fewer than 15 came from the northern counties of Yorkshire, Lancashire, Cumberland and Westmorland, as did 13 of 34 Squires of the Body; of 7 vacancies which occurred in the prestigious Order of the Garter during Richard's reign, 5 or 6 of them were filled by northerners; also, both as Protector and King, Richard was very much inclined to employ northerners for tasks of political delicacy: Ross, *Richard III*, pp. 56–7.

51. *Croyland Chronicle*, p. 496.

52. Pollard, 'Tyranny of Richard III', pp. 157–62.

53. Ross, *Richard III*, p. 120.

54. *CFR 1471–85*, pp. 222, 245; Shaw, *op. cit.*, vol. 2, p. 20.

55. *CPR 1476–85*, pp. 387, 393, 398, 399, 492, 563, 579; *Harleian MS 433*, vol. 1, pp. xxviii, 102, 288; R.M. Warnicke, 'Sir Ralph Bigod: A Loyal Servant to King Richard III', *The Ricardian*, vol. 6 (1984), pp. 299–303.
56. Seward, *op. cit.*, p. 148.
57. *Bishop Percy's Folio Manuscript*, ed. J.W. Hales and F.J. Furnivall, vol. 3 (1868), Ballad of Bosworth Field, p. 246, where Constable's presence at Bosworth (as a noble knight, of King Richard's Council) is noted.
58. Dockray, 'Sir Marmaduke Constable', pp. 263–4.
59. *PRO Lists and Indexes,* IX, where he is shown to have been sheriff of Yorkshire for two consecutive years 1471/2 and 1472/3; *CPR 1467–77*, p. 637, *1476–85*, p. 579; W.C. Metcalfe, *A Book of Knights Banneret, Knights of the Bath and Knights Bachelor* (1885), p. 7; Sutton and Hammond, *op. cit.*, p. 304–5.
60. *CPR 1476–85*, p. 368.
61. Seward, *op. cit.*, pp. 141–2.
62. *CPR 1476–85*, pp. 392, 394, 397, 398, 401, 425, 490, 492, 552, 563, 579; *Harleian MS 433*, vol. 2, p. 77.
63. *CPR 1476–85,* pp. 380, 445. Ashton also had an annuity of £20: *Harleian MS 433*, vol. 1, p. 100.
64. *Ibid.*, vol. 1, pp. 180, 251, 111, p. 154. Sir Robert Percy was also granted manors and lands in Cambridgeshire and, together with his son and two others, an annuity of £35: *Ibid.*, vol. 1, pp. 133–4.
65. *CPR 1476–85*, pp. 397, 399, 489, 491, 572, 574; *Harleian MS 433*, vol. 1, p. 147, vol. 4 (1983), p. 210. Warde was also granted manors in Sussex and Essex to the value of £30, appointed steward of various manors in Surrey, lieutenant of the forest of Wolmer and master of Herthounds: *Ibid.*, pp. 153, 127, 152–3, 149.
66. *CPR 1476–85,* p. 425; *Harleian MS 433*, vol. 1, pp. 113, 176.
67. *CPR 1476–85*, p. 410; *Harleian MS 433*, vol. 1, p. 113. Saville also served as a commissioner of array and justice of the peace in the county of Southampton, and received manors and lands in Hampshire, Wiltshire and Devon: *CPR 1476–85*, pp. 399, 572; *Harleian MS 433*, vol. 3 (1982), p. 155.
68. *CCR 1476–85,* p. 419.
69. *CPR 1476–85*, pp. 371, 399, 488, 493, 501, 577; *PRO, Lists and Indexes IX*, p. 124; *Harleian MS 433*, vol. 1, p. 236, 111, p. 142.
70. *CPR 1476–85*, pp. 398, 572. Markenfield was also granted manors and lands in Somerset worth some £100 per annum: *Harleian MS 433*, vol. 1, pp. 134–5.
71. PRO, E101/72/2/1035; Shaw, *op. cit.*, 11, p. 20.
72. Sutton and Hammond, *op. cit.*, p. 413–4; *Harleian MS 433*, vol. 1, p. 96, 11, p. 44; *CPR 1476–85*, pp. 400–1, 577; *PRO, Lists and Indexes IX*, p. 128. Also, in December 1483, he was a commissioner to enquire concerning treasons, insurrections, rebellions etc. in Nottinghamshire and Derbyshire, and, in March 1484, was granted manors, lands etc. in Staffordshire and Kent (for his 'good service against the rebels') worth in excess of £80: *CPR 1476–85*, pp. 393, 415; *Harleian MS 433*, vol. 1, p. 161.

73. *CPR 1476–85*, pp. 436, 437; *Harleian MS 433*, vol. 2, p. 41, 1, p. 162.
74. *Ibid.*, vol. 1, p. 282.
75. Dockray, 'Sir Marmaduke Constable', p. 264.
76. Sir Robert Harrington (died 1487), of Badsworth in the West Riding, had been both a retainer of Warwick in the 1460s and a member of Gloucester's council in the 1470s; he took part in both the 1475 expedition to France and the 1482 campaign in Scotland; in Richard III's reign, he was both a commissioner of array in Leicestershire and a justice of the peace there, steward and keeper of two parks in Loughborough (with an annual fee of £20), and in receipt of an annuity of £63.6.8; and he ended up fighting for the King at Bosworth and being attainted for his trouble by Henry VII: Coles, *op. cit.*, pp. 277, 308; PRO, E101/72/1/1010; Shaw, *op. cit.*, vol. 2, p. 18; *CPR 1476–85*, pp. 400, 489, 564; *Harleian MS 433*, vol. 1, pp. 77, 168–9; *Rotuli Parliamentorum*, vol. 6, p. 276a.
77. Sir Thomas Fitzwilliam continued in office as constable of Tickhill, served as a justice of the peace and commissioner of array in the West Riding, and was granted, *inter alia*, the manor of Kenwick in Norfolk: Somerville, *op. cit.*, p. 529; *CPR 1476–85* pp. 580, 399, 492; *Harleian MS 433*, vol. 3, p. 201, 1, p. 198. Sir John Conyers, as well as being made a Knight of the Garter, provided with an annuity of 200 marks per annum and granted the manors of Aldbrough, Catterick *et al*, served as a justice of the peace in the North Riding throughout the reign, on commissions to enquire into treasons, insurrections etc. in Yorkshire (in December 1483 and February 1484) and of array in the North Riding (May and December 1484), and on the Scottish border: Dugdale, *op. cit.*, vol. 2, p. 291; *Harleian MS 433*, vol. 1, pp. 92, 253; *CPR 1476–85*, pp. 393, 401, 425, 450, 579; Rymer, *op. cit.*, vol. 5, iii, p. 152.
78. Ross, *Richard III*, p. 44, n. 1.
79. C. Allmand, *Lancastrian Normandy 1415–50* (1983), pp. 247–8, stresses the support Henry V's expeditions to France received from Lancashire. Dr. Michael Jones has pointed out to me that Cheshire, too, provided important military support for both Richard II and Henry V, and that from at least the later fourteenth-century English Kings may well have viewed the north as a reliable pool from which fighting men could be drawn. This is not to argue, however, that Richard II, Henry IV and Henry V introduced northerners into central government in anything like the same way as Richard III.
80. Edward IV did deliberately build up a relatively few members of the baronage in particular areas, notably Humphrey Lord Stafford in the south-west, William Lord Herbert in Wales, William Lord Hastings in the midlands, and, after 1471, his own brother in the north; Henry VII, too, experimented in the north, following the murder of Henry Percy Earl of Northumberland in 1489, by appointing Thomas Howard Earl of Surrey as northern supremo. Neither King, however, attempted any significant sub-baronial colonisation by outsiders.
81. *Harleian MS 433*, vol. 1, Introduction, p. xxvi.
82. Opposition to Richard III had of course surfaced in the Buckingham rebellion before the 'invasion' of northerners, and may indeed have caused it.

83. C. Richmond, 'After McFarlane', *History*, vol. 68 no. 222 (February 1983), pp. 55–6, and see his paper in this collection.

84. Ballad of Bosworth Field, *loc. cit.*, pp. 233–58. Northern barons present at the battle included Lords Dacre (said to have 'raised all the North country'), Fitzhugh and Scrope of Bolton, as well as knights from northern counties other than Yorkshire and a considerable number of men from Nottinghamshire (where Richard III started his campaign). Also present, perhaps, were Sir Thomas Markenfield, Sir Christopher Warde, Sir Robert Plumpton, Sir William Gascoigne, Sir Richard Tempest and Sir Martin of the Sea (all Yorkshire knights): W. Hutton, *The Battle of Bosworth Field* (1813), pp. 208–111.

85. For the behaviour of Richard III's northern connection during the early years of Henry VII, see my paper on 'The Political Legacy of Richard III in Northern England' (forthcoming).

'A CURIOUS SEARCHER FOR OUR WEAL PUBLIC': RICHARD III, PIETY, CHIVALRY AND THE CONCEPT OF THE 'GOOD PRINCE'.

Anne F. Sutton

'. . . the some of all my labours hath restyd in this, to be a curyous sercher for our weal publyque, merry at home, laborious outward, besy to atteyne scyence, pyteous of them which has necessyte, namely to my fader, moder & kynne, welbyloued of my neyghbours, true to my frendes, obeysaunt & devoute in thynges relygious'

So spoke Flamineus, one of the two suitors arguing their merits and nobility before their lady in John Tiptoft's translation of *The Declamation of Noblesse*.[1] Between them, these contestants say much about the ideal conduct expected from the high-minded and the well-born. Tiptoft's translation was published by Caxton in 1481 and became extremely popular. We can be reasonably hopeful, if not certain, that Richard Duke of Gloucester read Tiptoft's vivid and humorous English prose.

There was an alarming plenty of books available to give advice on how the fifteenth-century prince should conduct himself and govern others, both in war and peace.[2] A selection can be made with Richard Duke of Gloucester in mind. It has been asserted recently that he followed bad examples of conduct among his peers[3] so it seems appropriate and necessary to examine the availability of good examples. It is good example, after all, that inspires imitation.

It should be first remembered, however, that Richard had a head start towards a virtuous and commendable life, at least in the minds of his contemporaries and doubtless in his own mind – he was of noble blood, the descendant of kings, saints, holy men and women. It was a generally held belief that nobility was to be equated with virtue, (and it is a fact that the ranks of the better born did produce the most medieval saints). More was expected of the noble because of his advantages of position. Riches, dignities and military training all could be used for evil but they could also dispose a man towards the best of goals. In the public eye, a noble was under pressure to set a good example, avoid shame and the hatred of his subjects. Advice for the noble flooded in from all sides and his very position and wealth were held to be great inducements to use his power positively and with hope – the great medieval virtue of magnanimity, great heartedness. The magnanimous or great hearted man loved to tackle great tasks and endeavoured to improve the world and leave it better than he had found it.[4] To go back to the enthusiastic Flamineus: 'I gaue my sylf hoolly & fully to the weal publyque of this cyty'.[5]

Princes were aware of the obligation of their position and they sought advice almost as assiduously as their clergy and servants offered it to them. History was an obvious source of good example and it was read enthusiastically in the hope of practical benefit – more than half of Edward IV's library was history. Royal children, like the future Edward V, had history on their curriculum in the hope of inculcating positive endeavour.[6] Richard himself owned at least two history books, a French Chronicle and the Story of Thebes.[7] Particular heroes were singled out for emulation such as Alexander or Joshua or any of the Nine Worthies. Alexander was especially praised as a conqueror and for his magnanimity, the indomitable spirit to accomplish his designs, besides liberality, mercy and prowess. He was Charles the Bold's inspiration, and it was not unusual for a prince to adopt such a specific model for his career just as he had his particular saint. Chastellain referred to Charles as a second Hector and 'dernier Alexandre' in the same spirit.[8] Nearer home for Richard there were the English models of Henry V, the victor of Agincourt, or Edward III, 'the house of very polycye and flowre of Inglond'.[9]

More important than the histories and the lives of heroes were the treatises and handbooks specifically designed to advise the prince. They are much underrated sources. One distinct group of such works is known as 'mirrors' of princes – mirrors in which the prince might find his image and understand what he ought to do and ought not to do. Mirrors began to proliferate in the thirteenth century and went through many redactions and editions between then and the sixteenth century. It is necessary to emphasise how seriously they were taken: Jean-Philippe Genet assures us that these tracts 'were appropriate to a system in which everything depends on the just and good . . . will of the ruler.'[10] The ideal was cast in a recognisable form and there was no doubt that the ideal could be achieved, with God's help. Not many princes were without a mirror or a related text: Edward III had one presented to him as soon as he became King, together with the lives of wise and prudent kings. Hoccleve wrote his *Regement of Princes* for Henry V. Several were written for Henry VI. Edward II, Margaret of Anjou, Edward of Lancaster, Edward IV and Edward V owned copies.[11] Certainly they did not always have the desired effect.

Richard appears to have owned the mirror 'masterpiece', a latin text of *De Regimine Principum* by Aegidius Colonna. The copy contains the arms of Richard, Duke of York, his father, and an erased legend calling it the illustrious book of the prince, the Duke of Gloucester. Richard is the Duke of

Gloucester most likely to have had his name erased.[12] This is one of the classic and most popular mirrors, written by a pupil of St. Thomas Aquinas.[13]

As Richard owned his book, Colonna's version of the perfect prince is of considerable importance for an assessment of good influences on Richard's life. Colonna's prince should have all the virtues and be deeply concerned about his realm. He should be prudent, dignified but sympathetic, and above all truthful. He must be energetic and just, tempered with mercy; courageous but not rash; moderate in all things; magnanimous and munificent in his undertakings, and a generous but careful rewarder of the deserving. He must love honour. He must be humble and friendly while commanding respect. He should have an equal as his wife who can share his secrets. Above all he must love the common good and the welfare of the state and not merely his own advancement. He should work to increase the virtue, education and wealth of his subjects, encourage wise men and priests, and choose the best councillors from them for their practical qualities and ability to speak the truth. The king's laws must be made known and observed and not lightly changed. Colonna is particularly notable for his stress on the law, the need for wise counsel, and the importance of towns and townspeople.[14]

Colonna's masterpiece gave Richard the perfect prince in Latin but if he wanted an English text he could turn to the popular *Game of Chess Moralised* by Jacques de Cessoles, translated and printed by Caxton in 1473 and again circa 1483. This text stressed the importance of law, with justices serving as councillors to the prince, the punishment of evil-doers and the value of the common people.[15] Another English text undoubtedly available to Richard was the hugely popular *Secretum Secretorum* (*The Secret of Secrets*), attributed innaccurately, but with great effect, to Aristotle. This was not a mirror proper but had much the same catalogue of advice for princes. There is much on 'largesse', the need to maintain a balance between giving and spending on the one hand and avarice and taxation on the other. The ability to take the wisest course of action will come with the prince's desire for 'good fame', the cultivation of the virtues and the abandonment of all vice. This is the secret of secrets. The prince must be prudent, religious outwardly and inwardly, cunning in the law, virtuous of body. He must help the needy, be merciful, never break faith, promote education and be just, (the God-like attribute of kings), and choose wise councillors.[16]

It is the personal virtue of the prince that is the theme of all these works.[17] He is the model for his subjects:

> 'and lyke as yovr rowme es moste of excellence, . . .
> so ovght yovr lyfe be clennest from offence,
> and shyne en vertve above yovr svbgectes all.'[18]

He answers to God and acknowledges his place beneath God and the law. There was an equal certainty that God would aid the prince in all his righteous courses.[19]

Nor did Richard or his contemporaries have to go out of their way to imbibe this advice as all the histories, lives of heroes and mirrors were a standard part of the education of a noble youth, the royal household itself providing the chief school of 'moral integrity and good manners'.[20]

There was a more entertaining way of acquiring knowledge of the good prince open to the wealthy Duke of Gloucester. The three great English poets of the late fourteeenth century had all written on the subject.[21] Chaucer's *Tale of Melibee* tells of how a prince learns to appreciate the wisest counsel. John Gower's works are loaded with pleas for individual virtue, good government and the correct administration of the law. For Gower, love is the basis of social concord and the true defence of the king, and it is the responsible king who motivates the whole of society.[22] In Gower we find the message of the *Secretum* in an English context. In book seven of the *Confessio Amantis*, one of the most popular books of fifteenth century England, Gower used this source[23] to present a simple five point programme for the good prince: 'Among the vertus on is chief, And that is trouthe . . . no double speche . . . to kepe his tunge and to be trewe'.[24] Secondly largesse, the economics of housekeeping and patronage.[25] Thirdly, the love of justice: 'What is a king in his ligance, Wher that ther is no lawe in londe?' He shall chooses wise judges and know his own laws.[26] Fourthly, pity shall make him gracious and a stranger to cruelty. Pity shall only be measured by the need of just war for defence and not glory. Wisdom shall guide him between the sometimes conflicting, demands of pity and justice. Fifthly, chastity in marriage.[27]

If Gower's argument is simple and in simple language the discussions on government in *The Vision of Piers Plowman* by William Langland are complex, set in an allegorical and mystical framework. I have argued elsewhere that Richard knew *Piers Plowman* well enough to quote from it and christen the castle of Nottingham his 'castle of care'.[28] Langland presents a compelling image of an harmonious society bound together by law, loyalty and love. Law controls man's relationship to man and ensures each receives his due livelihood. Loyalty goes beyond law and is the bond between man and man, responsible neighbourliness, keeping faith and truth. Love transcends both of these to the best of all conditions. The good king is responsible for the maintenance of this harmony under God, with Christ as his ultimate model.

'So comune cleymeth of a kyng thre kynne thynges,
Lawe, loue and leaute, and hym lord antecedent'[29]

Langland's king chooses to fulfill his coronation oath, has Reason and Conscience for his councillors, and throws Meed and Wrong into prison:

'Ich wolle haue leaute for my lawe; let be al ʒoure Ianglyng;
By leel men and lyf-holy, my lawe shal be demyd'[30]

The word 'loyalty' or 'leaute' carries several shades of meaning in *Piers Plowman*. Apart from the obvious meaning of 'faith-keeping' it bears the meanings of 'legality', 'uprightness' and 'obedience to the law'. It has also been convincingly argued by P. M. Kean that it means 'justice', the good life in the fullest sense, the 'virtue entire' of St. Thomas Aquinas. Once the world was governed in accord with this 'justice' or 'leaute' the world would be at peace.[31]

These subtleties are worth bearing in mind when it is remembered that 'loyalty binds me' was Richard III's motto. He would have called it his 'word' or 'reason'. If Richard read *Piers Plowman*, as it seems that he did, then it is interesting to speculate whether the poem's emphasis on the importance of loyalty in the structure of the body politic is of significance. I am not suggesting that 'leaute', in the sense of Aquinas' 'virtue entire' came across to Richard although he may well have had clerics fully able to expound both Langland and Aquinas to him. It is significant enough that loyalty in the sense of keeping faith and truth, was the cement of society in Langland, every man in his place fulfilling his duty and in harmony with his neighbour:

'And lyven as lawe techeth, done lewte to all,
Criste of his curteysie, shal conforte ʒou atte laste'[32]

The message is clear to any reader. To Richard loyalty was the stabilising element in society binding all men and the king. The medieval conviction that duties and obligations were reciprocal was a fundamental one. A man who fails in his loyalty therefore becomes the 'most untrue creature living'.

I must make a brief digression to deal with the doubt cast upon 'loyalty binds me' being Richard's main motto.[33] Most important it exists in Richard's own handwriting bracketed together with his signature on a document dateable to 1483, and in the decoration of his charter to the Waxchandlers of London of 1484. In the copy of the Wycliffe Bible which belonged to him occurs '*a vous me lie*', so close a variant of *loyaulté me lie* as to be certainly an earlier draft. It also exists among the Paston Letters in a hostile comment by Sir George Brown made in 1483 which has not received much attention: '*Loyawte ayme*. Hyt schal newyr cum howte for me'.[34] I do not think that there is much doubt that Richard's usual motto contained the word 'loyalty'. It is also perhaps worth noting that loyalty occurs in the mottoes of two families with which Richard was closely associated: The Parrs of Kendal had *amour avec loyaulté*[35] and Lord Dacre (d. 1525), who as a boy was one of Richard III's henchmen, and was the son of a Parr, used *forte en loiauté*.[36]

I must reiterate that these ideas of the 'good prince' did not exist in a vacuum. Public morality was merely an extension of private morality in the middle ages; the study of politics was the study of morals. The king's will had to be controlled by a desire to serve the good of the community, the 'common weal', and by obedience to the rule of natural law.

With such a flood of prose and verse no prince could avoid knowledge of the ideal. A king of England had the lessons reinforced for him at his coronation with a multitude of symbols and, above all, by his oath. The oath's clauses were ancient and extremely simple: maintain the church, administer justice, uphold the laws of England, and defend your subjects. This was the ideal reduced to its essence. The fifteenth century did not require greater complexity of expression, even a chief justice could say 'Lo! to fight and to judge are the office of a king.'[37] Richard III appears to have been impressed by the oath – it was translated into English for the first time for his coronation and he is known to have referred to its terms at least four times, twice specifically mentioning it by name. The most striking of these references is the long letter summarising the objectives of good government for the benefit of the Earl of Desmond. Richard wants the church to be upheld, his subjects protected, evil-doers punished and the peace kept so that the ruler 'may appere and be named a veray justicer aswele for his propre honnor and wele as for the common wele . . .'[38]

The ideal of a good government was of course a commonplace of most medieval kings' pronouncements. I have found, however, no specific reference to their oaths or a letter comparable to the one for Desmond among the pronouncements of Edward IV (hampered by the lack of convenient, printed collections of documents) or for Henry VII (in contrast extremely well served by Campbell, Pollard, and Hughes and Larkin) and both of them ruled for over twenty years.[39] The emphasis in Richard's pronouncements was, I maintain, personal to him.

Richard was not only subject to the moral instruction directed at princes but also to that directed at all laymen by the church. The Christian religion provided the ultimate guide for behaviour – all Christians had moral obligations, and the anointed king had the greatest:

> So were it good that he ther fore
> First un to rightwisenesse entende,
> Whereof that he hym self amende
> Toward his god and leve vice,
> Which is the chief of his office[40]

Apart from the religious instruction of the child, learning its psalter at the age of five,[41] the church provided constant reminders of the goal of the virtuous and the fate of the profane. This was done above all through sermons, another vastly underrated source. Sermons were the staple, weekly diet of the people and they could be a useful medium of propaganda, as we know from the sermons used to depose Edward V and publicise Richard III's title in London.[42] Sermons by lord chancellors at the opening of parliaments were a particularly appropriate vehicle for moralising on government: in 1461 the text was 'amend your ways and your doings', and in November 1485 Bishop Alcock encouraged Henry VII with the text *'intende, prospere, procede et regna'* and spoke of the two main regal virtues of piety and justice.[43] Predominantly sermons seem to have consisted of general, rather than specific, complaints about the evils of the world and, most relevant to this paper, the abuses by secular and spiritual leaders, the oppression of the poor and the crimes of officials. They urged, above all, that the poor be helped because the poor could not afford the law to protect them against the corrupt official or the harsh landlord to whom they were particularly vulnerable.[44] In their sermons the clergy were exhorting the rich, the 'better sort' of men as they were called, to fulfil the obligations placed on them by their wealth and rule justly.[45]

Richard's record in this area is well known. He actively promoted the court that was to become the Court of Requests where poor men might bring their suits at Westminster.[46] As both duke and king he attempted a benevolent rule in Glamorgan which aimed to assist the tenant and discourage the corrupt official.[47] His position as an absentee landlord in Wales contributed to a failure of his good intentions there, but I am led to suppose from this example and other regulations for the administration of his lands as king, that a similar policy would be found on Richard's other estates and most effectively where he was able to supervise personally. The control of the corrupt official must benefit the poor and friendless more than any other class in society and therefore all Richard's efforts in this direction should be seen as part of his concern for the poor. I will return to the corrupt official later.

The heart of the church's instruction to the laity was its insistence on piety, devotion to God and to the Church. As has been seen the advisors of princes were equally keen on a pious prince. Let us consider the inner life first.

Investigation into late medieval devotion is at an early stage but what is clear from such studies as do exist is that there was plenty of instructional literature available to the pious and literate person who wanted it. The active man was encouraged to sanctify his whole life in the service of God and cultivate an inner life, however little time he had to spare, under the careful supervision of the church. Apart from attendance at liturgical devotions or private recitations of offices he might observe a brief regime of daily devotion personally prescribed for him by a priest, or he might read one of many short tracts, in prose or verse, outlining themes of meditation on the Passion, the Sorrows of Mary, the transitoriness of life, the Virtues or the Paternoster. Certain privileged persons were licensed by their bishops to read the Bible in English or they might read the easier doctrine of Nicholas Love's translation of St. Bonaventura's *Life of Christ*, the popular *Mirror of our Lady* or any of the many lives and revelations of saints, notably St. Catherine of Siena, St. Bridgit of Sweden and Matilda of Hackenborn.[48] It was a very vivid piety with a strong emphasis on the Passion of Christ, acute visualisation of each of the Passion's stages, both in the primer itself (the book of hours) and in many verse renderings. There were specific cults of Christ's Wounds, the Cross and the Sacred Blood, besides the very popular devotion of the *Fifteen Oes* of St. Bridgit on fifteen specific moments of the Passion.[49]

Of Richard's personal piety we have several indications. He possessed religious texts: he owned an English Bible, like most great nobles and kings of the fifteenth century, and several portions of the the Old Testament in verse.[50] He and his wife (like his mother Cecily Neville) owned the book of Matilda of Hackenborn, a mystic of the Sacred Heart 'a beautiful and delicate creation of German mysticism.'[51] He had of course his own book of hours which contained prayers to the Cross, the Five Wounds, and the Fifteen Oes.[52] It also contained a prayer specifically composed for Richard while king, presumably by his confessor, John Roby, doctor of theology, a Franciscan and warden of that Order's house at Nottingham in the 1470s.[53] The prayer asks for help and protection from various ills, each request being linked to a relevant release from ills of saints or prophets.[54] This was an ancient and not uncommon form of prayer, but to acknowledge its derivative nature is not to denigrate the insight it affords into Richard's piety nor its sincerity and passion. Whatever the modern reader may feel it tells us of Richard, passion in religion was part of late fifteenth century piety.

A closely related element in this kind of devotion was the object of piety, such as an image of Christ on the Cross or a relic. There is no inventory of Richard's possessions but it is known he presented York Minster with a jewelled calvary containing relics of St. Peter.[55] He had also paid repect to a relic of St. Thomas Becket, the holy oil which had been given to that saint by the Virgin Mary for the anointing of future English kings. This Richard decreed should be kept in Westminster Abbey with the coronation relics of Edward the Confessor and he had it conveyed there by two bishops. He also made a proviso that he could have the oil back if he needed it, undoubtedly for access to its strength, its association with the saints.[56]

Richard's devotion to other saints can be glimpsed from the dedications at his religious foundations in the 1470s, his personal reason for the choice of each one being fairly easy to evaluate. Apart from the subsidiary saints referred to in the Middleham statutes, there are eight main saints for the three foundations of Queens' College, Middleham and Barnard Castle, with Christ and the Virgin Mary.[57] Of these St. George, St. Anthony and St. Ninian occur at Middleham and Queens'. St. George was an obvious choice for a prince of the house of York which developed his cult; he was patron saint of soldiers, the personification of chivalry and associated with the crusading ideal. St. Ninian (also to be found at the Barnard Castle foundation) was the apostle of the Picts and had a popular shrine at Whithorn in the Western March of which Richard was Warden. Again an obvious choice, and Richard had Ninian's collect specially added to his book of hours.[58] St. Anthony had lived in the desert 'twenty-four years and more without any company but the wild boar', the only beast that refused to threaten him at the order of the demons. The boar's ability to reject evil for good is an important characteristic for the animal supporting Richard's arms! Anthony was a healer of men and animals and his legend was painted on the stalls of Carlisle Cathedral during Richard's time in the north.[59] The history of St. Cuthbert adorns these stalls too, another of Richard's chosen patrons for Middleham College. Cuthbert was again an obvious choice because of his association with

Durham and the eastern march. Banners of his arms and of St. George decorated the ceremony of the investiture of Richard's son as prince of Wales.[60] Both St. Barbara and St. Katherine, the remaining Middleham saints, and St. Margaret at Barnard Castle were popular virgin martyrs. Barbara was patron of gunners and those in danger of sudden death and Katherine the patron of all ranks of scholars and learning. St. Margaret, the odd one out, was a patron of childbirth and persons dedicating churches to her had large assurances of a heavenly crown.[61]

Now to pass to the outward show of piety. Princes needed to give to the church in order to display their worldly position, to thank God for that position which He had given them, as Richard specifically says in his Middleham statutes. This both supported the church and set a good example to their subjects.[62] There were also profound religious reasons for giving, every individual's need of prayers to help him through this life and, above all, through purgatory in the next. It was an explicit obligation to provide such prayers for one's family too, in particular parents and blood relatives. The idea was that prayer for the living and the dead should be constant, the church being one unit composed of both the living and the dead.[63] The desire for such intercessionary prayers was the underlying reason for all foundations, usually more important than any educational or charitable consideration. All Richard's foundations fall into this category. Such chantry foundations, of whatever size, were also, it must not be forgotten, of considerable benefit to their locality. Working parishioners had greater opportunity to attend mass, an over-pressed priest of a large parish would be helped by the additional chaplain, and the laity benefited in general from a greater number of educated men among them.[64] This may well have been the case at Barnard Castle and was certainly so at Middleham where it was specifically planned that the College should take over the financial upkeep of the parish church from the parishioners.[65] The north and north–west of England were especially devoted to chantry foundations, perhaps because of their isolation and economic poverty, and one may justifiably wonder if these considerations reinforced Richard's inclination towards northern foundations. The service of an isolated community in the heavily forested area of Hawes, Wensleydale, was certainly intended by Richard III when he paid the salary for one year of a chaplain there. He was lord of the manor of Aysgarth (or part of it) and his care of its souls was very proper.[66]

Richard's foundations are an impressive record of his continuous good intentions throughout his adult life to maintain the priesthood, one of the objectives of a 'good prince' as well as a good son of the church. Improved facilities encouraged a better disposed and better educated clergy and the college was both the favourite means of achieving this and the ideal basis for a chantry in the fifteenth century.[67]

Richard's first foundation was at Queens' College, Cambridge, to which he made a grant in 1477 to support four priests studying theology and pray for Richard, his wife, son, parents, dead brothers and sisters and his associates killed at Barnet and Tewkesbury. The educational benefit is solidly there, if half a step behind: the grant encouraged learning and strengthened both college and university. Larger grants followed to Queens' in 1484 'to maintain the doctrine of the faith'.[68] Middleham College was again 'for the salvation of the living and the repose of the dead', the good estate of the king and queen, Richard's parents, siblings, and son. It extended the parish church by a college composed of a dean, six chaplains, clerks and choristers. The statutes laid down that the dean was to have a Cambridge degree, all the personnel were to be learned in literature and music, and established a scholastic link with Queens' College.[69] Of the projected Barnard Castle foundation only the licence of 1478 exists for a dean and twelve chaplains with prayers for Richard's family.[70] Richard was also generous to York intending an extension of St. William's College to house as many as 100 chantry priests of the Minster. A parallel benefit to the Minster was the grant of Cottingham to support the vicars choral and ensure that their full complement of thirty-six men could be maintained.[71] In London Richard raised the chapel of Our Lady beside All Hallows Barking by the Tower in London into a royal free chapel with a dean and six chaplains thereby extending the chantry established there by Edward IV for his parents and brothers.[72]

Against this background of these large intentions there were many other gifts, large and small. The pattern starts when Richard was duke. In 1474 he presented a bell to the shipmen's fraternity in Hull, and at some date he and his wife gave or contributed to the Last Judgement window at Great Malvern where he was lord of the manor.[73] As king he gave towards a window at Carlisle Cathedral Priory.[74] As lord of Wilberfoss in the East Riding he relieved the poverty of the nunnery there, and as lord of Middleham he remembered Coverham.[75] He protected the rights to pasture of the priory of Pontefract 'for the which we of duetie the rathere owe to defende the same in alle right. . .'[76] He was generous to the building programme of King's, Cambridge, and also to that of St. George's, Windsor, by removing there the profitable remains of Henry VI worth about £200 a year in pilgrims' gifts.[77] At the other end of the scale he paid annuities to the anchoresses at Pontefract and Westminster.[78]

Richard was not short of good examples of religious conduct in his immediate family. For the inner life the obvious inspirations were his mother and sister, Margaret, the former in particular a much cited example of the pious noble widow of her day. She, like her son, revered relics and objects of devotion, including a piece of the true Cross, and her devotions included reference to several of the Passion cults. In all she presented the image of a pious woman worthy of reverence, precisely the tone adopted by Richard in his letters to her, however conventional.[79] Margaret's piety as duchess of Burgundy might be less generally known to Richard but it was probably she who introduced the stricter order of friars, the Observantines, into England. She too owned devotional treatises including works on the 'medled lyf' directed at the lay person unable to enter the full religious life. She displayed concern over the education of the clergy and personally performed the corporal works of mercy.[80] Such piety generated further piety in the younger generations, so we can be sure that good example did have good effect. Of Richard's nieces, Bridget daughter of Edward IV entered a strict Dominican house, Anne de la Pole became Prioress of the austere order of Brigettines at Syon, and Margaret Plantagenet was revered for her piety.[81] Nor should we forget the formidable Beauchamp tradition of piety coming to Richard through his wife. Richard's book of hours is thought to be of Beauchamp origin. His wife's grandfather was generally considered an example of piety because of his pilgrimages to the Holy Land and Rome, his crusading and his subjection of heretics, and his son Henry, duke of Warwick, had been known to recite the entire psalter every day 'unless he had great business'.[82]

Another connection that may have had a pietistic influence on Richard in his teens and twenties was that of the Fitzhughs of Wensleydale, closely connected with the Nevilles, Parrs and Lovels. The Fitzhughs had a long standing family association with Jervaulx Abbey and either Richard Lord Fitzhugh or his father gave Richard of Gloucester a chronicle of the Abbey. An earlier Fitzhugh had been a founder of Syon with Henry V and had owned the autograph copy of the *Judica* by the northern mystic, Richard Rolle, an associate of both the Fitzhughs and of the Scropes, also of Wensleydale.[83]

There is one last important source of religious and educational influence on Richard of Gloucester, generally underrated but briefly mentioned by Professor Ross – that of George Neville, Archbishop of York. George was a well-educated man who maintained a learned household, patronised learning and was a notable benefactor of Oxford University. He was deeply concerned with the education of the clergy and was a practical and conscientious bishop.[84] He was one of the great figures of Richard's youth and, despite his political machinations, disgrace and imprisonment, never lost the loyal affection of several notable ecclesiastics, four of whom achieved greater prominence in Richard's service: Thomas Barret, sent on an important diplomatic mission to Ireland by Richard, Thomas Barowe, ducal councillor and later Master of the Rolls, Edmund Chaderton, ducal councillor and later Treasurer of the King's Chamber, and John Shirwood promoted to the bishopric of Durham.[85] Shirwood, probably, and Richard, certainly, were involved in getting George released to spend his last years (December 1474 to June 1476) administering his diocese.[86] Richard as duke and king can be seen, in some measure, as continuing George Neville's patronage of learning and the education of the clergy. In practical terms, he continued St. William's College, a project of George and his brother the Earl of Warwick, and he joined the Corpus Christi Guild of York, the establishment of which had owed much to George Neville.[87] In terms of his continuing George's promotion of learned men four notable examples have already been mentioned, of whom John Shirwood became Richard's proctor in Rome and was recommended for a cardinal's hat with particular emphasis laid on his learning. Thomas Langton, the brother of another long standing associate of

George Neville, was promoted by Richard to the bishopric of Salisbury, and was later to claim that he owed all his advancement to his learning; Thomas was himself a conscientious and enthusiastic promoter of education.[88] Other learned men approved of by Richard include John Doget, John Gunthorpe and Thomas Penketh, all educated in Italy. Doget acted as a chaplain and diplomat for Richard,[89] Gunthorpe was councillor and keeper of his privy seal,[90] and Penketh, an Oxford lecturer in theology and editor of the first printed text of Duns Scotus, was selected to make the St. Mary Spittal sermon on Richard's title to the throne at Easter 1484.[91]

Richard seems to have had a genuine interest in both learned clergy and the promotion of learning. On the same evidence why should it not also be assumed (contrary to the normal assertion) that Richard was a well-educated man who not only enjoyed the company of learned clerics but was perfectly capable of appreciating the learned disputations he chose to attend at Oxford in 1483? In further support of this contention one may add that *The Croyland Chronicle* tells us he had 'surpassing talents', and that the few books of his which survive are all plain undecorated texts, only desirable for their contents, and not lavishly illustrated ones which might have been more valued for their pictures.[92]

Such an interest in the church and the education of the clergy, advised by the mirrors of the princes, also repaid the prince in a practical way. The court was closely linked to the universities, particularly through the personnel of the royal chapel, and through this channel the king was supplied with diplomats, secretaries, chaplains, authors and councillors, essential to his government and prestige.[93] This practical side of piety bears greater examination. Richard's favoured clergy were energetic, conscientious administrators contributing to the common weal. They were also the king's natural councillors, the choice of wise and honest councillors being again of the deepest concern to the mentors of the 'good prince'. To take two examples from among the bishops closely associated with Richard as duke and as king. The northerner Richard Redman, Bishop of St. Asaph, was also known to Richard as the Abbot of Shap, Westmorland. He was an active visitor of his order of the Premonstratensians, restorer of his cathedral and arbiter in local disputes. He was one of the two bishops chosen by Richard to bear the coronation oil to Westminster Abbey.[94] Another northerner, Richard Bell, Bishop of Carlisle, was arguably the third bishop who owed his promotion to Richard, when he was Duke of Gloucester in 1478. He was another active, efficient administrator of a poor northern diocese. He decorated his cathedral and was a benefactor of Cambridge University.[95]

Bishop Alcock has left us a contemporary's opinion of what a bishop should be, to which we can compare Richard's bishops to their credit: of good behaviour, chaste, hospitable, a teacher, modest and the ruler of his house. Generally Alcock had a high opinion of the priesthood about him.[96] Recent research has tended to reinstate the pre-Reformation church, and its bishops in particular, and to reinforce Alcock's opinion. The ideal bishop, we are also told, was expected to have good birth, virtue and learning, and he should also ,erve the crown.[97] Piety was desirable but it was not the sole or main requirement, it did not ensure reliable clergy any more than a pious king ensured reliable, good government. The practicalities were made sure of first.

These practicalities of patronage, of personnel and foundations are also reflected in Richard's general pronouncements to the church. He, like Edward IV, at his own volition confirmed the church's liberties. He also took seriously his power and duty as a 'good prince' to direct the clergy in virtue, as can be seen in his often quoted letter to a bishop, probably to all his bishops, asserting that 'our principalle entent and fervent desire is, to see vertue and clennesse of lyving to be avaunced encresed and multiplied/ and vices and alle othre thinges repugnant to vertue . . . repressed and adnulled/ And this perfitely folowed and put in execucion/ by persones of highe estate . . . not oonly enducethe persones of lower degree to take thereof example . . . but is also pleasurable to God.'[98] The bishop was exhorted to use his ecclesiastical courts to this end, and, by implication, to set a good personal example like all persons of high estate, including the king. Just as the late fifteenth century bishops have been rehabilitated spiritually and acquitted of hypocrisy so Richard can be acquitted of hypocrisy: 'to prove they were misguided is not to prove that they were malicious or insincere.'[99] Richard was acting as was proper in a 'good prince'; he was actively encouraging virtue, the prerequisite of social harmony.

The third education undergone by such as Richard, Duke of Gloucester, was that of the knight, an education endorsing that of the prince, for Christ was the model for the perfect knight as he was for the perfect prince. Like the prince, the knight's duty was to protect the weak, fight for justice, keep the peace and serve the common weal. The chivalric code of behaviour did not allow evil conduct and shamed those who committed crimes. Good birth was, again, considered to incline those who had it towards the achievement of honour.[100] The education of a knight[101] was similar to that of a prince: the reading of history and the study of the lives of good knights from Joshua to Richard Beauchamp, 'the father of courtesy'. They read the lives of their 'stars' in all seriousness and they in turn expected that their own exploits be recorded by the heralds of their own day.[102] Caxton was certain of the value of emulation and listed heroes including Henry V and ancestors of Queen Anne Neville when dedicating Lull's *Order of Chivalry* to Richard III. He urged the King to get his young men to 'rede Froissart', an author much in favour of the upright knight, the just war, and the protection of the weak, whether cleric or labourer.[103]

The romances were taken with equal seriousness by their medieval readers and it has even been argued that they were the main encouragement of noble conduct. Richard owned a prose version of one of the standard late fourteenth century knightly romances, *Ipomedon*, in which the hero sets out to be the best knight in the world for the love of his lady. This presented him with the special virtues of knighthood in their full glory. Prowess and loyalty were paramount with largesse, courtesy and pity not far behind. Prowess is the indomitability and magnanimity already mentioned and, in this context, courage in battle. Loyalty is, again, a complex word covering fidelity to one's word, a person and a cause, as well as a quality of soul with strong religious overtones. (In parenthesis Richard's remembrance of his brothers in arms killed at Barnet and Tewkesbury in the prayers of his foundation at Queens' College, should be noted.) Pity is compassion, a desire for justice and fair dealing.[104]

Richard held the supreme chivalric post of constable of England from the age of seventeen (1469) and would have been expected to know the theories and practice of arms and knightly conduct, as expressed in Lull's *Order of Chivalry*, in Vegetius' *De Re Militari*, of which Richard is known to have commissioned a copy,[105] or in Bonet's *Tree of Battles*, a legal hand-book on how to conduct a war justly, which John Howard considered essential reading on the Scottish campaigns of 1481. War was not considered an evil in Richard's day – there was such a thing as a just war – the evils that might attend a war were the result of abuse and might be avoided by loyal knights, a good commander of moderate temper, and regularly paid, well disciplined soldiers.[106] Richard, like John Howard, appears to have taken Bonet's advice to heart during the Scots campaign of 1482 – a competent campaign (as Dr. MacDougall describes it) of moderate and disciplined conduct. He was allotted money for 20,000 men for four weeks only and for 1,700 men for a further two weeks. He observed this time limit: he captured Berwick, occupied Edinburgh without sacking it (evidence of the discipline exercised over his forces) and secured agreements that were realistic in the unforeseen and disastrous political circumstances of not having James III to negotiate with.[107] Discipline and moderation were the qualities most desired in a commander by the authors of medieval military treatises.[108]

The constable's other duties concerned his court of law, particularly for matters of *lese majesté*, and the oversight of the heralds. Of both a little is known. Ordinances of 1478–80 which have been attributed to Richard urge that the heralds, among other things, frequent good company, cultivate good manners and eloquence, study books of arms, and record the feats of arms and ceremonies of their own day. Richard himself owned two rolls of arms and he can be glimpsed enforcing his herald's rights to their fees at the marriage of Anne Mowbray and Richard Duke of York. His concern for the heralds continued when he was King with a charter of incorporation as well as the gift of Cold Harbour for their headquarters.[109] These activities must be taken to represent a genuine interest resulting from his office, and contrasts markedly with the uninterest of his successors as constable and king.

Most of his judicial duties were conducted by deputies and the clerk to the constableship and promoter of business concerning the king's majesty,[110] but in important cases he was certainly involved, such as the executions after Tewkesbury. Another case, more in the category of farce, occurred in 1473 and contributes to the impression that Richard's attention to his duties was sensible and conscientious. It concerned a private quarrel between two London goldsmiths who were neighbours. The quarrel reached such levels of abuse that treason was spoken and the King ordered the constable to investigate. The constable examined the two men, realised the true nature of the case and remitted it to its natural arbiter, the Goldsmiths' Company, much to that Company's relief.[111]

One last concern of the knight must be mentioned: the Crusade. Richard owned a copy of Chaucer's *Knight's Tale* and would have been familiar with Chaucer's picture of that knight's illustrious crusading career. Maurice Keen has convincingly argued that this crusading knight was no obsolete ideal when Chaucer wrote, citing numerous contemporary English families who provided crusaders to Spain, the Mediterranean and Prussia, the Lovells, Scropes, Morleys and Rythers – all families well known to Richard in their descendants.[112] Richard also knew John Kendale, turcopolier of Rhodes and knight of St. John, who was conspicuous in raising money for the war against the infidel and appointed by Richard to present his obedience to Innocent VIII.[113] George Neville was a well known enthusiast for a crusade, the late fifteenth-century Popes were constantly urging action, and Caxton in his 1481 dedication of his *Last Siege of Jerusalem* to Edward IV encouraged 'every Cristen man' to a crusade.[114] The crusade was still the 'highest expression of chivalrous dedication'[115] in Richard's day and he too is known to have expressed interest in the subject. He spoke to the German Von Poppelau of the joys of driving back the Turks from Hungary, he made a royal free chapel of the chapel where Richard I's heart was supposed to be buried and where another crusading King, Edward I, had placed an image of the Virgin Mary in response to a vision promising him victory if he did so, and he made sure that Westminster Abbey would return to him the coronation oil which legend said would anoint the English king who would regain the Holy Land.[116]

The overwhelming plea of the mentors of the prince and knight was for a positive pursuit of virtue, a prerequisite of social harmony. They longed for the right and fair regulation of society by those who governed, a recognition of the mutual obligations between different sections of the community (rich and poor, buyer and seller, citizen and foreigner, lord and liegeman) and justice in its fullest sense of the weal publique.

Law was the obvious means to enforce social harmony in an imperfect, sinful world – the first of William Langland's trinity of law, loyalty and love. Of Richard's education in the law nothing is known. It is possible he attended an inn of court in his teens; the inns were becoming recognised as one of the best educations available.[117] A royal duke was able to employ lawyers at need to prosecute cases and compose documents but if he was wise he understood the principles involved. With or without a period at an inn his own ducal council would have provided an early forcing school of experience for Richard. By the time he was king he would have been familiar with the complexities of the land law, the difficulties of securing title and the endless squabbles that might arise over an inheritance. His ducal council became a valuable source of arbitration in such matters, as can be seen in the Clervaux, Place dispute over boundaries settled in 1478 'tendering the peace and weal of the country where the said parties inhabit and also gladly willing good concord.'[118] This judicial role of his council answered a desperate need of people when the existing legal processes could not provide a solution. Richard's concern for peaceful arbitration and judicial solutions continued when he was king, shown above all by his continuation of his ducal council in the north under the Earl of Lincoln. He laid down articles for the council: none of its members were to speak 'for favour, affection, hate, malice or mede' but only as the king's laws and 'good conscience' required and with impartiality; any one on the council connected with a case under considera- tion was to leave the room while it was in hand; no land cases were to be decided without the consent of the parties involved; it was to sit regularly and hear all complaints brought before it; and disturbances of the peace were to be dealt with swiftly.[119] A comparable exercise was Richard's extension of the royal council's existing responsibility to hear the suits of the poor and friendless men mentioned already. This was the king's duty 'to provide for the administration of justice to all his subjects' in operation.[120] Richard's practice followed his theory spelled out on the first day of his reign in King's Bench when he called his justices before him and strongly urged them to administer the law without delay or favour.[121] His proclamation to Kent in 1483 urged men to bring their complaints before the King and another, 1484–5, urged the same 'for the love that he hath for the ministracion and execucion of Justice for the comowne welthe of this Royaulme the whiche he mooste tendrethe.' Men did come and the promise was kept, as Thomas Langton's famous letter about Richard's first progress specifically assures us.[122]

Richard can thus be seen to have observed the king's primary, every day duty of caring for his subjects through the administration of justice. There is, however, another aspect of the king's justice to be considered. Kingship was a combination of heady, God-given authority and of moral obligation. On the one hand, the king was the fount of justice and indispensable to the English 'constitution', and on the other, when he accepted the divine vocation of his office he bound himself to give justice, defend the people and act on proper advice and consultation with his subjects. On the one hand he had great privileges, the law and its officers were his servants, on the other he had to acknowledge his justices' superior knowledge of the law, to observe the due processes of the law and to go to parliament if he wished to make or break a law. If he did not he could justifiably be called a tyrant.[123] Richard clearly accepted this principle during his consultation with his justices in the Star Chamber: 'this is the King's will to wit, to say "by his justices and by his law" is to say one and the same thing.'[124] This comment by the king was made in response to a specific decision that fines for the offence of misprision were to be set by the royal justices in the future. Richard was also clearly intending a remark of wider significance – after all he could have briefly stated his agreement and no more. The offence of misprision, misbehaviour of officials in their office, was an ideal one from which to draw a general principle of his support for the good administration of the law.

Richard's parliamentary legislation concerned with the law was of the same order. There are five relevant statutes of which the most important concerned the legal instruments of the use and the fine[125] and aimed to quiet title and, in the case of the use, to stem the flood of petitions to the chancellor over dishonest feoffees.[126] The other three statutes allowed bail for persons imprisoned for felony on suspicion, encouraged justices of the peace to inquire into all such arrests, raised the standard of juries empanelled at the sheriff's tourn, and facilitated the correction of dishonest officials at pie powder courts. These last three statutes benefited the king's lowest and least sufficient subjects and were aimed primarily at corruption in the legal system. This is so predominantly and generally the concern of Richard's administration that it cannot really be doubted that it was he who gave this legislation its character. This is not to discount the importance of his justices' wishes, nor the undoubted contribution by his new lord chancellor to the statutes on the use and the empanelling of juries, nor the fact that general reform of the empanelling system had been an issue for years.[127] It is merely to point out that it was the climate of Richard III's council which made these particular statutes possible in 1484. The tribute of Lord Chancellor Francis Bacon that Richard was 'a good lawmaker for the ease and solace of the common people' is moderate, fair and exactly right. His comment has been subject to over enthusiastic exaggeration by 'fans' of Richard, but it is equally not to be dismissed.[128] Bacon was an eminent and subtle lawyer and he did not lightly give praise were none was due. He worked in the legal system only 100 years after Richard and before the great changes of the seventeenth century.

One of the most fundamental problems for an administrator was the control of the corrupt or lazy official, one of the standard subjects of abuse in medieval literature. He harmed the king and those of his subjects least able to defend themselves. Some of Richard's statutes dealt with this problem, and in his well known session with his justices in the Star Chamber two of the cases he brought to their attention were concerned with official malpractice – one the method of punishing a dishonest justice of the peace who had acted contrary to a jury's decision, the other the correction of men who had connived to alter a court record. The reporter of this session specifically tells us that Richard was 'perturbed' that such cases could arise.[129] Richard also intervened personally when the law was not involved as when he dismissed Richard Bele from a privy seal clerkship, Bele having bribed himself into the job.[130] His regulations to secure honesty on his council in the north and on his Glamorgan estates when duke (already mentioned) were part of a general policy. He set standards for his receivers, wanting well disposed, educated men of sufficient wealth in the office so that they would be less vulnerable to corruption. His orders for the administration of the honour of Tutbury similarly demanded that able persons of good character be appointed annually as bailiffs and ordered proclamation to the effect that any complaint against past officials would be heard and the offender punished.[131] His statute on the tourn juries ensured that the men empanelled were worth 20s. a year. This policy of placing the well-to-do man in office on the assumption that such a man will be less selfish and less open to corruption (his very wealth placing an obligation upon him to rule well) accords precisely with the advice given by the mentors of princes.[132]

There was another group who benefited from strong, honest and uncapricious government, the people who lived in towns. They were more vocal in their demands than the poor and they were of more political importance to the prince. Richard's treatment of towns is, I believe, as revealing of his basic attitude to the problem of ruling as his activity in the sphere of justice. Under the guidance of Susan Reynolds we are now more able to understand civic government in the terms that a fifteenth century man would have used. We can no longer dismiss it as 'oligarchic' in a pejorative sense and unworthy of our attention. The citizen of Richard's day both wanted and expected rule by the 'better' sort of his fellows (invariably the rich and successful), for the benefit of all.[133] And the 'better' sort of citizen could potentially be very good indeed, to quote John Colet, Dean of St. Paul's in the words of his friend Erasmus: 'there was no absolute certainty in human affairs but for his part he found less corruption in such a body of citizens than in any order or degree of mankind.'[134] Aegidius Colonna, author of Richard's mirror of a prince, was equally well aware of the value of the citizen.[135] Richard too had first hand experience of such citizens, their value to the realm in terms of armed men and cash as well as their worth of character, their aspirations and problems. As Duke he had joined the main civic guild of York, he had spoken for the city on several occasions and he had led their men in war.[136] As King his charters and grants went mostly to the towns he had known as Duke and, vice versa, they were the towns most likely to beseech him for favours: York and Chester had their fee farms reduced, Pontefract and Llandovery were incorporated, and Scarborough (his castle since 1474) received county and sea port status, civic government under a mayor and the manor of Falsgrave to increase its territory.[137] Extending a town's powers over a hinterland seems to have appealed particularly to Richard, perhaps because of the extension of potentially beneficent government, and, of course, he knew the precedent of York having such a perquisite (as did Lincoln under a grant of 1466). He increased Lincoln's area of control,[138] he gave Gloucester such an area when he incorporated that town, Scarborough has been mentioned, and he offered the City of London the borough of Southwark with £10,000 to build a wall round it.[139] Richard made it clear too that no one, not even the Prince of Wales, should come between the king and his towns when he wrote to Southampton condemning the giving of liveries and any outside interference in its franchises: 'Forsomoche as it is fulle according and righte welethy that the commonaltee of every Citee or Towne be hoole and of one wille and agrement in alle causes concernyng the same.'[140] However ineffectual they proved in the event, these gifts and orders reflect the aspirations of both the

King and his towns and cities. Richard was not unique among kings in valuing civic authorities but his encouragement of them is remarkably intensive.

Townspeople also took a particular interest in two qualities urged upon the 'good prince': largesse and virtuous living. They eyed the king's housekeeping because they were liable to be called to assist. They expected him to spend, to maintain a sumptuous household and give liberally to deserving servants and to the poor in alms, but also to avoid both indebtedness and avarice. Moderation was the demand of the mirrors of princes. Richard had an excellent example to follow in Edward IV whose achievements included the reform of his household (Richard had probably sat on the advising council) and solvency by 1478.[141] Richard continued Edward's household policy by assigning additional issues of lands to his household (one of the most reliable sources of income) and he recognised generally the value of keeping as much land as possible in his own control,[142] both measures intended to ensure that he could pay his way. Evidence of Richard's financial reorganisation remains in the well known memorandum advising certain expedients, including additional bypassing of the Exchequer on the lines initiated by Edward. Richard wanted to ascertain 'yerely of the hole revenues of alle his livelod & what thereof is paid and what is owing & is whos defaute', the essential prerequisite of financial efficiency.[143] He started his reign with certain financial difficulties: he had probably lost some of Edward IV's treasure, he had no customs income (a very major slice of the king's revenue) until parliament could grant it, and he had had to pay for a double coronation and the crushing of a rebellion. He also had to try to avoid Edward IV's bad example in terms of finance. The sin of avarice had encouraged Edward to accumulate a treasure and to acquire such bad habits as the benevolence, gifts from the wealthy at demand, the cause of considerable opposition, in London at least, by 1482.[144] Richard did manage to refuse several gifts of money from towns both before and after Buckingham's rebellion,[145] and he then deprived himself by statute of the benevolence. London was the prime encourager of this abolition and it seems possible that it was delight over this statute that moved the Pewterers' Company of London to write 'And God save kyng Rechard' in their minutes of 30 January 1484.[146] Edward's other enterprising means of raising money, such as trade and fines, remained open to Richard, but, by this statute, he was formally acknowledging the principle, firmly held by his subjects, that they should be consulted over their obligation to assist the king with money, by aid or loan.[147] Again, this was the proper course for a 'good prince' who was also king of England.

Now to pass on to the desirability of the good prince being of a virtuous habit of life. Aegidius Colonna and the other mentors of princes advised on the desirability of a good wife and the observance of the marriage vows. Edward IV's well known incontinence in marriage meant that he could justifiably be attacked in Richard's parliament as 'lede by sensuality and concupiscence',[148] indeed it was his very lack of virtue (a pre-contract with one woman followed by a clandestine marriage with another) that had made his children bastards and gave Richard his moral claim to the throne. In contrast, Richard while he was duke had a good reputation for a virtuous private life and as king could exhort his clergy to promote clean living and expect to be taken seriously. His peccadilloes are accepted as having occurred before marriage by his two, very different, biographers, Ross and Kendall.[149] Virtuous living like piety did not guarantee good kingship, however, as the example of Henry VI showed, but they might be thought to incline their host towards right in preference to wrong.

It was another decorative quality of the good prince that eluded Richard early in his reign (later its lack also tarnished his marital record) – good reputation or honour, 'worth more than gold or silver.'[150] This loss of reputation was not incurred by his taking the throne – there were solid enough reasons for that – but by the later rumours that he had murdered his nephews, which rumours in their turn encouraged those of 1485 accusing him of his wife's death and the desire to marry his niece. Richard would have known only too well from the mirrors of princes and his knightly education of the value of honour. The sins of every individual contributed to the troubles of the state and the sins of the prince (real or rumoured) were proportionately more responsible for any disharmony in the state. In Richard's reign one can actually see the morality of the mirrors inexorably worked out in real life. Rumours of such a character attached to the prince, even if localised and concentrated in the south of the country, were inevitably seen to create the disharmony of rebellion and invasion. An unknown cleric of Henry VII's reign mentions in a sermon how important it was for a king to be 'in reputacion and favour of the peple' for otherwise malice and disorder arise 'as it was like to have bene in this reem within fewe yeres'.[151] It is bitterly ironic that a prince who 'contents the people where he goys best that ever did prince'[152] and followed the *Secret of Secrets* should have been caught out by one of its wisest precepts, the preservation of good reputation. This irony is, I am sure, one intellectual reason why Richard and his reign continue to fascinate so many.

There exist three independent comments by contemporaries on Richard's policy as duke and as king. The first comes from Mancini concerning the period before 1483: 'He kept himself within his own lands and set out to acquire the loyalty of his people through favours and justice. The good reputation of his private life and public activities powerfully attracted the esteem of strangers.'[153] The second was made before Richard left York on his 1483 progress by Thomas Langton, Bishop of St. David's. A much misused comment on which Professor Griffiths has recently made the best, indeed the only recent, clear-headed statement giving both Richard and Langton their real due.[154] Langton was a highly educated, brilliant man who undoubtedly knew Richard before he was King. He was also a good, benevolent, caring man whose words should not be dismissed as mere time-serving. One of Langton's protégés Richard Pace, has left a delightful memorial of him as the enthusiastic patron of the school he had established in his household: 'And most of all he delighted in hearing the boys repeat to him in the evening what they had learned that day from the schoolmaster. And in this examination he who did well was nicely complimented and given something he wanted. For that best of masters had always on his lips the saying that worth thrives on praise. And if a boy seemed dull, but willing, he did not treat it as a fault, but with kindness urged him on . . .'[155] The letter of such a man praising Richard is particularly important. In it he is responding to Richard's earliest expression of his intentions as king and to seeing him actually fulfilling the traditional role of the prince: 'He contents the people wher he goys . . . many a poor man . . . have be relevyd and helpyd by hym and his commands in his progresse.' Langton is responding with enthusiasm in the successful period after the coronation, after a comparatively easy 'active assumption of power' and before Buckingham's rebellion darkens the scene. About nine months later in May 1484 a foreigner reacted to Richard in a remarkably similar and enthusiastic way, without the long acquaintance with the King that Langton had. The German, Von Poppelau, referred to Richard as having 'a great heart' (*ein grosses herz*) – in other words the princely virtue of magnanimity, the desire to do great things and in particular those which benefit the common weal.[156] To return to Langton: 'On my trouth I lyked never the condicions of ony prince so wel as his; God hathe sent hym to us for the wele of us al . . .'

On the preceding evidence I would argue that Richard conformed to the models presented to him of the 'good prince' and consciously initiated policies in that image as both duke and king. It was an image directed to the common weal. If such an image was propaganda as we are told (and all governments have their propaganda) then it was admirable propaganda, and there is no evidence to make us suppose it insincere. It can be found before his accession and after it. It was not initiated to retrieve a lost reputation as Polydore Vergil and Professor Ross assert,[157] rather the loss of reputation was Richard's one failure in his active policy of being a 'good prince'.

Notes

1. R.J. Mitchell, *John Tiptoft, 1427–1470* (London 1938), p. 236. Tiptoft's text is a version of the old dispute over the equation between virtue and nobility. Flamineus puts the case of the less well born man who holds that virtue lies in the individual soul, in opposition to the noble by mere blood and wealth. The virtues he describes are, however, of the one basic ideal.
2. L. Renwick and H. Orton, *The Beginnings of English Literature to Skelton 1509* (London 1966), 3rd ed., p. 98.
3. This is one of the most constantly reiterated themes of C. Ross, *Richard III*, London 1981, pp. 14, 23, 31, 32, 34, 36–7, 78–80, 87, 144, 175, 228–9. Also

M.A. Hicks, 'The Warwick Inheritance – Springboard to the Throne', *The Ricardian* vol. 6, no. 81 (1983), pp. 174–180.

4. Alexander Murray, *Reason and Society in the Middle Ages* (Oxford 1978), pp. 272–3, 336–8, 351–66. Murray argues convincingly that the more generally held medieval belief was that nobility was naturally inclined to virtue. He argues from evidence of the period before 1400 but much is applicable to the fifteenth century. See also S.L. Thrupp, *The Merchant Class of Medieval London* (Michigan 1948), pp. 302–3.

5. Mitchell *op cit.*, p. 235.

6. R. Firth Green, *Poets and Princepleasers. Literature and the English Court in the late Middle Ages* (Toronto 1980), pp. 135–140.

7. The French Chronicle, BL. MS. Royal 20 CVIII, which bears his signature on f.134b, and The Story of Thebes by Lydgate. P. Tudor-Craig, *Richard III Catalogue of the National Portrait Gallery Exhibition 1973* (revised edition 1977), p. 63 (item 154).

8. Joshua was among the books of the Old Testament which Richard possessed in verse, *NPG Catalogue op. cit.*, p. 63 (item 154). George Cary, *The Medieval Alexander* (Cambridge 1948), p. 230.

9. G.L. Harriss, 'Henry V and Government', Reading symposium 8 July 1983, argued that Henry V set out to be the ideal king. Edward III occurs with Alexander and Solomon as a shining example to the House of York in the preamble to Edward IV's Black Book of his Household, A.R. Myers, *The Household of Edward IV* (Manchester 1959), p. 84.

10. J.P. Genet, 'Political Theory and the Relationship in England and France between the Crown and the Local Communities', in *The Crown and Local Communities in England and France in the Fifteenth Century*, ed. J.R.L. Highfield and R. Jeffs (Gloucester 1981), p. 24, and his *Four English Political Tracts of the Later Middle Ages*, Camden Society, 4th series, vol. 18 (1977), pp. ix–xix. Firth Green, *op. cit.*, pp. 149–163.

11. J.J.G. Alexander, 'Painting and Manuscript Illumination for Royal Patrons in the Later Middle Ages', in *English Court Culture in the Later Middle Ages*, ed. V.J. Scattergood and J.W. Sherborne (London 1983), pp. 141–2. Firth Green *op. cit.*, pp. 140–1. Derek Pearsall, *John Lydgate* (London 1970), pp. 70–1, 297. Genet, *Four English Political Tracts, op. cit.*, p. 41. Nicholas Orme, *English Schools in the Middle Ages* (London 1973), pp. 22–3.

12. *NPG Catalogue op. cit.*, p. 65 (item 157). Richard's father is reputed to have had a good understanding of latin and there is no reason to suppose Richard did not, indeed his interest in the learning of others encourages a belief that he too was inclined to learning.

13. Genet, *Four English Political Tracts op. cit.*, p. x. L.K. Born, 'The Perfect Prince: A Study in Thirteenth and Fourteenth Century Ideals', *Speculum*, vol. 3 (1928), pp. 488–491, 499.

14. Born *op. cit.*, pp. 488–491.

15. For a summary of Cessoles, Born *op. cit.*, pp. 491–3. Facsimile of Caxton text, introduction by N.F. Blake, Scolar Press (London 1976).

16. Genet, *Four English Political Tracts op. cit.*, p. xvi. M.A. Manzalaoui, *Secretum Secretorum, Nine English Versions*, Early English Text Society OS. 276 (1977), pp. xxiv–xl, 32–45, 69–71, 74–80.

17. Born *op. cit.*, p. 504.

18. R.H. Robbins, *Historical Poems of the Fourteenth & Fifteenth Centuries*, New York 1959, no. 97, Advice to the Several Estates II, lines 42, 44–5 (pp. 233–4).

19. Charles T. Wood, 'Law, Sovereignty and the Holy Spirit 1294–1534. England in comparative context.', p. 3 of typescript of unpublished talk given at the 1980 Annual Meeting of Law and Society Association, Wisconsin, June 1980.

20. N. Orme., 'The Education of the Courtier', in *English Court Culture, op. cit.*, p. 63 (translating Fortescue) and Firth Green *op. cit.*, chapter 3, 'A Lettered Court.'

21. Minor, anonymous works also abounded on the art of governing but these were not certainly available to Richard, e.g. Robbins *op. cit.*, nos. 95 and 97.

22. G.C. Macaulay (ed.), *The Works of John Gower* (Oxford 1901), vol. 4, *Vox Clamantis* line 999: *amor defensio regis*. John H. Fisher, *John Gower. Moral Philosopher and Friend of Chaucer* (New York 1964), pp. 183–4.

23. M.A. Manzalaoui, '"Noght in the Registre of Venus": Gower's English Mirror for Princes,' *Medieval Studies for J.A.W. Bennett*, ed. P.L. Heyworth (Oxford 1981), and A.H. Gilbert, 'Notes on the Influence of the *Secretum Secretorum*,' *Speculum*, vol. 3 (1928), pp. 84–93.

24. *The Works of John Gower*, vol. 3, *Confessio Amantis, VII*, lines 1725–39.

25. *Ibid.*, lines 1985–2176.

26. *Ibid.*, lines 2698–9, 2748–53, 3029–3102.

27. *Ibid.*, lines 3103–3266, 3518–3626, 3807–3940, 5365–5397.

28. Anne F. Sutton, 'Richard III's Castle of Care' *The Ricardian* vol. 3 no. 49 (1975), revised version in *Richard III, Crown and People*, ed. J. Petre (London 1985), pp. 303–6.

29. W.W. Skeat (ed.) *The Vision of William concerning Piers, the Plowman . . .* by William Langland, 2 vols. (Oxford 1886), vol. 1, C iv, lines 381–2.

30. *Ibid.*, C v, lines 174–5.

31. Anna P. Baldwin, *The Theme of Government in Piers Plowman*, D.S. Brewer (Cambridge 1981), pp. 5–6, 15, 18, 53. P.M. Kean, 'Love, law and *lewte* in *Piers Plowman*', *Review of English Studies*, vol. 15 (NS.) 1964, pp. 16–261 and especially pp. 255–7 on 'lewte' as 'justice'. Her argument continues in 'Justice, Kingship and the Good Life in the Second Part of *Piers Plowman*', in *Piers Plowman: Critical Approaches*, ed. S.S. Hussey (London 1969), pp. 76–110.

32. *Piers Plowman*, B xiv, lines 147–8.

33. Ross, *Richard III op. cit.*, plate 18a, asserts that Richard's 'usual' motto was *tant le desiere* which exists in two sources: an heraldic scrapbook of arms and mottoes of which Richard's boar and this motto is one 'scrap' (BL. Add. MS. 40742, f.5 illustrated *NPG Catalogue op. cit.*, illustration no. 46); and as *tant le desieree* in Richard's copy of *Ipomedon*, with his signature (Longleat MS. 257, f. 98b, see *NPG Catalogue*, p. 63 item 154). The role of this motto is as hard to assess as it is to translate satisfactorily. Princes could use several mottoes

particularly when taking part in courtly entertainments which demanded such fancies. For a more detailed discussion see the author's note in *The Ricardian*, vol. 7, no. 89, June 1985, pp. 74–5.

34. BL. MS. Cotton Vespasian F XIII. *NPG Catalogue* p. 29, item 59. Guildhall Library: Waxchandlers' Charter 1484, MS 9517. N.Davies (ed.), *The Paston Letters and Papers of the Fifteenth Century* (Oxford 1976), vol. 2, p. 443. See also P.M. Kendall, *Richard III* (London 1955), pp. 113, 181.

35. S.E. James, *The Parrs of Kendal 1370–1571*, unpublished Ph.D. thesis, Cambridge 1977, e.g. pp. 86, 94–5, 115, 117, 124 for some of the Parr connections with Richard. See also C. Ross, 'Some "Servants and Lovers" of Richard in his Youth', *The Ricardian* vol. 4, no. 55 (1976), pp. 2–4, for Richard's loyaltys to Parr supporters.

36. R.S. Ferguson, 'The Heraldry of Naworth', *Transactions of the Cumberland and Westmorland Archaeological and Antiquarian Society*, vol. 4 (1878–9), p. 496. Anne F. Sutton and P.W. Hammond, *The Coronation of Richard III* (Gloucester 1983), p. 330.

37. Sutton and Hammond *op. cit.*, pp. 2–5.

38. *Ibid.*, pp. 3–5, on oath and citing Richard's references to his duties. The two specific references to the oath by Richard are in a proclamation at Leicester October 1483 'remembering the profession of mercy and justice made by him at his coronation' (T. Rymer, *Foedera etc.*, vol. 12 (London 1714), p. 204) and in a letter to York September 1484 'the administracion of justice wherunto we be professed' (R. Davis, *Extracts from the Records of the City of York* (London 1843), p. 190). For the letter to the Earl of Desmond, R. Horrox and P.W. Hammond (eds.), *BL. Harleian Manuscript 433*, vol. 3 (London 1982), p. 109, and see also A.B. Ferguson, *The Indian Summer of English Chivalry* (Durham, N. Carolina, 1960), p. 141.

39. Both Edward and Henry can be found rehearsing the usual concerns of the ideal king: protection, justice, peace and prosperity. For Edward IV, see M. Bateson (ed.), *The Coventry Leet Book*, part 2, EETS. OS. 135 (1908), p. 373, *The Rolls of Parliament* vol. 5, p. 622. For Henry VII's urging of his subjects to complain to him personally, see P.J. Hughes and J.F. Larkin, *Tudor Royal Proclamations: The Early Tudors 1485–1553* (Yale 1964), no. 17 (to which may be compared Richard III's proclamation to Kent, *BL. Harleian MS. 433 op. cit.*, vol. 2 (Upminster 1980) pp. 48–9), and W. Campbell (ed.) *Materials for a History of the Reign of Henry VII*, vol. 1 (Rolls Series, 1873), pp. 93–4.

40. *Works of John Gower, Confessio Amantis op. cit.*, VIII, lines 3068–3072. And compare K. Pickthorn, *Early Tudor Government: Henry VII* (Cambridge 1934), p. 6, on the long credit of the sacred king.

41. T. Stapleton (ed.), *The Plumpton Correspondence*, Camden Society (1839), p. 8.

42. A.R. Myers, *English Historical Documents 1327–1485* (London 1969), pp. 625, 821. Anne F. Sutton, 'Richard III's tytylle and right: a new discovery', *The Ricardian*, vol. 4, no. 57 (1977), p. 2, and correspondence on same, vol. 4, no. 59 (1977), p. 28.

43. Campbell *op. cit.*, vol. 1, pp. 110–112.

44. G.R. Owst, *Literature and the Pulpit in Medieval England* (Cambridge 1933), pp. 228–231 and ch. 9, and J.W. Blench, *Preaching in England* (Oxford 1964), pp. 231–263.

45. Susan Reynolds, 'Medieval Urban History and the History of Political Thought', *Urban History Yearbook 1982* (Leicester 1982), pp. 14–23, a stimulating and lucid explanation of what the townspeople expected of government.

46. A.F. Pollard, 'The Growth of the Court of Requests', *English Historical Review*, vol. 56 (1941), pp. 300–303.

47. *Glamorgan County History*: vol. 3 *The Middle Ages* ed. T.B. Pugh (Cardiff 1971), pp. 203–4.

48. John H. Hirsh, review of *A Check-list of Middle English Prose Writings of Spiritual Guidance* by P.S. Jolliffe (Toronto 1972), in *Medium Aevum* vol. 44 (1975), pp. 318–320. And his 'Prayer and Meditation in late Medieval England: MS. Bodley 789,' *Medium Aevum* vol. 47 (1978), pp. 55–66. W.A. Pantin, 'Instructions for a Devout and Literate Layman,' in *Medieval Learning and Literature. Essays presented to R.W. Hunt*, edited J.J.G. Alexander and M.T. Gibson (Oxford 1976), pp. 398–413. N.D. Hurnard, *Studies in Intellectual Life in England from the middle of the fifteenth century to the time of Colet*, unpublished D.Phil. thesis, Oxford 1935, pp. 145–165. Hurnard saw the mid fifteenth century as neglectful of the layman's need for religious literature but this is being overturned by recent research.

49. For a recent essay on late medieval English piety, J.A.W. Bennett, *Poetry of the Passion* (Oxford 1982), Ch. 2, and especially pp. 59–63 for the desirable and practical effect of this piety on conduct. Alexandra Barratt, 'The Prymer and its Influence on fifteenth century English Passion Lyrics', *Medium Aevum* vol. 44 (1975), pp. 264–279. And see Blench *op. cit.*, pp. 258–263.

50. *NPG Catalogue op. cit.*, p. 63 (item 154).

51. C.A.J. Armstrong, 'The Piety of Cecily Duchess of York: A Study in late Medieval Culture', in *For Hilaire Belloc on his Seventieth Birthday* ed. D. Woodruffe (London 1942), p. 86. *NPG Cataloge*, p. 27 (item 52).

52. M.R. James, *The Manuscripts in the Library at Lambeth Palace* (Cambridge 1900), p. 652, item 474, ff.131, 145b. Richard's College at Middleham celebrated a mass of Jesus, James Raine, 'The Statutes . . . for Middleham College 1478', *Archaeological Journal* vol. 14 (1857), p. 165.

53. A.B. Emden, *A Biographical Register of the University of Oxford to 1500* (Oxford 1957–9), p. 1580. There is disappointingly little known of Roby.

54. Text and translation of prayer, *NPG Catalogue op. cit.*, pp. 96–7. And see Ross, *Richard III*, p. 129.

55. N.P. Tanner, *Popular Religion in Norwich with special reference to the evidence of Wills, 1370–1532*, unpublished D.Phil thesis, Oxford 1973, pp. 179–182, on the popularity of such objects. James Raine, *York* (London 1893), pp. 88–9.

56. Sutton and Hammond *op. cit.*, pp. 7–9.

57. W.G. Searle, *History of Queens' College Cambridge*, Cambridge Antiquarian Society Octavo Publications no. 9 (1867), vol. 1, p. 89. William Atthill, *The

Collegiate Church of Middleham, Camden Society 1847, p. 8. *Victoria County History of Durham*, vol. 2 (London 1907), pp. 129–130. D.H. Farmer, *Oxford Dictionary of Saints* (Oxford 1978), *passim*, and Tanner *op. cit.* on the cult of saints, pp. 164–170.

58. *BL Harleian Manuscript 433*, vol. 1 (Upminster 1979), p. 201. Dedications to Ninian are mostly in Scotland and North England with a cult at Ripon, Bishop Dowden, 'Note on the foundation of Richard III at Queens' College Cambridge 1477, illustrating the cult of St. Ninian', *Transactions of the Scottish Ecclesiological Sociey*, vol. 1 (1903), p. 156, and Thomas Lees, 'St. Ninian's Church, Brougham,' *Transactions of the Cumberland and Westmorland Archaeological and Antiquarian Society* OS. vol. 4 (1880 for 1878–9), pp. 421–2. M.R. James *op. cit.*, p. 651 (item 474), f.1 for Ninian's collect and f.2 for a *memoriae* of St. George. And see the statutes of Middleham generally for Ninian's importance to Richard, cited above n. 52.

59. C.G.V. Harcourt, *Legends of St. Augustine, St. Anthony and St. Cuthbert painted on the back of the stalls in Carlisle Cathedral* (Carlisle 1868), pp. 17, 21. The rather mawkish idea that the Tanthony pig, the weakest of the litter, was the association that linked Richard (a child once expected not to live) to St. Anthony, seems far less preferable than the wild boar's rejection of evil for good.

60. B. Colgrave, 'The St. Cuthbert Paintings on the Carlisle Cathedral Stalls', *Burlington Magazine*, no. 73 (1938), p. 17. Sutton and Hammond *op. cit.*, pp. 80–1.

61. *Memoriae* of Katherine and Barbara were in Richard's book of hours, M.R. James *op. cit.*, p. 651, item 474, f.15. There is also a tradition that Memling painted Richard's sister, Margaret, as Saint Barbara, and certainly his mother owned an *agnus dei* with an image of the saint on it, Armstrong *op. cit.*, p. 92.

62. Sandra Raban, *Mortmain Legislation and the English Church 1279–1500* (Cambridge 1982), pp. 131–2. 'Statutes . . . for Middleham College', p. 161 (note 52 above)

63. Tanner *op. cit.*, pp. 207–8. Alan Krieder, *English Chantries. The Road to Dissolution* (Harvard 1979), pp. 6–7, 92. John Bossy, 'Blood and Baptism: Kinship, Community and Christianity in Western Europe from the fourteenth to the seventeenth centuries', in *Sanctity and Secularity: The Church and the World, Studies in Church History*, vol. 10, ed. D. Baker (Oxford 1973), p. 136.

64. Krieder *op. cit.*, pp. 53–5, 69. Despite the crown's dislike of alienation into mortmain both Edward IV and Richard III tolerated it, not with the excessive permissiveness of Henry VI, but at the rate of about 6–7 licences a year, with fines on just over half of these at the rate of 3–5 times the annual value of the land. Henry VII raised the fines to 7½–10 times and the licences dropped to less than 2 a year, Raban *op. cit.*, p. 47, and Krieder, pp. 81–2. This policy was felt most keenly by the less wealthy would-be founder and by the communities that failed to benefit. Henry himself was, of course, a lavish founder for the benefit of his own soul and those of his relatives, notably his chapel at Westminster and the enormous Savoy Hospital.

65. 'The Statutes . . . for Middleham College', p. 170 (note 52 above).

66. Krieder *op. cit.*, pp. 15, 91. *BL Harleian Manuscript 433*, vol. 2, p. 118. *Victoria County History of Yorkshire: North Riding*, vol. 1, pp. 201, 205. Another similar gift was 5 marks towards the building of Windermere church, *BL Harleian Manuscript 433*, vol. 1, p. 201.

67. A.H. Thompson, *The English Clergy and their Organisation in the later Middle Ages*, Oxford 1947, pp. 146–160.

68. Searle, *op. cit.*, pp. 87–101.

69. *Ibid.*, pp. 88–9. 'Statutes . . . for Middleham College' *op. cit.*, pp. 161–2 (note 52, above), and see NPG Catalogue *op. cit.*, p. 47 (item 111).

70. *Victoria County History of Durham*, vol. 2, pp. 129–130. At some date Richard apparently contributed to the fabric of the parish church as his boar appears in the stonework of one of the windows.

71. G.E. Aylmer and Reginald Cant (eds.), *A History of York Minster* (Oxford 1977), pp. 97–8 and n. 196; p. 93 and F. Harrison, *Life in a Medieval College: The Story of the Vicars-Choral of York Minster* (London 1952), pp. 109–111.

72. Rosemary Horrox, 'Richard III and All Hallows Barking by the Tower', *The Ricardian*, vol. 6, no. 77 (1982), pp. 38–40.

73. *Victoria County History: East Riding*, vol. 1: *Hull*, p. 398. Ducal arms seen in the window by William Habingdon, James Nott, *Malvern Priory Church* (Malvern nd.), pp. 25, 35.

74. C.M.L. Bouch, *Prelates and People of the Lake Counties: A History of the Diocese of Carlisle 1133–1933* (Kendal 1948), pp. 129–130. Prior Gudybour put up this window as he did the painted stalls referred to above.

75. *CPR 1476–85*, p. 375. *Victoria County History: East Riding*, vol. 2, p. 191. *BL. Harleian MS. 433*, vol. 2, p. 20.

76. *Ibid.*, vol. 2, pp. 30–1.

77. *Ibid.*, vol. 2, pp. 207, 131, W.J. White, 'The Death and Burial of Henry VI: Part 2', *The Ricardian* vol. 6, no. 79 (1982), pp. 110–113. *BL. Harleian MS. 433*, vol. 2, p. 210.

78. For the spiritual value of anchorites to the community, Tanner *op. cit.* (note 55), p. 129. *BL. Harleian MS. 433*, vol. 1, p. 88, vol. 2, p. 171 (Pontefract) and vol. 1, p. 128, vol. 3, p. 196 (Westminster). Alice Rippes the anchoress of Westminster had been Margaret Multon's predecessor at Pontefract, *Rolls of Parliament*, vol. 5, p. 546b.

79. Armstrong *op. cit.* (note 51), *passim*. Pantin *op. cit.* (note 48), p. 412. And see Ross, *Richard III*, p. 128.

80. David Knowles, *The Religious Orders of England*, vol. 3 (Cambridge 1959), pp. 10–12. Kathleen Chesney, 'Notes on some Treatises of Devotion intended for Margaret of York (MS. Douce 365)', *Medium Aevum*, vol. 20 (1951), pp. 29, 33. Armstrong, pp. 76, n. 5, 83–6, 90–2.

81. Armstrong, pp. 88–9.

82. *Ibid.*, p. 74 n. 3. Pantin *op. cit.*, p. 402.

83. Richard Fitzhugh was first cousin to Richard's wife, his two sisters married Francis Lovel, Richard's friend, and Sir William Parr, and a younger brother

went into the church under George Neville's patronage. *NPG. Catalogue op. cit.*, p. 79. Gillian Keir, *The Ecclesiastical Career of George Neville 1432–76*, unpublished B.Litt. thesis Oxford 1970, p. 177–8. H.E. Allen, *English Writings of Richard Rolle* (Oxford 1931), pp. lvi n. 1, 83. Ross, *Richard III*, p. 48, refers to the close Fitzhugh connection but not its religious implications.

84. Ross, *Richard III*, p. 134. Keir, *op. cit.*, pp. 15–21, 62, 71–6, 123, 181. For another high opinion of George Neville, R.G. Davis, 'The Epsicopate', in *Profession, Vocation and Culture in Later Medieval England, Essays in Memory of A.R. Myers*, ed. C.H. Clough (Liverpool 1982), p. 61.

85. Keir, *op. cit.*, 103, 180. Barrett's embassy, *BL. Harleian MS. 433*, vol. 3, p. 109. Chaderton, Emden, *Oxford, op. cit.* pp. 382–3, and *Testamenta Eboracensia*, vol. 4, Surtees Society vol. 53 (1868), pp. 67–8. Barowe, A.B. Emden, *A Biographical Register of the University of Cambridge to 1500* (Cambridge 1963), pp. 40–41.

86. Keir, *op. cit.*, p. 146, 154–5, 233.

87. *Ibid.*, pp. 94, 153–4.

88. R. Weiss, *Humanism in England during the Fifteenth Century* (Oxford 1957), pp. 149–150. J. Wegg, *Richard Pace, a Tudor Diplomatist* (London 1932), pp. 4–5. P. Brown, 'Thomas Langton and his tradition of learning', *Transactions of the Cumberland and Westmorland Archaeological and Antiquarian Society*, NS. vol. 26 (1926), pp. 158–160, 166–8.

89. Weiss *op. cit.* pp. 164–7. Hurnard *op. cit.* (note 48), pp. 358–398.

90. Emden, *Cambridge, op. cit.*, pp. 275–277.

91. Hurnard *op. cit.*, pp. 22–3. *The Ricardian*, vol. 4, no. 59 (1977), p. 28 (*op. cit.* no. 42 above). Penketh received an annuity from Richard III, *BL. Harleian MS. 433*, vol. 1, p. 263.

92. Ross, *Richard III*, pp. 76, 132–5 on Richard and learned men, p. 149 for his doubt on Richard's ability to understand learned disputations, and p. 229 for his general doubt on Richard's intelligence. H.T. Riley (ed.) *The Croyland Chronicle* (London 1854), p. 470.

93. Firth Green *op. cit.* pp. 87–8.

94. F. Gasquet (ed.), *Collectanea Anglo Premonstratensia*, Camden Society 1904, vol. 1, pp. xix–xx. F.W. Ragg, 'Two Documents relating to Shap Abbey', *Transactions of Cumberland and Westmorland Archaeological and Antiquarian Society*, NS. vol. 9 (1909), pp. 276–81. Sutton and Hammond *op. cit.*, p. 388.

95. B. Dobson, 'Richard Bell, prior of Durham (1464–78) and bishop of Carlisle (1478–1495)', *Transactions of the Cumberland and Westmorland Archaeological and Antiquarian Society*, vol. 65 (1965), pp. 207, 209–10.

96. Blench *op. cit.*, pp. 75, 241.

97. A.R. Myers, *English Historical Documents 1327–1485*, introduction, pp. 51–89. R.G. Davis 'The Episcopate', *op. cit.* (n. 84), pp. 51–89, esp. pp. 56, 63.

98. Myers, *English Historical Documents*, no. 406 and F.R.H. Du Boulay, *Registrum Thome Bourgchier* (Oxford 1957), p. xxxii. *BL. Harleian MS. 433*, vol. 1, p. 136, vol. 3, p. 139. Ross, *Richard III*, p. 138 is notably hostile, ascribing every word of Richard to hypocrisy.

99. Davis, 'The Episcopate', *op. cit.*, p. 52. See below n. 149.

100. The value of good birth, see M. Keen, *The Laws of War in the late Middle Ages* (London 1965), pp. 254–7, S.J. Miko, 'Malory and the Chivalric Order', *Medium Aevum* vol. 35 (1966), pp. 211–2, and Caxton's epilogue to his edition of Lull's *Order of Chivalry, The Prologues and Epilogues of William Caxton*, ed. W.J.B. Crotch, EETS. OS. 176 (1929), p. 84.

101. The main sources used for the eduation of a knight are: M. Vale, *War and Chivalry* (London 1981), ch. 1; A.B. Ferguson, *The Indian Summer of English Chivalry* (Durham N. Carolina 1960), ch. 2; M. Keen, 'Chivalry, Heralds and History', in *The Writing of History in the Middle Ages. Essays presented to R.W. Southern* (Oxford 1981), pp. 400–1.

102. e.g. Writhe's 'Garter Book' of Richard's time, Keen, 'Chivalry' *op. cit.*, pp. 405–6.

103. C.T. Allmand (ed.), *Society at War* (Edinburgh 1973), pp. 21–27.

104. *Ipomedon* was based on an Anglo-Norman original. For this romance and its fellows see Lee C. Ramsey *Chivalric Romances* (Bloomington 1983), Ch. 3, 'The Best Knight in the World'. Gervase Mathew, 'Ideals of Knighthood in late-fourteenth-century England', in *Studies in Medieval History presented to F.M. Powicke*, edited R.W. Hunt, W.A. Pantin and R.W. Southern (Oxford 1948), pp. 357–360. *NPG Catalogue op. cit.* p. 63 and Renwick and Orton *op. cit.*, p. 422, for the version owned by Richard. C. Ross, 'Some Servants . . .' *op. cit.* n. 35 above. The offences for which a knight might be expelled from the order of the Garter were against loyalty and prowess: heresy, treason and flight from battle, E. Ashmole, *The Institution, Laws and Ceremonies of the most noble Order of the Garter* (London 1672), p. 621.

105. D. Bornstein, 'Military Manuals in fifteenth century England', *Medieval Studies*, vol. 37 (1975), pp. 469–73, gives a summary of Vegetius. *NPG Catalogue*, p. 57 (item 190), BL. Royal MS. 18 A xii.

106. G.W. Coopland, *The Trees of Battles of Honoré Bonet* (Liverpool 1949), pp. 21–5 and n. 43 on its circulation and influence. N.A.R. Wright, '*The Tree of Battles* of Honore Bouvet and the Laws of War' in *War, Literature and Politics in the late Middle Ages, Essays in honour of G.W. Coopland*, ed. C.T. Allmand (Liverpool 1976), pp. 13–15, 18–19.

107. N. MacDougall, *James III. A Political Study* (Edinburgh 1982), pp. 154, 168–70. And see Ross, *Richard III*, pp. 45–7.

108. Keen, *Laws of War op. cit.*, pp. 239–247. See also Christine de Pisan's summary of the attributes of a good commander (cited Bornstein *op. cit.*, pp. 475–6) among which moderation and slowness to anger are very important.

109. A. Wagner, *The Heralds of England* (HMSO, 1967), pp. 67–8, 75, 130.

110. *CPR 1467–77*, p. 110, *CPR 1476–85*, p. 343.

111. T.F. Reddaway and L. Walker, *The Early History of the Goldsmiths' Company 1327–1509* (London 1975), p. 152.

112. *NPG Catalogue*, p. 63. M. Keen, 'Chaucer's Knight, the English Aristocracy and the Crusade' in *English Court Culture* (note 11), pp. 45–61.

113. Biography of Turcopilier, *The Ricardian*, vol. 5, no. 73 (1981), p. 368.

114. Keir, *Ecclesiastical Career of George Neville*, pp. 188–9, 193, 221. Crotch, *Order of Chivalry*, p. 48.

115. Keen, 'Chaucer's Knight' *op. cit.*, p. 60.

116. Dominic Mancini, *The Usurpation of Richard III*, ed. C.A.J. Armstrong (Oxford 2nd ed. 1969), p. 137. R. Horrox, 'Richard III and Allhallows' *op. cit.*, p. 38. Sutton and Hammond *op. cit.*, pp. 7–8. A remembrance of Richard's crusading enthusiasm may also be expressed in *The Song of the Lady Bessy, NPG Catalogue op. cit.*, p. 44.

117. E.W. Ives, 'The Common Lawyers', in *Profession, Vocation and Culture in Later Medieval England. Essays dedicated to the Memory of A.R. Myers*, ed. C.H. Clough (Liverpool 1982), pp. 198–9.

118. A.J. Pollard, 'Richard Clervaux of Croft: A North Riding Squire in the Fifteenth Century', *Yorkshire Archaeological Journal*, vol. 50 (1978), pp. 162–3. And see Ross, *Richard III*, p. 55.

119. *BL. Harleian MS. 433*, vol. 3, p. 107. Compare Henry VII's similar efforts, K. Pickthorn, *Early Tudor Government: Henry VII* (Cambridge 1934), p. 39.

120. *Ibid.*, p. 39. E.W. Ives, *The Common Lawyers of Pre-Reformation England* (Cambridge 1983), p. 194.

121. *The Great Chronicle*, ed. A.H. Thomas and I.D. Thornley (London 1938), p. 232.

122. *BL. Harleian MS. 433*, vol. 2, p. 49, vol. 3, p. 124. For Langton's letter, see below n. 153.

123. Pickthorn *op. cit.*, pp. 51, 58. S.B. Chrimes, *English Constitutional Ideas in the fifteenth century* (Cambridge 1936), esp. pp. 61–2. Reynolds *op. cit.* (note 45), p. 22. Ives, *The Common Lawyers of Pre-Reformation England*, esp. chapter 10.

124. M. Hemmant (ed.), *Select Cases in the Exchequer Chamber before all the Justices of England*, vol. 2, Selden Society vol. 64 (1948), p. 90. Compare Ives *op. cit.*, p. 260 and n. 57. Ives' comment seems to be vitiated particularly if the relevant case of Sir Thomas Cook's fine for misprision is taken into account, see Anne F. Sutton, 'The Administration of Justice wherunto we be professed' in *Richard III, Crown and People* (London 1985), p. 362–3 (reprinted from *The Ricardian* vol. 4, no. 53, 1976).

125. The importance of Richard's statute on the fine (cap. 7) was admitted when it was re-enacted in 4 Henry VII after its too hasty abolition. C.A.F. Meakings, *Final Concords*, Surrey Record Society 1946, pp. xxvi–vii, for the purpose of the statute.

126. J.W. Bean, *The Decline of English Feudalism 1215–1540* (Manchester 1968), discusses the beneficial purpose of Richard's statute on the use, pp. 177–8. Ross does not appear to be aware of this section of Bean's work when discussing and dismissing the 1484 statute, *Richard III*, pp. 187–9.

127. Chrimes *op. cit.*, pp. 184–5 for Chancellor Russell's speech opening parliament referring to the problem of the corrupt empanelling of juries – of course the King could have instructed Russell to mention this issue. For the desire for reform of the jury in the 1470s, WAM 12235 and the seminar paper by D.A.L.

Morgan given at the Insitute of Historical Research, London, 11 March 1982. Ross' comments on the sheriff's tourn are overstated probably following Plucknett. No parliament would make a statute for an 'obsolete' court as he states. In 1484 the tourn, although in decline, could still be very oppressive to the lowest classes if maladministered. A better jury might curb this. By 1641 the tourn was indeed 'out of use' because of the sale of sheriffwicks. See John Wilkinson, *A Treatise . . . concerning the Office . . . Coroners and Sheriffs* (London 1641), p. 95 for both its potential power of coercion and its decline. See Potter's *Historical Introduction to English Law*, ed. A.K.R. Kiralfy (London 1958), p. 96 for a sounder appreciation of the tourn's position after the 1462 Statute. A record of an active tourn may be found for 1502–3, under Sir Gervase Clifton, Nottingham University Manuscripts Department: Middleton Ms. Mi M112.

128.   Bacon cited by H.G. Hanbury (Vinerian Prof. of English Law, Oxford) 'The Legislation of Richard III', *American Journal of Legal History*, vol. 6 (1962), p. 95. Hanbury remains the only detailed examination of Richard's statutes. Some of his commentary is undoubtedly naive but it is apparently his pro-Richard conclusions that have earned him a hail of criticism most vehemently expressed by Prof. Elton (review of Ross' *Richard III*, *TLS*, 22.1.1982, p. 70). Professor Ross holds more moderate views but is too dismissive of several of the statutes and of Bacon's superior knowledge (*Richard III*, pp. 187–9).

129.   Hemmant *op. cit.*, pp. 86–94. Ives, *The Common Lawyers op. cit.*, pp. 259–60, 313, comments that the King's anger was unusual.

130.   *BL Harleian Manuscript 433*, vol. 2, p. 36.

131.   *Ibid.*, vol. 2, pp. 119–20, 117, and see vol. 1, p. xxix for the conflict of local and financial interests that might result from such good intentions being put into practice. Such problems should not however be taken to mean that good intentions were useless. When there was such a conflict of interests tending to oppress the weaker subject it was, even more essential for the king to *intend* and enforce benevolent government as he was the sole authority able to intervene effectively. A 'good prince' had to consciously maintain his position and reputation as the fountain of justice.

132.   Reynolds *op. cit.*, pp. 21–2. George Ashby in his *Active Policy of a Prince* specifically advises the appointment of men of middle estate as more competent and less greedy (like himself), EETS. ES. 76 (1899) pp. 32–3, 38 (verses 91, 92, 116).

133.   Reynolds *op. cit.*, pp. 20–2.

134.   Letter to Jonas Jodocus 16 September 1519.

135.   Born *op. cit*, p. 488.

136.   Davies *op. cit.*, pp. 52–5, he spoke to Edward IV over the appointment of their common clerk, pp. 84–91, his involvement in the problem of fishgaths. He gave them 'good and benevolent lordship' *ibid.*, p. 125. Comparable is Richard's ducal encouragement of Cardiff, Pugh, *Glamorgan County History*, p. 348.

137.   *BL Harleian MS. 433*, vol. 1, p. 201 (Pontefract), p. 256 (Llandovery); pp. 249, 274, vol. 2, p. 216 (Scarborough). *VCH North Riding* vol. 2, pp. 539, 542, 551.

Scarborough's need and his own need to build a fleet may have influenced Richard, Peter Heath, 'North Sea Fishing in the Fifteenth Century: The Scarborough Fleet', *Northern History* vol. 3 (1968), *passim*

138. Francis Hill, *Medieval Lincoln* (Cambridge 1948), pp. 282, 285.

139. N.M. Herbert and others, *The 1483 Gloucester Charter in History* (Gloucester 1983), pp. 11, 53. Anne F. Sutton, 'Richard III, the City of London and Southwark', in *Richard III, Crown and People, op. cit.*, pp. 289–95 (reprinted from *The Ricardian* 1975).

Richard is also remarkable for his grants towards city defences and walls, mostly seaside towns: Plymouth (*BL. Harleian MS. 433*, vol. 1, p. 108); Tenby (*ibid.*, vol. 1, p. 109); Sandwich (*ibid.*, vol. 1, p. 128); Dartmouth (*ibid.*, vol. 1, p. 167, vol. 3, p. 194); Newcastle-upon-Tyne (*ibid.*, vol. 1, p. 189); Brecon (*ibid.* vol. 2, p. 131). And the offer of £10,000 to London to help wall Southwark.

140. *BL Harleian MS. 433*, vol. 2, p. 19. Of his nine orders against the unlawful giving of liveries five went to towns (I except the several orders to Kent towns and Canterbury in the aftermath of Buckingham's rebellion).

141. Firth Green *op. cit.* (note 6), pp. 17–18, 24, 28, 30–2. Myers *op. cit.*, pp. 15, 31–9. Wolffe, *The Crown Lands 1461–1536* (London 1970), p. 102.

142. Wolffe, *Crown Lands*. p. 64.

143. *BL. Harleian MS. 433*, vol. 3, pp. 118–120. Wolffe, *Crown Lands*. p. 59.

144. The Croyland Chronicler gives details of Edward's other ways of increasing his income, pp. 474–5. Ross, *Edward IV* (London 1974), pp. 371–387, on Edward's finances and p. 386 on the danger of his financial policies making him unpopular. Sutton, 'Richard III, the City of London and Southwark' *op. cit.*, p. 292.

145. Anne F. Sutton and R.C. Hairsine, 'Richard III at Canterbury', in *Richard III, Crown and People op. cit.*, p. 343. Ross, *Richard III*, p. 152, says mistakenly that offers of money were not made after the 1483 progress.

146. C. Welch, *History of the Worshipful Company of Pewterers of London* (London 1902), vol. 1, p. 57.

147. G.L. Harriss, 'Medieval Doctrines in the Debates on Supply 1610–29' in *Faction and Parliament*, ed. Kevin Sharpe (Oxford 1978), pp. 78, 95, 99, and his 'Aids, Loans and Benevolences', *The Historical Journal* vol. 6 (1963), pp. 1–19, for the nice balance between obligation, compulsion and consent in these transactions. Also Reynolds *op. cit.* for the importance of consultation.

148. *Rolls of Parliament*, vol. 6, p. 240.

149. Mancini, *op. cit.*, p. 62. See above n. 99. Ross, *Richard III*, pp. 136–8 makes a virulent attack on Richard's virtuous life as hypocritical, in the tradition of Polydore Vergil, cf. Kendall, *Richard III*, p. 321.

150. Keen, 'Chivalry' *op. cit.*, p. 413.

151. Blench *op. cit.*, p. 116 quoting BL. Harleian MS. 2247, f. 1.

152. Langton's letter, J.B. Sheppard (ed.), *The Christ Church Letters*, Camden Society 1877, p. 46.

153. Mancini *op. cit.*, pp. 62–5.

154. R.A. Griffiths, 'Richard III: King or Anti-King?' in *The 1483 Gloucester Charter in History*, pp. 32–5. *Christ Church Letters op. cit.*, p. 46. Compare Ross's hostility to Langton, *Richard III*, pp. 151–2.

155. Jervis Wegg, *Richard Pace. A Tudor Diplomatist* (London 1932), pp. 4–5.

156. Given in Armstrong's edition of Mancini *op. cit.*, p. 137. And see M. Greaves, *The Blazon of Honour* (London 1964), p. 17.

157. Charles Ross, 'Rumour, Propaganda and Public Opinion', in *Patronage, the Crown and the Provinces* (Gloucester 1981), pp. 25–8. This continues as one of the constant themes of Ross, *Richard III*, pp. xxvi, 127, 130, 146, 147 ff., 173, 175, 188.

THE SONS OF EDWARDIV: A CANONICAL ASSESSMENT OF THE CLAIM THAT THEY WERE ILLEGITIMATE

R.H. Helmholz

This paper deals with a narrow, but not unimportant, question relating to the accession of Richard III in 1483: Were there legal grounds supporting the claim made on Richard's behalf that the sons of Edward IV were illegitimate? The argument advanced was that there had been a contract of marriage between Edward and Lady Eleanor Butler prior to the time Edward married Elizabeth Woodville, the mother of the sons, and that this contract rendered the children illegitimate. This claim of bastardy was made in Parliament, and it was inserted on the rolls in the Act of Settlement in order to support Richard's claim to the English throne.[1] It alleged that the realm had suffered great and demonstrable harm because of the unlawful union between Edward and Elizabeth, and it claimed that no children of that union had the right to rule. The second continuation of the Croyland Chronicle put the legal argument as follows:

> It was set forth . . . that the sons of King Edward were bastards, on the ground that he had contracted a marriage with one Lady Eleanor Butler before his marriage to Queen Elizabeth; added to which, the blood of his other brother, George, Duke of Clarence, had been attained; so that, at the present time, no certain and uncorrupted lineal blood could be found of Richard, Duke of York, except in the person of . . . Richard, Duke of Gloucester.[2]

The union in question here had been entered into during May of 1464, when Edward IV married Elizabeth Woodville,[3] in what Professor Ross has called an 'impulsive love-match of an impulsive young man.'[4] The actual marriage was not a solemn act of State. It was celebrated clandestinely, that is privately, in the presence of a small group of witnesses. There was no formal

'Church' wedding and no reading of banns. The King's advisers were in fact entirely unaware of what he had done at the time. However, Edward publicly recognized Elizabeth as his wife during the following autumn, and she was subsequently crowned in May of 1465. The union produced ten children, of whom three are of dynastic importance: Elizabeth (b. 1466), Edward V (b. 1470) and Richard (b. 1473).

It was this fruitful and long-accepted marriage that Richard IIIs supporters attacked as adulterous and unlawful. The Bishop of Bath and Wells had revealed that the children were illegitimate, because at the time of the marriage Edward had already entered into a contract of marriage with Lady Eleanor Butler. That pre-contract had also been consummated; indeed there is a suggestion that the lady's seduction had been Edward's goal. Accordingly, the Bishop said, in the eyes of the Church this contract rendered the subsequent marriage invalid and its children illegitimate. Lady Eleanor had died in 1468, and could not give evidence. But, at least according to Commynes, the Bishop recited the facts from what he claimed was his personal knowledge.[5]

The supporters of Richard III seized upon this story to help justify his assumption of kingship. It was not, of course, the only justification, but it was given some weight at the time and it deserves the careful attention of the historian who seeks to assess, or to understand, the claims and the character of Richard III. The ultimate truth or the falsity of the pre-contract story are unfortunately impossible to assess at this distance. The facts were controverted at the time,[6] and the passage of 500 years has only rendered unravelling the threads more difficult. Perhaps we can say that the pre-contract story is plausible but not proved.

What *can* be accomplished more satisfactorily is assessment of the strength of the legal arguments. Assuming that the story was true, did Richard IIIs supporters have a case? Under the law as it stood in 1483, would the establishment of such a pre-contract as alleged on the Rolls of Parliament have rendered the children of Edward IVs union with Elizabeth Woodville illegitimate? This narrow legal point is important, because it can shed some light on the psychology of the actors in the historical drama. It certainly would have been possible for any partisan of Richard III to believe honestly in the existence of the pre-contract between Edward IV and Lady Eleanor. Such clandestine marriages were of common occurrence in medieval England, and this one is not wholly inconsistent with what was known about Edward's character. However, if the existence of such a pre-contract were legally irrelevant, it would have been an act of cynicism, pure and simple, to base a claim to kingship upon it. A partisan may succeed in convincing himself of the likelihood of many facts, but if those facts do not add up to a valid legal claim, the partisan will be acting dishonestly or disputing the law's validity if he pushes forward with the claim. Was this the situation Richard IIIs supporters found themselves in?

The answer to this question given by most modern historians is that this was in fact the situation in 1483. It has been treated most fully by Mortimer Levine in an article published in *Speculum* in 1958.[7] He more recently reiterated his conclusions in a book called *Tudor Dynastic Problems*.[8] Some of Levine's conclusions were briefly though effectively challenged by Mary O'Regan, in an article appearing in *The Ricardian* for 1976,[9] but on the whole Levine's conclusions represent the received opinion about the question. At the least, they are the necessary starting point for examination.

The conclusion of Professor Levine was that, even if true, the story of the pre-contract would not improve Richard IIIs claim to the throne. This was for four reasons. First, although the pre-contract might bastardize the first child born to Elizabeth and Edward, it would not affect the boys Edward V and Richard, since they were born after the death of Lady Eleanor in 1468. Since it was *their* legitimacy which the Parliamentary petition attacked and upon which the immediate succession depended, Richard's claim is out of court. Second, the initially secret nature of the marriage with Elizabeth, stressed in the Parliamentary petition as a determinative factor, was in fact legally irrelevant. Under the medieval canon law, clandestine unions were valid and binding, although they were considered sinful and subjected the parties to penance. Third, the long public recognition of the validity of the King's marriage with Elizabeth, a recognition shared by the highest authorities of Church and State, rendered the claim legally suspect if not invalid. It was raised after their death and was thus made too late to be considered. And fourth, the matter could not rightly have been raised in Parliament. If raised at all, it must have been in an ecclesiastical court, to whose exclusive jurisdiction matrimonial causes belonged. Therefore, even if the story inserted on the rolls of Parliament about Edward's prior contract with Lady Eleanor Butler were true, still this would not be legally sufficient to bastardize Edward V and Prince Richard. It would not survive what lawyers call a demurrer, and it could not improve Richard IIIs claim to the English throne. It was therefore a disingenuous and cynical argument on the part of his supporters.

1. *The Impediment of 'Pollution' by Adultery*

First, did the fact that Lady Eleanor Butler died in 1468 render Edward's existing union with Elizabeth Woodville valid after that date? Levine assumes that it did. Even if the marriage had been adulterous in 1464, once the first wife had died, by definition there could be no objection raised against the second marriage's validity. This analysis is of course correct under modern law. Bigamy ends once one of the two spouses dies. However, the modern assumption distorts the situation under the medieval canon law applicable to Richard IIIs argument. In fact he had the stronger case.

Under medieval canon law, adultery, when coupled with a present contract of marriage, was an impediment to the subsequent marriage of the adulterous partners.[10] It was not simply a matter of having entered into an invalid contract. The parties to it rendered themselves incapable of marrying at any time in the future, because under the canon law one was forbidden to marry a person he had 'polluted' by adultery where the adultery was coupled with either a present contract of marriage or 'machination' in the death of the first spouse.[11] Thus, to use the language of the schools, if Sempronius, being validly married to Bertha, purported to marry Titia and consummated this second, purported marriage, Sempronius and Titia would not only have entered into an invalid union and committed adultery, they would also have incurred a perpetual impediment to marrying after Bertha's death. This is precisely the situation (it was alleged) of Edward IV and Elizabeth Woodville. The canon law forbade him ever to marry her, because he had 'polluted' her by adultery.

Stated this way, the result seems harsh, even unfair. This harshness was recognized by the medieval canonists themselves. They tempered the rules about the consequences of adulterous 'pollution' in several ways, and we should recognize that even under the medieval canon law there would have been arguments possible in favour of the legitimacy of the second marriage with Elizabeth Woodville. Most strikingly, the canonists held that since the purpose of the rule was to protect existing marriages and to discourage adultery, the prohibition did not apply if the second spouse were unaware of the prior marriage.[12] If Titia, in the example above, knew nothing of Sempronius' prior marriage with Bertha, she would not be committing adultery knowingly. Hence it would be unfair to make the impediment perpetual as to her. This made sense. To require a divorce between Titia and Sempronius after Bertha's death would penalize a party who had acted in good faith, and would not deter adultery in any meaningful sense.[13] In fact, it would put a weapon (the ability to secure a divorce) into the hands of a conscious, and perhaps unscrupulous, adulterer if Sempronius were allowed to divorce Titia by alleging his own prior marriage as a perpetual impediment.[14] Thus, in the case at issue, if Elizabeth Woodville had been innocent of any knowledge of Edward IVs prior marriage contract with Lady Eleanor Butler, it would follow that there would have been no impediment to the second union after Lady Eleanor's death in 1468. The argument depends on facts which would have to be proved. We know nothing of Elizabeth Woodville's state of mind. For present purposes, however, the essential point is that Richard IIIs claims were not subject to dismissal out of hand.

Of course, even assuming Elizabeth's innocence in 1464 one might raise the nice legal point that they should have been required to undertake a new marriage ceremony after Lady Eleanor's death. Medieval canonists discussed the point, and it would be possible to do the same today, delving into such questions as whether sexual relations repeated after the death of the first spouse amounted, in law, to sufficient ratification of the prior contract to amount to a new marriage.[15] There would be something to be said on both sides of the question as it related to Richard IIIs argument. It might even be worthwhile to follow the canonists down this path, except for the fact that it is rendered unnecessary because of the clandestine nature of the marriage between Edward and Elizabeth. This is the second point in the allegations made by Richard III found in the Parliamentary claim.

2. The Effects of Clandestinity

The question in law is whether the legitimacy of the children born to Edward IV and Elizabeth Woodville was undermined by the clandestine nature of their marriage contract. Professor Levine dismisses the matter. Under the canon law of marriage, he reasons, clandestine marriages were indisputably valid and binding on the parties.[16] Only after the Council of Trent on the Continent, and much later in England, was marriage before the parish priest a requisite for the union's validity. Therefore, the fact that the marriage was not contracted *in facie ecclesie* could have no effect on the validity of the union which produced the children.

Levine's general understanding of marriage law during the Middle Ages is certainly correct. The Church courts in England, as elsewhere in the West, treated clandestine marriages as valid and specifically enforceable, even though such marriages were contrary to the canonical rules and subjected the participants to penitential discipline.[17] However, this argument moves too quickly to the conclusion that the children were legitimate. It does not follow that the legitimacy of the children was not affected by the fact of clandestinity. The canon law did not treat the question of legitimacy as dependant simply on whether or not the parents were validly married, as we generally do today. Instead, the medieval canon law created a number of subsidiary rules, not dependant simply on whether or not the parents were validly married, which rules were to be used in determining questions of legitimacy.[18]

Most of the canonical rules worked in favour of the children's legitimacy. The application most famous to English historians is legitimation by subsequent marriage of the parents, a soft-hearted principle that earned the disapproval of the English baronage at the Council of Merton in 1234.[19] There were others, probably the most important of which in practical application was the rule that when children were born of a marriage which was later dissolved because of an existing impediment such as affinity or consanguinity, the children were neverthless legitimate unless the parents were aware of the impediment at the time the children were conceived.[20] This rule depended on the good faith of the parents, it being felt that no penalty should accrue from their ignorance of facts which would render the marriage invalid. What to do when one party knew of the impediment and the other did not was a problem that exercised the talents of the medieval canonists. One opinion held that the child was legitimate for purposes of inheritance from the good faith parent, illegitimate as to the other. But this solution was thought inelegant, and the *communis opinio* favoured treating the child as legitimate as long as one parent had been ignorant of the impediment.[21]

These rules obviously bear on the question of the legitimacy of the children born to Edward IV and Elizabeth. Under them, if both of them were aware of the existing contract with Lady Eleanor Butler, then their children were illegitimate. We do not know what proof on this question would have revealed, and perhaps it is idle to raise the question. But in this context it does not matter greatly, because, even assuming ignorance on Elizabeth's part, the canon law held that the rule favouring legitimacy applied only when the marriage had been contracted *in facie ecclesie*. The children of Edward IV and Elizabeth would be illegitimate under the canon law, precisely because they had entered into a clandestine marriage.[22] The favour shown to children, in other words, was available only when their parents had contracted marriage according to the laws of the Church. Thus clandestinity, far from being irrelevant to this question, was a central point in determining the question of the legitimacy of Edward IVs children.

This rule excluding legitimacy was less arbitrary than it might seem. A central reason for discouraging clandestine marriages was to prevent marriages between people between whom an impediment existed. Thus, the reading of the banns was considered important in medieval law because it attracted public attention and would lead naturally to the public disclosure of possible impediments. Secret marriages were suspect because they provided a way around this useful requirement of publicity. Hence, since in these circumstances the legitimacy of the children depended ultimately on the good faith of the parents, it made some sense to create an exception to the general rule favouring legitimacy where the parents had married contrary to the rules of the Church. One who alleges good faith must show good faith by his or her actions. To marry otherwise than according to the laws of the Church raised a presumption of bad faith. This was precisely Elizabeth and Edward's situation. They had not married *in facie ecclesie*. They had done so hastily and secretly. Had they followed the Church's rules, it could have been argued, the pre-contract would have come to light. Therefore, under the law as it existed in 1483, the Parliamentary claim rightly made a point of clandestinity. The lack of marriage publicly contracted *in facie ecclesie* was enough, in most circumstances, to render the children of the union illegitimate.

3.   *The Effect of the Passage of Time*

The third point against Richard IIIs claim is that it came too late. As Professor Levine rightly says, the parents of the princes 'had lived together openly and [were] accepted by the Church and the nation as man and wife.'[23] Therefore, he argues, any possible claim of bastardy would be barred by the passage of time, the death of the parents, and the prior public recognition of the validity of the marriage. This argument is not frivolous. The canon law held that long-time public cohabitation created a presumption of a valid marriage, and that legitimacy of the offspring of such a union could be presumed from the same outward facts.[24] Many legal disputes are settled by presumptions, and the difficulties of proof might have made the dispute at issue here a perfect candidate for such disposition. Again, Levine begins with a right understanding of the canon law.

Nevertheless, on this point as well, Richard IIIs claim stands up in law (always assuming that the pre-contract story was true). There are three reasons under the medieval canon law why his claim cannot be dismissed as legally insufficient to state a cause of action. First, the presumption of validity existed only where the marriage had been contracted *in facie ecclesie*.[25] Again, the canon law's favour extended only to parents who had obeyed the precepts of the law. Second, the canon law specifically allowed the question of bastardy to be raised after the death of the parents in order to determine questions of inheritance. Several decretals found in the *Liber Extra* of Pope Gregory IX dealt with suits brought in precisely such circumstances.[26] Third, a principle of the canon law held that, if an act were inherently wrong, its continuation over a long period could not make it right.[27] Adultery would not be excused by its continuation. It became the greater sin by being repeated.

All of these three points applied to the marriage between Edward IV and Elizabeth Woodville. Their marriage had been contracted clandestinely and therefore their children could not take advantage of the canon law's presumption of legitimacy from long cohabitation. There was a valid question of inheritance at issue, that is the right to succeed to the crown of England, and therefore the decretal law specifically permitted raising the issue of illegitimacy after the death of the parties involved. The allegation made in Parliament was that the union between Edward IV and Elizabeth Woodville was adulterous, and therefore called for denunciation. If true, the facts presented a case of continued wrongdoing that the canon law singled out for special condemnation. Whatever we may think today about the propriety of raising the claim at such a late date, or whatever we may suspect about the motivation of Richard IIIs supporters in doing so, it simply cannot be said that his claim can be dismissed as coming too late. The medieval canon law allowed the matter to be raised when it was.

4.   *The Jurisdictional Question*

The fourth issue raised by the claim of illegitimacy is a jurisdictional one: The English Parliament was a secular assembly and had no power to determine a question properly triable only before an ecclesiastical court. Parliament was, in Levine's phrase, 'an assembly of doubtful status' before which to claim that Edward V and Prince Richard were bastards and incapable of succeeding to the English throne.[28] Therefore, Richard IIIs claim must be dismissed. Whatever its force in substantive law, the claim was inadmissible on jurisdictional grounds.

There is merit to this argument. The letter of the medieval canon law favours the view that whenever a question of legitimacy of birth arose, it should be tried by the Church, not by a secular court.[29] Yet the situation raised a difficult question, even under the canon law. The underlying question in dispute in most such cases, certainly in the one raised by Richard IIIs claim, had to do with a secular matter, rights of inheritance under feudal law. Rights of inheritance, the canon law conceded, belonged to secular determination. Hence the Church's role was strictly a subsidiary one, provided only to assist the secular courts in determining a preliminary legal question. Therefore, under a specific decretal of Pope Alexander III, the proper procedure was to suspend the secular trial whenever a question of legitimacy was raised, and refer the matter to the proper ecclesiastical tribunal, which would determine the limited question of bastardy and certify its answer to the secular court.[30] The secular court could, in turn, finish the case. Judgment belonged to the secular forum. The procedure was time consuming but workable. Analogous systems exist in later legal practice.[31]

It is evident that the authors of the Parliamentary petition were sensitive to the strength of the argument that the Church had the exclusive right to determine the preliminary question of legitimacy. They sought to meet it by inserting on the Parliament rolls the claim that the illegitimacy of Edward IVs children was a matter of public notoriety. This might have had the effect, under some readings of the medieval canon law, of transferring the onus of going forward to the children themselves.[32] That is, where a matter was sufficiently well known, its truth might be presumed. As one decretal stated the law: 'If the crime is so public that it may rightly be called notorious, in that case neither witness nor accuser is necessary.'[33] Thus the petition notes that the putative marriage between Edward and Elizabeth Woodville was invalid, 'as the common opinion of the people and the public voice and fame is throughout all this land.'[34] This was not idle rhetoric. The petition raised a legitimate canonical argument that the truth of the facts it alleged could be presumed, at least until the contrary was shown. Coupled with an offer of proof, the claim was evidently meant to anticipate the argument that Parliament was without authority to decide the question of legitimacy.

It is a measure of the canon law's importance in England at the time that the supporters of Richard III chose this argument. They might well have adopted a more direct approach. They might have attacked the whole basis for canonical jurisdiction over the question by stressing that a secular, not a spiritual matter, was ultimately at stake and by pointing out that in many areas of Western Christendom the canonical procedure just outlined was virtually a dead letter by the end of the fifteenth-century. On the Continent, the practice of sending questions of bastardy to the Church courts had long since disappeared. As the *glossa ordinaria* to Alexander IIIs decretal acknowledged: 'But today in this kingdom the secular judge takes cognizance in all cases, and there is no recourse to the Church.'[35] The canonical procedure had become a matter of theory only, one which even the most prominent canonists were unwilling to push. Thus, to have asserted Richard IIIs rights before a lay assembly would merely have been to bring English practice into line with what happened regularly on the Continent.

The weakness of this more direct argument was that in 1483 English common law still recognized the validity of the canonical rules. Recourse to the ecclesiastical courts where a question of illegitimacy was raised in the course of secular inheritance litigation was the common practice.[36] There were a few exceptional cases where the common law courts would retain jurisdiction—that of children born before the marriage of their parents being the most celebrated—but the usage applied under English common law was essentially in accord with the canonical rule. Whatever Continental practice then was, English practice followed the canon law more closely, and this clearly posed a dilemma for Richard IIIs supporters. They sought to address it by laying emphasis on the supposed notoriety of the illegitimacy of the children. Given English practice, it may have seemed their only recourse. That it posed a real problem for the members of Parliament as well is suggested by the *Croyland Chronicle*. As Levine notes, the *Chronicle* tells us that Parliament was at first unable to give a definition on the matter, and at length presumed to do so only out of fear.[37] On this fourth point, therefore, there was something to be said on both sides of the case. But the stronger argument under the canon law, confirmed by English practice, lay with Richard IIIs opponents.

Conclusion

Except perhaps on the jurisdictional question, therefore, the position stated on the Rolls of Parliament in favour of Richard IIIs claim to the Crown made good legal sense. It would have survived a demurrer. Its ultimate weight depended, as stated at the outset of this paper, on the truth of the underlying facts. Had there been a pre-contract of marriage between Edward IV and Lady Eleanor Butler? And even on the law, in each of the questions there was room for argument on both sides. As so often happens, a lawyer's analysis of a question leads on to further questions. But certainly it should be recognized that under the medieval canon law as it stood in 1483, the claims of illegitimacy against Edward IVs children could not be dismissed out of hand.

When this is said, however, to modern minds there remains something very unattractive about the case, and I think this is more than the normal layman's reaction to *any* strict legal argument. It does not seem just to bastardize the sons of Edward IV as Parliament did. I suppose that it is as well to state this directly in concluding, because even under contemporary canonical standards there was something seemingly unfair about summarily depriving the defenders of those children of the chance to prove their legitimacy before a proper court. What is most suspect about the deprivation was the lack of a fair hearing. It was quite wrong to preclude them from securing a chance to present their case. On this subject the canon law of the time was clear. Richard's supporters would have had to meet the force of this argument by stressing the urgency of the situation. To have opened the case up to the exigencies of litigation would have invited delay of a quite intolerable sort. Affairs of state had to prevail over full exploration of the issues. This is not a dilemma our own age has solved.

However, there is an additional reason that most modern historians react so strongly against Richard's position. It points to the root of the problem. We regard illegitimacy in a different way from most medieval men. They were more hard-headed about it than we are. This is true in three ways. First, the medieval law did not shrink from visiting the sins of the parents on the children. The attitude of mind which regards this as right has receded in recent years, and we are more apt to regard all claims of bastardy as tainted on this account.[38] Medieval men did not. Although they recognized that the children of an adulterous liaison were personally blameless, and although the canon law accorded them favourable presumptions in a number of situations, still it did not seem wrong to deprive such children of inheritance rights for a fault that was not theirs. As one canonist put it, after stating the equitable factors favouring the child of an adulterous union, 'Neverthless . . . in detestation of such a crime and in hatred of the parents, the child is considered illegitimate.'[39]

Second, the medieval law was willing to follow logical arguments to their conclusions in the area of family law to a far greater extent than we are. Humanity and happiness have become the goals of modern family law. To allow them to be subverted by a 'drily logical' doctrine now seems patently indefensible. The medieval canon law, however, did not take that view. It often forced men and women to live with the logical consequences of their domestic acts. Thus, if Edward IV and Lady Eleanor Butler had contracted marriage, they were bound to live with the results as fully as we would be bound to follow a decision we had freely made about financial matters, even where the decision had unfortunate consequences against the authorities of the Inland Revenue. There were, of course, some tempering principles even under the medieval law. It is a difference of degree. But it is a real difference nonetheless.

Third, the medieval canon law was more sensitive than is modern law to the differences between what can be proved in a public court and what is ultimately true. For legal purposes, we are largely satisfied with the former, ignoring (or pretending to ignore) the latter. However, *both* were taken seriously by the medieval canonists, and the result was a legal system under frequent pulls in opposite directions. The question under discussion in this paper provides a good example. Suppose the story of the pre-contract were true, but that its existence rested solely on the word of the Bishop of Bath and Wells or even (as Richard III's supporters alleged) on widespread public notoriety. It would therefore be difficult to prove in court. What result should follow? Should men's lives be ruled by external proof or by what they know to be the truth? In general the canonists held that external proofs must determine the matter, but they were uncomfortable with the outcome, because they recognized that the law thereby worked an ultimate injustice. In the 'forum of conscience' the opposite result should obtain. This (unresolved) tension was a continuing problem for the canonists, and it meant that they could feel the merit of the arguments in favour of Richard III more strongly than we can.

With the other two factors, this last point gives additional reason for the historian to avoid rejecting out of hand the claim of illegitimacy put onto the Rolls of Parliament. If the modern historian attempts to think the thoughts of men of the fifteenth-century, he will be sensitive to the ultimate superiority of what the parties knew to be the truth, even where they could not prove it in a public court. The ease with which the claims of Richard III's supporters have been rejected is more a product of modern habits of thought than it is the result of study of the law applicable at the time. That is the canon law. Under that law the Parliamentary claim stated a legitimate cause of action.

Notes

1. *Rotuli Parliamentorum* (1783), vol. 6, pp. 240–242.
2. *Ingulph's Chronicle of the Abbey of Croyland*, ed. H.T. Riley (1854), p. 489.
3. See Charles Ross, *Richard III* (London 1981), pp. 89–91; Paul Murray Kendall, *Richard the Third* (London 1955), pp. 257–62.
4. Charles Ross, *Edward IV* (London 1974), p. 86.
5. See Philippe de Commynes, *Memoires*, ed. J. Calmette and G. Durville. (Paris 1924–25), vol. 2, pp. 232, 305.
6. The bill was stigmatised as 'faux et seditious' in proceedings brought before all the Justices assembled in the Exchequer Chamber during Henry VIIs first year. Year Book, 1 Henry VII, 5, pl. 1.
7. Mortimer Levine, 'Richard III – Usurper or Lawful King?', *Speculum*, vol. 34 (1958), pp. 391–401.
8. Idem, *Tudor Dynastic Problems, 1460–1571* (London 1973), pp. 29–30.
9. Mary O'Regan, 'The Pre–contract and its Effect on the Succession in 1483', *The Ricardian*, vol. 4, no. 54 (1976), pp. 2–7.
10. See *Decretales Gregorii IX*, Lib. IV, Tit. 7 (X 4.7.1–8) in *Corpus Iuris Canonici*, ed. E. Friedberg (1879), vol. 2, pp. 687–90. John J. Donohue, *The Impediment of Crime* (1931); A. Esmein, *Le mariage en droit canonique* (1891), pp. 384–93.
11. E.g., Antonius de Butrio, *Commentaria in Libros Decretalium* (Venice, 1578) ad 4.7.2 (*Significavit*), no. 1: 'Si vivente prima legitima uxore quis contrahat cum secunda, et eam cognovit, etiam prima mortua secundam habere non potest.'
12. *Idem*, ad X 4.7.7 (*Veniens*), no. 1: 'Si quis vivente prima secundam huius rei nesciam duxit uxorem, mortua prima remanet cum secunda.'

13. *Idem*, ad X 4.7.7 (*Veniens*), no. 2: '. . . et sic ignorantia excludit adulterium, et omnem penam imponendam, et sequelam adulterii.'
14. E.g., Hostiensis, *Lectura in Libros Decretalium* (Venice 1581) ad X 4.7.1 (*Propositum*), no. 1: 'Doloso petente, non datur divortii sentencia.'
15. E.g., Panormitanus, *Commentaria in Libros Decretalium* (Venice 1605) ad X 4.7.7 (*Veniens*), no. 1: 'Si quis vivente prima, secundam huius rei nesciam duxerit uxorem, mortua prima, licite remanet cum secunda novo consensu interveniente.' A full discussion would require treatment of the difference between tacit and explicit consent, and of the possible role of sexual relations as raising a presumption of consent. Also involved in the actual case would have been the factual question of when the knowledge of the prior contract with Lady Eleanor had come to Elizabeth, Edward's Queen. See, e.g., Hostiensis, *Lectura* ad X 4.7.1, no. 1.
16. See *Tudor Dynastic Problems*, supra note 8, at 29.
17. See my *Marriage Litigation in Medieval England* (1974), pp. 25–31.
18. A separate title of the Gregorian Decretals was devoted to the subject; see X 4.17.1–15, in *Corpus Iuris Canonici*, supra note 10, pp. 710–17.
19. See *Councils & Synods with other Documents relating to the English Church II: A.D. 1205–1313*, ed. F.M. Powicke and C.R. Cheney (1964), Pt 2, pp. 198–200; F.W. Maitland, Introduction to *Bracton's Notebook* (1887), pp. 14–17.
20. *Glossa Ordinaria* ad X 4.17.10 (*Referente*) s.v. *referente*: 'Si scientes inter se impedimentum, matrimonium contrahunt, illegitima est proles eorum.' See also Antonius de Butrio, *Commentaria* ad X 4.17.6 (*Tanta est*), no. 9.
21. See *Glossa Ordinaria* ad X 4.3.3 (*Cum inhibitio*) s.v. *si ambo*: '. . . monstrum enim esset si aliquis esset partim legitimus et partim illegitimus.'
22. X 4.3.3 (*Cum inhibitio*); Panormitanus, *Commentaria* ad X 4.17.14 (*Ex tenore*), no. 9: 'Ultimo circa ignorantiam conclude quod aut matrimonium est clandestinum et ignorantia parentum non prodest.'
23. Levine, *Tudor Dynastic Problems*, supra note 8, at p. 29.
24. *Glossa ordinaria* ad X 4.17.11 (*Pervenit*) s.v. *Si est ita*: '. . . eo ipso quod parentes istius in facie ecclesie contraxerunt approbante ecclesia simul fuerunt usque ad mortem praesumitur legitimum matrimonium inter eos quare filii legitimi sunt habendi quousque contrarium ostendatur.' See also G. Mascardus, *De Probationibus*, (Venice 1593), vol. 1, concl. 342, no. 5, with authorities given therein.
25. Panormitanus, *Commentaria* ad X 4.17.11 (*Pervenit*) no. 4: '[H] ic autem papa non admittit probationes de impedimento, dummodo possit constare quod in facie ecclesie contraxerunt.'
26. E.g., X 4.17.3 (*Causam quae*); see also *glossa ordinaria* ad X 4.3.3. (*Cum inhibitio*) s.v. *voluerit*: '. . . post mortem etiam admittitur accusatio propter bona.'
27. E.g., Panormitanus, *Commentaria* ad X 4.7.5 (*Cum haberet*), no. 4: 'Nota tertio quod diuturnitas in peccato non minuit peccatum sed augmentat.'
28. Levine, *Tudor Dynastic Problems*, supra note 8, at p. 29.
29. See my 'Bastardy Litigation in Medieval England', *American Journal of Legal History*, Vol. 13 (1969), pp. 362–67 for a fuller development of the argument following.
30. X 4.17.5 (*Lator praesentium*).

31. See J.H. Baker, 'Ascertainment of Foreign Law: Certification to and by English Courts prior to 1861', *International and Comparative Law Quarterly*, Vol. 28 (1979), pp. 141–51.

32. G. Mascardus, *De Probationibus*, supra note 24, Vol. 2, Concl. 791, no. 10: 'Secundo limitabis, ut usque eo non procedat quin saltem transferat onus probandi contrarium in adversarium.'

33. X 3.2.8 (*Tua nos duxit*).

34. *Rot. Parl.*, Vol. 6, p. 240.

35. *Glossa ordinaria* ad X 4.17.4.

36. See William Clerk, *The Trial of Bastardie* (1594).

37. *Croyland Chronicle*, supra note 2, pp. at 495–96.

38. See generally Jenny Teichman, *Illegitimacy: an Examination of Bastardy* (1982), pp. 153–74.

39. *Lectura* ad X 4.17.6 (*Tanta est vis*), no. 2: 'Nichilominus cum enim in matrimonium peccaverat uterque ex certa scientia adulterium committendo in destestationem tanti criminis et parentum odium proles illegitima censebitur.'

THE SONS OF EDWARD IV:
A RE-EXAMINATION OF THE EVIDENCE
ON THEIR DEATHS AND ON THE BONES
IN WESTMINSTER ABBEY

P.W. Hammond and W.J. White

This paper discusses the fate of the sons of Edward IV, how they apparently vanished from the Tower of London during the reign of their uncle, Richard III, and what was said about them in that reign, and subsequently. It does not discuss, except incidentally, who, if anyone, murdered them, and is concerned solely with what people believed had happened. Secondly, it presents an historical and scientific discussion of the bones found in the Tower in 1674, and shows why bones so found in the past should have been identified with such alacrity as those of the Princes, perhaps influencing Tanner and Wright, the modern investigators of the 1674 bones into giving them a spurious veneer of respectability. The conclusions of Tanner and Wright are discussed, as are the findings of modern research on the influence of diet, disease, etc upon the height and apparent ages of children. Also considered are tests which might now be applied to the Tower bones to age, date and sex them conclusively.

The main events between 9 April 1483, the date of Edward IV's death, and 6 July 1483, the coronation day of Richard III, are too well known to need discussing in detail in this context. It is probably sufficient to say that by about 19 May Edward V (then aged 12½ years) was residing in the Tower, presumably in preparation for his coronation (at this date still fixed for 22 June), and his brother Richard of York (aged nearly 9) joined him there on 16 June. The coronation of Edward V was then postponed until 9 November, and subsequently cancelled by his uncle's accession on 26 June.[1] From this day the two sons of Edward IV had no official position in the realm, and little that is unequivocal is heard concerning their continued existence. There are however two definite reports of their being seen.

The first of these reports is that of Domenico Mancini to Angelo Cato, Bishop of Vienne. This was written in the late autumn of 1483, describing events up to Mancini's departure from England a few days after Richard's coronation on 6 July. Mancini was an Italian, a priest, and had been in England from late in 1482.[2] From the evidence of his report he seems to have had informants at Court, probably only minor functionaries, and there is less evidence of this during the Protectorate and reign of Richard of Gloucester. He apparently spoke no English, which must have restricted his ability to gather information, but presumably spoke Latin with churchmen and educated laymen, and Italian with Genoese merchants. He may have known and conversed with Pietro Carmeliano, the Italian court poet (see below), and he certainly conversed with Dr John Argentine. Argentine was doctor to Edward V, was also a priest and, as important, may have known some Italian (he certainly knew Latin). His evidence gives us one of the few examples of Mancini's ability to procure 'inside' information.[3]

Mancini says that Argentine reported (presumably to Mancini) that the young King was expecting death. According to Mancini Argentine was the last attendant allowed access to the young King, and reported that Edward and his brother were withdrawn into the inner apartments of the Tower after Lord Hastings was executed and 'day by day began to be seen more rarely behind the bars and windows, till at length they ceased to appear altogether'. Mancini goes on to say that after Edward's removal from sight there were rumours that he was dead, but that he had not been able to confirm this.[4]

Mancini's reference to the Princes no longer being seen presumably refers to a date just before he left England in mid-July. This is compatible with the other unequivocal reference to the boys after Richard's accession. This is from the *Great Chronicle* of London, which says that in the mayoralty of Sir Edmund Shaa (29 October 1482–28 October 1483) 'the childyr of Kyng Edward were seen shotyng and playyng in the Gardyn of the Towyr by sundry tymys'.[5] These sightings may be dated between 16 June, when Richard of York joined his brother, and the apparent disappearance of the brothers in July reported by Mancini.

There are two references in the Signet Office docket book later than July 1483 which have been taken to refer to Richard's nephews, but both are almost certainly references to others. The first is a warrant for the delivery of clothing to 'the Lord Bastard' dated 9 March 1485, and the second an ordinance for regulating the King's Household at Sheriff Hutton, dated 24 July 1484. This states *inter alia*, 'My lord of Lincolne and my lord Morley to be at oon brekefast, the Children togeder at oon brekefast', and that no livery should exceed the allowance except to 'my lord and the Children'.[6] Sheriff Hutton housed the King's Council of the North under the Earl of Lincoln, Richard's nephew, and it has been argued that 'the Children', obviously of high rank, must include the sons of Edward IV, and that the 'lord Bastard' must be the elder of those sons.[7] By the act of *Titulus Regius* Edward's sons were undoubtedly bastards, and Markham argued that young Edward was still Earl of March and Pembroke, making him a lord. However, on Richard's accession to the throne his nephews undoubtedly became incapable of holding any honour (unless newly granted), and despite Markham's protestations any bastard son of a king was liable to be called a 'lord bastard'. It has recently been shown that John of Gloucester, Richard's illegitimate son, was so called for example.[8] As to 'the Children': the probably explanation of this phrase is that Richard had collected at Sheriff Hutton many of his nephews (and nieces, ignored by Markham) and possibly his own illegitimate children too. We know that at least Elizabeth of York and Edward of Warwick were there in 1485. All these children would share the rank of the Earl of Lincoln, as 'the Children' obviously do.[9]

Other arguments have been used to attempt to prove that Edward and Richard of York were alive after the summer of 1483. For example, it has been suggested that they must have been alive in November 1483 when the Duke of Buckingham was executed, on the grounds that if they had then been dead Richard would have siezed this opportunity to accuse Buckingham of their murder, whoever had murdered them. Alternatively, if Richard had wished to murder them then he would have done so, and accused Buckingham of the deed.[10] This is a very slight argument indeed, and need not detain us. Another argument which has been tentatively put forward is that the curious reference of Vergil to a 15 year old Edward being removed from Sheriff Hutton on the orders of Henry VII in 1485 relates to Prince Edward of York and not to Edward of Warwick, as Vergil says. The former was 15 in 1485, the latter only 10. However Vergil probably did not know how old Edward of Warwick was in 1485, this being the most likely explanation of the mistake.[11] It could also be said that the statement in Ricart's *Kalendar* for the year 1484 that 'this yere the two sonnes of King E. were put to scylence in the Towre of London' means that they were alive until then, but the years being used are in fact mayoral years, beginning on the 15th September. The rest of the entry for 1484 deals with the great flood and storms of autumn 1483, and ends with the execution of the Duke of Buckingham, i.e. the events of 1483. Since the *Kalendar* was probably written up somewhat after the events being described Ricart may not have been quite sure in which mayoral year he heard the rumours, and it is probable that 1483 is meant. It is also of interest that the accession and coronation of Richard of Gloucester is reported without comment.[12]

Finally, it has been argued that Edward and Richard of York lived on until the reign of Henry VIII, concealed in the household of Sir Thomas More.[13] This theory depends on subjective interpretations of a form of code concealed in a painting by Holbein, but has no objective backing, and will not therefore be discussed here. It is of course true to say that it was firmly believed by many at the time that one or both of Edward IV's sons had survived Richard III's reign, witness the success of the pretenders in gathering support, of whom the major examples are Lambert Simnel and Perkin Warbeck.[14] Such a prominent actor in events as Sir William Stanley was reported to have said that if Perkin Warbeck were indeed the son of Edward IV he would never fight against him, which implies some doubt on his part as to whether or not Edward's sons were both dead.[15] So widespread does the belief in the continued existence of the Princes appear to have been that William Parron, personal astrologer to Henry VII apparently felt it necessary in his almanac for 1500 to affirm that both Princes were dead before 1485. This general belief was later reported by both Vergil and More.[16]

The rumours to the effect that the Princes were still alive were in fact only part of those circulating from the time of Richard III's accession to the throne or before. As noted above, by early July 1483 rumours that Edward and Richard were dead were reported by Mancini. The existence of these rumours is further demonstrated by that reported in the recently discovered London chronicle. This was probably written contemporaneously with the events described, and says that the Princes were put to death in the Tower in 1483.[17] These rumours had already begun circulating by about the middle of June as seen in the cryptic memorandum amongst the Cely papers. It is worth quoting in full to show the state of confusion existing at that time:–

'There is a great rumour in the realm. The Scots has done great in England. Chamberlain is deceased in trouble. The Chancellor is proved false and not content. The Bishop of Ely is dead. If the King, God save his life, were deceased, if the duke of Gloucester were in any peril, if my lord prince, God defend, were troubled, if my lord of Northumberland were dead or greatly troubled, if my lord Howard were slain.'[18]

This seems to be saying that Edward V may be dead, and possibly his brother too. It was obviously written after Hastings' execution on the 13th June and before Richard put forward his claim to the throne, and may have been written by Sir John Weston, Prior of St John's,[19] and a councillor of Edward IV and Henry VII, if not of Richard III. Sir John should have been well aware of the true course of events. That he apparently was not, even thinking that the Bishop of Ely was dead, shows how much confusion there was in London; those outside an inner circle obviously had no idea of what was happening, and at such a time rumours begin to spread. It would only have been surprising if they had not.

Many instances of the spread and persistence of rumour in the late middle ages may be found. There were for example the false rumours, persisting as late as 1414, saying that Richard II was still alive, or those concerning the death of the Earl of Warwick in the Tower circa 1487. The rumours of the survival of Charles of Burgundy after the Battle of Nancy in 1477, and indeed of Richard III after the Battle of Bosworth are also noteworthy.[20] Professor Ross discussed the speed with which such rumours spread in the fifteenth century, their often seditious nature, and the difficulty of stopping them once started. He also stressed the credulity of the 'commons', who apparently had no difficulty in believing the most unlikely stories. He instanced for example the otherwise sober annalist who, in his record of the year 1462 notes as fact a vast international conspiracy with forthcoming foreign invasions directed against England.[21] This paranoid attitude towards foreign invasion is also illustrated in the phrase 'the Scots had done great in England' of the Cely memorandum. That rumours existed was obviously no proof that an event had occurred, (we know that Edward and Richard of York were alive in June 1483 for example), nor even that it was likely to have occurred or to occur. It may be noted here that none of the writers who reported the death of the Princes was doing more than reporting rumour, with the possible exception of Sir Thomas More, and with this exception none of them produced, or had produced for them, any corroborative evidence.

It thus appears that from mid June 1483 rumours were circulating, in London at least, that the nephews of Richard III had been murdered. Richard is in fact accused by Vergil of spreading rumours of their death himself. Vergil says that Richard 'permytted the rumor of ther death to go abrode to thintent (as we may well beleve) that after the people understoode no yssue male of King Edward to be now left alyve, they might with better mynde and good will beare and sustayne his government'.[22] Rumours circulating about this time are also reported by the Croyland Chronicler (possibly John Russell, Chancellor to Richard III, writing April–May 1486), saying that while Henry Duke of Buckingham was at Brecon in August–September 1483 'it was spread about that the said sons of King Edward had perished (by what violent means is unknown)'.[23] Certainly the Yorkists had made use of similar tactics before, e.g. the false rumours concerning the death of Henry VI spread before the battle of Ludford Bridge,[24] and they made considerable use of propaganda. In this instance though we may doubt if Richard was responsible, since the likely effect of such rumours would be to unite his enemies against him, as in fact did happen. These rumours were still current at Easter 1484 according to the *Great Chronicle*, which has 'afftyr Estyrn much whysperyng was among the people that the Kyng hadd put the Childyr of Kyng Edward to deth'.[25] The difficulty experienced by fifteenth century governments in stemming rumours has been mentioned above, if no effort was made to do so they would continue to circulate. Richard III of course apparently did nothing to stop them, unless the 'false and contrived invencions' which he refuted in London in March 1485 included these.[26]

This gossip, or propaganda, was soon known on the Continent. In a speech to the Estates General in January 1484 at Tours, Guillaume de Rochefort, Chancellor of France explicitly accused Richard III of murdering his nephews. This information may possibly have come from Mancini, he and the Chancellor may have been acquainted.[27] The tenor of this speech congratulated the French on their loyalty to their kings, and the continuity of their royal succession, in contrast to the disloyal English, who frequently deposed and murdered their kings. He was urging support for the government of the young king, 13 year old Charles VIII. This theme was relatively common in fifteenth century French government pronouncements.[28] Foreign charges of murder must not be seen in isolation, the information from England was being used for its political message to Frenchmen, and not for its moral message to them or to anyone else. Truth was not a necessary part of the message.

There is one piece of evidence to show that the French may have heard of the death of Edward IV's sons before the death of Louis XI on the 30th August. We owe this information to a genealogical roll of about 1513.[29] This says that a Thomas Warde, Doctor of Physick and Chaplain to Edward IV, was sent to France in 1482 to collect the subsidy from Louis XI (the date must be an error for 1483 as Edward received the subsidies for 1482), and was still in France when Edward died. Louis nevertheless paid the usual amount, plus an extra 1000 crowns. Before Warde could leave France however Louis 'was certifyed how that Richard Duke of Gloucester the protector had put his neviews to scilence and usurped the crowne upon thayme with great tyrany', and Warde was arrested and not released until later. This is an entirely circumstantial story, which could nonetheless be true. Edward certainly sent Garter King of Arms to France in February 1483, and Warde may have been part of this embassy. A Thomas Warde, possibly the same man, was employed in France by Richard III in May 1484, and a man of this name was employed on diplomatic business in 1486, 1487 and 1488.[30]

Thus, as has been seen, within the lifetime of their uncle there was a belief that his nephews were dead. It was also believed that he had murdered them. Neither of these propositions was necessarily true, but they appear to have been acted upon as if they were. We are told that the later stages of the Buckingham uprising were avowedly to set Henry Tudor on the throne, switching from the original purpose of freeing the Princes from the Tower.[31] This belief is enshrined in the Act of Attainder passed against Richard III in 1485 by Henry VII's first parliament. In this act he is accused of the 'shedding of infants' blood'.[32] Much ink has been expended in explaining the significance of these words, but it seems plain enough that it is an accusation of murdering his nephews. It has been suggested that the phrase is commonplace in mediaeval attainders, but this is not so. So far as can be discovered it is unique. John Tiptoft was accused on the scaffold of cruelty in putting children to death, but this is a reference to the two sons of the Earl of Desmond whom he may, or may not, have had executed. He was not attainted.[33] There appear to be no other similar references. Nevertheless, the wording in the attainder of Richard III is odd. If Henry Tudor had possessed definite evidence it would be expected that a definite charge would be made. It might almost be said that at this point Henry was merely repeating current rumours. He was definite enough in 1494 when instructing his envoys concerning the identity of Perkin Warbeck, ordering them to state categorically that Richard of York and his brother Edward had been murdered by their uncle Richard.[34]

Following the death of Richard III and his attainder it became safe as well as congenial to the government of Henry Tudor to openly express a belief that Richard had murdered his nephews. There are no fewer than four authors, writing within about two years of his death (the number perhaps reflecting how widespread the rumours were), all mentioning the death of Edward IV's sons. Three of these authors say they were dead and accuse Gloucester of murdering them. They are Dafydd Llwyd, a Welsh bard, Peitro Carmeliano, an Italian, court poet to Edward IV, Richard III and Henry VII and Diego de Valera, a Spanish diplomat and courtier.[35] The fourth is the Croyland Chronicler, who nowhere unequivocally says that the Princes were dead. In the main body of his work he says that there was a rumour that they had died violently. A curious poem near the end of the work, of which the Chronicler does not in fact claim authorship, concerning the three King Richards of England, says '*fratris opprimeret proles*'. This may mean 'destroy his brother's children', but not necessarily.[36] If John Russell was indeed the author, a man who could be expected to know what had happened, this lack of specificity is puzzling. It is analogous to the sentence used in the Act of Attainder.

English writers for the next 25 years or so maintain this general belief that Richard III was responsible for murdering his nephews. Is is interesting to note that within this period none of them give any details of how the murder was carried out. This applies to the brief notes in the Ashmolean Manuscript as well as to Rous and André. The statement of the latter that the boys were put to the sword (*nepotes quoque clam ferro incautos feriri jussit*) may be meant metaphorically.[37] The town chronicles are similarly brief, with the exception of the *Great Chronicle* (of London), dealt with separately below. Most of them are related, more or less loosely, as versions of the main London Chronicle, but there are others such as Ricart's *Kalendar* (see above) and the very late Chronicle of King's Lynn.[38]

During this time there were also a number of reports on the Continent about Edward and Richard of York. One of them (the French Chancellor) has already been mentioned, and apart from Commynes, whose description of events in 1483 (written circa 1490–96) is brief and bears some resemblance to the story as told by the English chroniclers (although he seems unsure whether Richard or the Duke of Buckingham murdered the Princes[39]), they are noticeably more detailed than the English sources. One very early report, that by Diego de Valera, has already been briefly referred to. This was written early in 1486, and says that Richard poisoned his nephews with herbs while Edward IV was campaigning in Scotland. In a later version he added that Richard also poisoned his brother. This extraodinary story possibly came from Spanish merchants sailing from Bristol.[40] The Dutch *Divisie Chronicle*, written about 1500 gives the interesting suggestion that Richard's nephews were starved to death, or possibly murdered by the Duke of Buckingham. It adds that 'some say' that Buckingham spared one of the children 'which he had lifted from the font and had him secretly abducted out of the country'. This appears to be unique in its explanation of the origins of the career of Perkin Warbeck.[41]

With Jean Molinet, probably writing about this time, we come to a much more detailed description of events, the first such. Perhaps here we begin to see the usual effect of distance and time on a rumour, interestingly shown in the sixteenth century descriptions of the misdeeds and bad character of James III of Scotland.[42] Molinet describes the most affecting scenes between the royal brothers and between Richard of York and the murderers. He states that the Princes died five weeks after the younger was imprisoned (i.e. about the end of July) and that they were put to death by the 'Captain of the Tower', being smothered, possibly between two quilts. He also mentions the possibility that they were starved (or suffocated) in a dungeon. However they died, they were first buried in a secret place, and later exhumed and given royal obsequies.[43] It is of interest to note that rumours continued to develop on the Continent. Martin du Bellay, writing in the middle of the sixteenth century tells us that Richard had his nephews murdered and gave out that they had died by accident, by falling from a high bridge within the Tower.[44]

At this point it is necessary to return to the English chroniclers, specifically to the *Great Chronicle*. From this we see that at some time before about 1512, when it was being written down, some of the embroidered versions of the story seem to have returned to this country. This begins a process interestingly similar to what happened with the descriptions of the murder of Edward of Lancaster, when details apparently added by foreign writers were taken up by native writers and embroidered further with great enthusiasm. The author of the *Great Chronicle* gives far more detail than any previous English writer. He says that the general opinion was that Edward's sons were dead, but that there were many theories as to how they had died. Suggestions are given that they were drowned in malmsey, stabbed, poisoned or smothered between two feather beds. For the first time a name is given to the murderer, Sir James Tyrell, or it might have been an old, unnamed servant of Richard III.[45] There were thus a number of different rumours still in circulation. Polydore Vergil, possibly writing slightly later, in 1512–13, gives a great deal more detail. He only gives one version of the death of the Princes, but this contains the outline of the well known story improved by More and later by Shakespeare. Vergil has Sir Robert Brackenbury, Lieutenant of the Tower (reminiscent of Molinet's Captain of the Tower) ordered to carry out the murder. On Brackenbury's refusal Richard commits the deed to Sir James Tyrell, who carries it out. Vergil goes on to say 'with what kinde of death these sely chylren wer executyd yt is not certanely known'.[46]

More wrote his *History of Richard III* about 1514–18, i.e. probably after Vergil had finished the first draft of his work. It seems possible therefore that More could have seen this draft, and thus the passage on the death of the Princes. Certainly More's description of their death is in essence an expansion of Vergil's bare description, containing elements also seen in the *Great Chronicle* and Molinet, i.e. an account of who did it (Sir James Tyrell), when, where, how (by suffocation in bed clothes interestingly enough) and how after an original clandestine burial the bodies were later reburied in a manner more fitting their royal birth.[47] The story is well enough known, and it is not necessary to discuss it in detail, except in a number of specific aspects.

It may first of all be asked where More obtained his information. His account contains a mass of circumstantial detail which it might be argued shows the essential truth of the whole story, since the detail shows some knowledge of how the royal Household of the fifteenth century operated. Such an argument could be used to demonstrate the truth of most historical novels. However it is worth asking where More obtained the other details of his description of the murders from. We may conjecture that he sifted them from the many rumours current at this time, demonstrated by the *Great Chronicle*. More himself gives the answer: 'but in the meanetime for this present matter, I shall rehearse you the dolorous end of those babes, not after every way that I have heard, but after that way that I have heard by suche men and by such meanes, as me thinketh it wer hard but it should be true', i.e. from rumours and oral tradition.[48] However he also claims as a source the confession of Sir James Tyrell. Having this one would not expect him to need the others. Be this as it may, Tyrell is said to have confessed to the murder of the Princes when in the Tower accused of treason. This would have been in 1502, when he was accused of aiding the Earl of Suffolk, Yorkist claimant to the throne. The confession is not referred to by writers before More (e.g. the *Great Chronicle* or Vergil), and it appears not to have been published by Henry VII. In addition Tyrell was not accused of murdering Richard's nephews in the attainder passed against him in 1504.[49] It thus seems probable that such a confession never existed, and that the whole of More's description of the Princes' death was cullled from the rumours which we have seen were circulating, and from his fertile imagination. That More was not writing history in any modern sense has been demonstrated very convincingly by Dr Alison Hanham, who shows that his authority as a source of historical information is, in general, negligible.[50]

One final point in More's description must be discussed, and this is the part of his story where he says that the bodies of the murdered Princes were hidden in the Tower 'at the stayre foote, metely depe in the grounde under a great heape of stones'. He goes on to say that they were subsequently moved to a 'better' location 'because thei wer a kinges sonnes',[51] (or possibly thrown into the Thames in a weighted coffin), the actual course of events known only to a priest who was now dead. This latter point is presumably to explain why the bodies had not yet been dug up and exhibited by Henry VII. However this has not prevented bones discovered under or near a staircase (or anywhere else) in the Tower being attributed to the sons of Edward IV, although such discoveries most certainly do not bear out More's account.[52]

That human remains should be found buried at the Tower of London is unremarkable given the enormous turnover of residents at the site during the middle ages. Multiple bone-finds would have been expected from such a site and this has been the experience at the Tower. As is well known the discovery of bones in 1674 had been foreshadowed by the finding of other skeletons at the Tower during the preceding one hundred years. It is not solely More's legacy that the successive relics should be graced initially with a royal identity since as seen above earlier sources agree upon the Tower of London as the last place in which the two princes were seen in one another's company. Each fortuitous excavator at the Tower was thus to regard his own find as the solution to a regal mystery until those skeletons inurned in 1678 were ennobled by royal decree: the 'most certain indications' (*indiciis certissimus*) – or, rather, a selective interpretation of More – rendering them '*Reliquiae Edwardi Vti Regis Angliae et Richardi Ducis eboracensis*'.[53] In a sense the false starts given by the discrete pairs of child-skeletons found earlier paved the way for the avid reception of the 1674 set.

Thus, the remains of a single individual – subsequently to be dismissed as a refugee from the Tower menagerie – were graced initially with the identity of one of the ex-royal personages concerned: 'certain bones like to the bones of a child being found lately in a high desolate turret were supposed to be the bones of one of these princes; others are of the opinion that this was the carcase of an Ape kept in the Tower', as Sir George Buc said in 1619.[54]

A find of potentially earlier date is mentioned by Aubrey de Maurier, (quoting Maurice, Prince of Orange)

> '. . . the Tower of London being full of Prisoners of State . . . as they were troubled to find room for them all, they bethought themselves of opening a door of a Chamber that had been walled up for a long time; and they found in this chamber upon a bed . . . halters about their necks . . . the skeletons of King Edward V and the Duke of York, his brother, whom their Uncle Richard the Cruel had strangled [sic] to get the crown himself [Queen Elizabeth] ordered the door to be walled up as before. Nevertheless . . . this door having been opened some time since, and the skeletons being found in the same place, the King of England . . . has resolved to erect a Mausoleum to their memory, and have them buried in Westminster Abbey among the Kings.'[55]

Yet another seventeenth-century discovery appears to be recorded on the flyleaf of a 1641 edition of More, belonging to one John Webb

> 'August ye 17th 1647 . . . when ye Lo: Grey of Wilton and Sir Walter Raleigh were prisoners in ye Tower, the wall of ye passage to ye King's Lodgings then sounding hollow, was taken down and . . . was found a little roome about 7 or 8 feet square, wherein stood a Table and uppon it ye bones of two children supposed 6 or 8 years of age which by ye aforesayd nobles and all present were credibly beleeved to bee ye carcasses of Edward ye 5th and his brother the Duke of York.'[56]

The reported finds of so many sets of 'Princes' bones prior to the 'authentic' discovery during the late seventeenth century pose many questions. How many separate finds are there? Are some of the reports merely confused accounts of the same discovery – or even a re-discovery? The de Maurier and Webb accounts may be considered compatible in several features and may record the same discovery. Some historians regard bones found in such a place, i.e. the 'little roome', as better princely candidates than those found in 1674.[57] Professor Ross dismisses the theory that the skeletons were those of the Princes since they were too young and the 'two young victims, apparently boys [sic], had been left to die . . . in a walled-up room' when there is 'no evidence that the fifteenth century practiced this particular form of cruelty.'[58] It seems evident, however that the immurement described was not the cause of death (which, from the presence of 'halters' about the necks was apparently by strangling) but merely a method of concealing the already dead and indeed laid out bodies. Similarly, Ross claims that 'we know the fate of almost all those for whom imprisonment in the Tower eventually brought death'.[59] This is perhaps rather overstating the case. At least one other Plantagenet Prince, Henry Pole, son of Lord Montague, imprisoned in the Tower in 1539, vanished without trace,[60] and a great many bones were exposed when the Tower of London moat was drained and cleared in 1830–40.[61] Furthermore, the skeleton of yet another child, (a male between thirteen and sixteen years of age), was found during the archaeolgical excavation of the Inmost Ward of the Tower in 1977.[62] The importance of this most recent find (firmly dated to the late Iron Age) is manifold. This discovery re-emphasises that there has been a human presence upon the site for more than two thousand yeas, underlining recent theories concerning the potential great antiquity of the bones in the urn and exposing the unreliability of their dating (assumed, hitherto, to be mediaeval).[63] Moreover, had this unfortunate youth been disinterred three hundred years earlier, who doubts that here would have been Edward V?

The discovery of the bones in 1674 is relatively well documented. Several apparently first-hand accounts agree upon the discovery of human remains during the demolition of a stone staircase which gave access to the Chapel of St John in the White Tower. However, the precise location of this archaeological deposit is never specified; instead there is, thereafter, a lamentable tendency to introduce material evocative of the More tradition (the 'Bloody Tower', the wooden 'chest' or coffin, the 'great heap of stones' . . .). Thus, an anonymous eye-witness reported

> 'This day I, standing by the opening, saw working men dig out of a stairway in the White Tower, the bones of those two Princes who were foully murdered by Richard III . . . they were small bones, of lads [sic] in their teens and there were pieces of rag and velvet about them . . . Being fully recognised to be the bones of those two Princes they were carefully put aside in a stone coffin or coffer'.

The scraps of 'velvet' appear to have been introduced as emblems of regality, whereas textiles were absent from the contents of the urn when examined in 1933 despite the fact that material of the requisite date ought to have survived, (compare the cloth of gold found in the coffin of Edward IV and the linen shroud in that of Anne Mowbray). Similarly, this account speaks of the remains being stored temporarily in a 'stone coffin or coffer' and hence may be the source of the belief that the bones had been found in a coffin, although John Knight, Principal Surgeon to Charles II, apparently an eye-witness, is quoted as saying 'about Ten Foot in the ground were found the Bones of Two Striplings in (as it seem'd) a Wooden Chest, which upon the survey were found proportionable to the Ages of those Two Brothers, viz. about Thirteen

and Eleven Years. The Scull of one being entire, the other broken . . .'[64]
Similarly, John Gybbon, Bluemantle Pursuivant, wrote in the College of Arms
copy of *A Catalogue of the Kings . . . of England*:– 'Friday July 17 Anno 1674
in digging down some foundacions in ye Tower, were discovered ye bodies of
Edw V and his Brother murdered 1483. I my selfe handled ye Bones
Especially ye Kings Skull. Ye other wch. was lesser was broken in ye
digging.'[65]

The secondary sources supply greater detail. Thus, a royal warrant to Sir
Christopher Wren, as 'Surveyor General of His Majesties Workes', issued in
February 18th 1674/5 commissions 'a white Marble Coffin for the supposed
bodies of ye two Princes lately found in ye Tower of London.'[66] The project
was executed by Joshua Marshall, King's Master Mason, for the year 1678, by
which time the urn was installed, ironically, in the Henry VII Chapel. The
inscription upon this reliquary described the place where the bones were
found as *alte defossa in ruderibus scalarum*, and Wren himself supplements
this with:–'. . . about ten feet deep in the ground . . . as the workmen were
taking away the stairs, which led from the royal lodgings into the Chapel of
the White-tower.'[67]

The skeletal remains in the urn have been subsequently accepted as
authentic by many historians chiefly because they had been encountered
under circumstances that appeared to match More's description, even though
belying the latter's further assertions. However neither the scene of the
alleged murder nor the site of burial are specified in More, who summed up
the extraordinary perambulation of the corpses thus:– 'these two noble
princes . . . privily slaine and murdered, theyr bodies cast god wote where.'[68]
The persistence of many different, mutually exclusive fates for the Princes'
corpses in More's work ought to act as a counterweight to the widespread
uncritical acceptance of the authenticity of the set of bones examined in 1933.
As said above, the finding of skeletons anywhere near a staircase belies
More's tale of a secondary burial by a priest. Tanner had seized upon the
'stayrefoot' site aforementioned as worthy of greatest credence because
Gairdner believed that it was founded on the confession of two of the
murderers.[69] In fact although More says that Sir James Tyrell directed the
burial, even specifying the site for it, Tanner quotes More on the inability of
the 'murderers' to state what became of the bodies of their victims.[70]
Inconsistencies such as these fail to inspire confidence in Thomas More's
account as an authoritative report.

Tanner also records a local tradition at the Tower that the Princes were
murdered in the Garden Tower (known more recently as the Bloody Tower).
He goes on to say, in attempting to rebut a further rumour that the priest
exhumed them from beneath the Garden Tower and reburied them beneath a
staircase at the White Tower, 'Possibly the murder took place in the Bloody
Tower and the bodies were carried to the foot of the White Tower for burial.'
This suggestion reveals an ignorance of the topography of the Tower in the
fifteenth century. The difficulties in transporting the bodies by the necessary

indirect route, and by night, (let alone in secret), around the outside of the curtain wall, skirting the twelth to thirteenth century ditch, and finally striking east and south through the then extant Coldharbour Gate, are considerable and must be stressed. In fact, rather than the Garden Tower, a more plausible location for the sojourn of the Princes from July 1483 was the more secure Lanthorn Tower. This was Henry VII's own residence at the Tower by the year 1500.[71] In fact the location in which the bones were found in 1674 remain inadequately known. Nonetheless, the context in which these bones were said to have been discovered was to be of crucial importance both to their tentative identification and affirmatory preservation in 1678 and the *sine qua non* of the positive identification claimed for their second exhumation in 1933.

The apparent gap (1674–78) in the known history of the Bones has in itself troubled several writers and it raises serious doubts that the skeletons interred in 1678, are necessarily those unearthed at the Tower of London four years earlier – and all this quite apart from the widely acknowledged purloining of a good many of the bones.[72] Circumstances under which skeletal remains with the required characteristics might have been substituted are not easy to envisage, but it is apparent from Sandford's account of the discovery that the skeletal remains had been treated with less than regal reverence by their initial excavators. Tanner glosses over any such discontinuity, claiming that the skeletons remained in the custody of Sir Thomas Chicheley, Master of the Ordnance, at the Tower until early in 1675 when the decision was made to re-inter them in Westminster Abbey. He adds that they then seem to have been stored temporarily in the vault of the tomb of General Monck (d.1670) in the Henry VII Chapel.[73] There is confusion over events from 1674 to 1678, however, for a former Dean of Westminster, (in his standard work upon the royal burials in the Abbey), maintained that the remains of the 'York Princes' were not transferred from the Tower into General Monck's vault until the year 1678.[74] Such uncertainties have given rise to doubts that the skeletons examined in 1933 were those disinterred in 1674. It has been argued that the skeletons in the urn must be those discovered in 1674 because Wright found that the skull of the younger child was broken, (see Gybbons account, above). However Wright's report goes on to reveal that he in fact found both skulls to be broken in 1933, (differing merely in the region in which damage had occurred). Thus, the skull of the elder child had also suffered, the facial parts being broken away – a fact which Wright treated as of great significance in attempting to confirm the identity of the Princes with these skeletons – yet such damage had gone unmentioned by Gybbon who claimed to have handled 'ye Kings Scull' in 1674. This exhumation by Professor Wright and Lawrence Tanner resulted from per for the disinterment of the bones in 1933. It has had the regrettable consequence of setting the stamp of apparent authenticity upon the remains investigated. Their methods will be discussed because of the far-reaching nature of the conclusions that they felt able to draw: that the urn contained the remains of two children, who were identifiable with those commemorated on the inscription thereon and that 'there is at least a reasonable possibility that the traditional story of the murder, as told by More, is in its main outlines true.'[75]

To begin with the above conclusion was not reached independently or without a knowledge of the persons alleged to be represented by the skeletal remains. Indeed, the over-riding presumption throughout the investigation, that the remains examined were of the missing sons of Edward IV has been admitted by Lawrence Tanner himself.[76] Thus, it would appear that the conclusions reached had been influenced by feed-back in support of a pre-judged issue. In the scientific sense the anatomist who had estimated the ages at which the two children had died had not been working 'blind'. Instead Wright had been aware, at the outset, whom the skeletons were presumed to represent and his report reveals an acquaintance with Sir Thomas More and particularly with the tale including murder, manner thereof, initial place of burial, and significantly, the ages of the Princes at the time. What conclusions might have been reached had the argument been from *Molinet* or even the *Great Chronicle* as the source?

William Wright, (Dean and Professor of Anatomy at the London Hospital Medical School and Hunterian Professor of Anatomy at the Royal College of Surgeons), was undoubtedly one of the foremost anatomists of his day. At this distance, however, one can only express astonishment at the incomplete nature of the examination of the skeletal remains attributed to the lost sons of Edward IV when the princely allowance of six days' investigation had been granted in order that the requisite osteological and biometric data might be collected. In the absence of definite evidence as to the date of death Wright made no attempt to resolve the remaining crucial question of the gender of the deceased yet he expended a great deal of effort in speculation about the cause of death.

It can freely be admitted that Professor Wright had very little material to go on at that time. This argues eloquently for caution in interpretation. Whether or not Tanner and Wright made optimum use of the resources available to them is a question to be examined in detail here and, in parallel, the skeletal material studied will be regarded as if discovered anew. Moreover, in a re-appraisal of Wright's data and findings, suggestions will be made as to how, with the benefit both of hindsight and of scientific studies carried out in the interim, further information might be extracted. Professor Wright's material will be re-examined in the following sequence: age, sex, height, family relationships and pathology (disease, including cause of death).

If the skeletons are those of the Princes, the question of age can be approached by date of burial, and the problem concerning how long the skeletons exhumed in 1674 had lain buried ought to have been one of the great imponderables of the 1933 study. Instead, with enviable precision, Tanner felt able to quote the date of death to the nearest month. This may appear impressive until one realises just how the date was arrived at. Extrapolation from the dates of birth deduced by Tanner, using the ages at death estimated by Wright (themselves open to criticism and with little allowance for error), produced the date for decease: August 1483. Nevertheless, Professor Wright's age-estimates constitute the strongest part of their case. These were based upon the teeth (including the mapping of the empty sockets and X-raying the jaws for unerupted teeth) and upon certain aspects of the development of the skeleton. In retrospect such an approach appears to be vindicated by the study of the skeleton of Anne Mowbray, Duchess of Norfolk, (d. 1481), coincidentally wife of the younger of the two princes. Certain anomalies apart, the state of eruption of her teeth is consistent with her known age at death, which is one month short of nine years old.[71]

Hence, one can have few quibbles concerning what Wright and his dental specialist, (Dr George Northcroft, President of the Dental Association and British Society of Orthodontists), were attempting to do – only querying perhaps the absolute figures that they arrived at and the precision with which Tanner and Wright considered that they could be regarded. More recent exten-sive studies (to be discussed) tend both to multiply the possibilities and to em-phasise the continuing problem of the lack of precision inherent in such analyses.

Paul Murray Kendall, quoting the opinions of Dr Arthur Lewis, orthodontist, and Professor Bertram Kraus, anthropologist, was the first to point out the intriguing possibility that the skeletal remains ascribed to the Princes were younger than Tanner and Wright estimated them to have been (see table 1). The results tabulated here, serve to increase the doubts concerning the identification of the remains.[78]

Authority	Dental Age (years)		Reference
	Elder child	Younger child	
Northcroft	12–13	9–11 (10)	Tanner & Wright
Lewis	11–13 (11½)	—	Kendall
Kraus	<12 (9)	—	Kendall
Bradford	>11 (12?)	7–11½	Ross
White	<12? (9–13)	7–11 (9)	Present study

Table 1: Some Age Estimates for the Bones, Based Upon Tooth Eruption Studies.

Figures in parenthesis indicate the 'best guess'. (Note that if these were the remains of the Princes then the ages-at-death required for death in August 1483 were almost thirteen, and exactly ten years of age, respectively).

Simple dental eruption studies are inadvisable as a criterion for the determination of the age at which a child died because they are capable of producing such a wider scatter of results. Instead age-estimation in skeletons now relies heavily upon the consideration of tooth development as a whole, this being considered far more accurate than the use of age-standards based merely on the state of eruption of the teeth or on the growth of the long bones during childhood.[79]

The medical terminology employed by Tanner and Wright has led to some difficulties in the interpretation of their results. However, where dental development is concerned, Wright appended Dr Northcroft's estimates of the extent of the tooth-root development in the jaws of the two deceased.[80] For the older of the two children too few teeth survived to permit an accurate assessment of age-at-death. Northcroft attempted to map the jaws by means of the dentition apparent from the empty sockets and using the sole extant tooth for the elder child: the partly-formed crown of a third permanent molar (or 'wisdom tooth') found loose in the urn. Tooth development provides the picture of a child between the ages of nine and thirteen and the presence of a third molar, with the crown one-third formed, allows even closer ageing attempts.[81] Thus, Professor Bradford considered that this 'would put the child at more than eleven years . . . if one assumes that the child is about average . . . the best guess would be twelve years old'. Certain published tables show a constant difference between the sexes, however, such that if the child is female the state of the tooth concerned would permit the deceased to be a girl no more than eleven years old, on average.[82] For the younger child, however, Northcroft's precise description allows all teeth to be scored giving rise to a calculated age of eight-and-a-half years (or only eight years if female) based upon tooth development.[83] Nevertheless, an unfortunate aspect of all such attempts at age-determination remains the lack of absolute precision possible, the degree of uncertainty being put at plus or minus two years of the figures quoted above. That is to say that in the general run of dental patients children from two years younger, to two years older than the ages stated would be found all showing the above pattern of teeth and all would be considered 'normal'.[84]

The only other criterion for ageing employed by Wright was the absence of fusion in the growing bones. He offered evidence that because the odontoid process of the second cervical (neck) vertebra (the 'axis') was unfused in the elder child the child was definitely less than thirteen years of age.[85] This categorical avowal threw into disarray the specialists to whom Kendall had referred Wright's report for expert comment. Dr Lyne-Pirkis affirmed that this inference was incorrect. Professor Kraus went further and stated that: 'Fusion of the apex to the odontoid process takes place between four and six years of age. This would indicate merely that the child is under four years of age.'[86] The confusion would appear to have arisen because the anatomists were arguing from different ends of the same bone, as it were. Thus this bone, the axis, possesses two centres of ossification, and fusion of one of these does occur between the ages of four and six, as Kraus asserts; the other (fusion of the apex) takes place by the age of twelve.[87] Modern anatomical knowledge concerning the development of the odontoid process of the axis would appear to make it possible in the spirit of the 1933 study to say 'with confidence' that the elder child had not yet attained the age of twelve and therefore could not have been Edward V. In fact, with the lesson of the Piltdown forgery, no osteologist now would presume to be so dogmatic or incautious.

Further light may be cast on the age of the deceased when they died by measurements made upon their bones. Attempts have been made to apply studies of bone growth in living children to child skeletons obtained from archaeological excavations. The latter type of investigation is most relevant of course when entire populations rather than isolated skeletons are available, and where hence the average of modern measurements may be compared with the ancient average.[88] Thus, so far as individuals such as the 'Princes' are concerned, all that can be done is to apply the published growth standards to the bone lengths printed by Professor Wright. The most useful of the latter measurements is the length of the diaphysis; i.e. the length of the shaft of the child's limb bone, measured between the epiphyses (the points at the two ends of the long bone at which new growth is occurring). Average 'diaphyseal length' has been published for various bones based upon investigations of living children of known ages. Using this published information, the data obtained by Wright tend to support ages for the two children concerned of about *ten* and *eight* years, (on average), respectively (Table 2). Measurements from the skeleton of Anne Mowbray are included for comparison.

Child	Bone length (mm)		Age
	Humerus	Ulna	
Elder	242	193	10
Younger	222	182	8
Anne Mowbray	187	148	6

Table 2: Age-estimates for the Juvenile Skeletons, Based Upon the Measured Diaphyseal Lengths for the Bones of the Arm.

The picture is not quite this simple, however, since ancient juvenile skeletons regularly reveal an apparent lag in growth behind modern children when present in sufficient numbers for the ancient and modern averages to be compared.[89] That this was so during the fifteenth century is demonstrated strikingly by measurements made during the as yet unpublished investigation of the remains of Anne Mowbray. Although she is known to have been almost nine years of age when she died her 'skeletal age' apparent from the size of her bones is closer to the modern average for a six-year old.[90] This emphasises the need to compare 'like with like' and that, therefore, the comparison of the growth of mediaeval children with that of their better nourished modern counterparts is not necessarily valid. Indeed, the influence of such factors as diet, disease, social class and so on upon 'skeletal growth' is the subject of a growing body of research which will be considered later. When this is taken into account the discrepancy between 'skeletal age' and 'dental age' for the two individuals studied by Wright appears less than at first sight, although the margin by which one child is the senior appears much reduced.[91]

Further research on the remains from the urn ought to encompass the measurement of those bones ignored in 1933.[92] However, the overall assessment would be governed by the allowance of a generous margin for error of plus or minus two years of the real age required by anthropologists.[93] This does not influence the difference in age between the two children though, and this age-difference now appears smaller than that previously accepted. Identification of the remains as those of the 'Princes' requires that one of the two children is almost three years older than the other, whereas consideration of skeletal age and size appears to shrink the age-gap to between eighteen months and two years.

Professor Wright's report was at its most sound with the age-determination of the two skeletons since statistical uncertainties inherent in ageing techniques make it possible that the deceased were of the ages he claimed. However, the same uncertainties render his categorical assertion of the ages untenable. This is a most unsatisfactory state of affairs, when the estimated age at death and the presumed identity for the remains are inextricably linked and provide the sole means by which the dating of the burials was considered possible.

If the evidence for age at death represents the strongest part of Wright's case for the identification of the skeletal remains as the Princes, the weakest is the absence of any discussion of the possible gender of the deceased in the 1933 investigation. His failure to assign sex to the remains was a mistake that Wright, himself, admitted in private and is hardly a trivial drawback to the research, since the demonstration that but one of the skeletons was female would have negated the conclusions.[94] That the deceased were male is taken for granted throughout the investigation. Indeed, it is symptomatic of the pre-judged nature of the whole inquiry that, by the second page of his report, Wright is already referring to the deceased as males (that is, when he is not addressing them by name) and on no evidence at all. He finds no room for any comment on gender determination in sub-adult skeletons, nor even for a dismissal of such a discussion owing to potential difficulties with such evidence. Indeed, it is not true as is so often asserted that it was not possible (or is not now possible) to estimate the sex of the skeletons of pre-pubertal children for the relevant research had been commenced long before Wright's investigation.[95] A subsequent work has claimed that the sex of human skeletal remains may be estimated 'with great confidence, even in the child'.[96] Sex-determination via the pelvic remains of juveniles and infants is now performed regularly and, so far as the bones in the urn at Westminster Abbey are concerned, information ought to have been sought in the right ischium and both ilia of the elder child and the surviving ilium of the younger.[97] Apart from the various shapes and angles involved the occurrence of a pre-auricular sulcus (a depression on the pelvis) would be of considerable interest for although its absence does not confirm the male sex (the pelvis of Anne Mowbray, for example, did not exhibit it) its presence serves to confirm that skeletal remains are female.[98] Wright made no mention of such a feature in the skeletons that he ascribed to the 'Princes' and, from other evidence, he does not appear to have been seeking it.

A newer method of determining gender that should be mentioned here is the apparently elegant demonstration that juvenile remains are male if 'skeletal age' does not exceed 'dental age' or female if it does.[99] This method of checking the sex of juvenile skeletons was not available in 1933 and takes advantage of the well known fact that, on average, females are further developed than males throughout childhood, so that girls tend to exhibit a greater 'skeletal age' than boys of the same 'chronological age'. However, as was discussed earlier, it has been established that the skeletons of English mediaeval children tend to show evidence of growth retardation; this would invalidate such an approach to sex-determination. This is shown in the recently studied skeleton of Anne Mowbray. Her 'skeletal age' rather than being greater than her 'dental age' (nine) was a mere six years.

Finally, there are differences between the sexes in the sizes of the crowns of the teeth. In general the crowns of certain teeth are larger in boys than in girls. Although some of these comparisons concern the milk teeth and so cannot be applied to the Princes (no such teeth were found in the urn), the permanent teeth become of value from the age of six years onward.[100] The latter teeth were rare amid the contents of the urn but fortunately the type of tooth considered the most useful in gender-determination, the lower permanent canine tooth, survives (unerupted) in the jaw of the younger child. Moreover, if Northcroft's published X-ray of the relevant portion of the lower jaw of the child is to scale there is the intriguing possibility that because the canine crown is less than seven millimetres in diameter this individual was female![101] This is something that may be checked readily and rapidly by careful re-X-raying of this particular jaw bone.

The estimation of standing-height during life based upon measurements made upon the long bones of juvenile skeletons is problematical and few modern anthropologists or forensic pathologists would presume so to do. However, William Wright's calculations will be accepted for the purposes of discussion of physical stature in the fifteenth century. Initial objections to the heights for the two children quoted by Wright, i.e. 4'10" (147 cms) and 4'6½" (138 cms), were that they were too tall to have been the sons of Edward IV of the ages (twelve-and-three-quarters and ten years old, respectively) required if death had occurred in the late summer of 1483 as claimed by Tanner and Wright.[102] Here, once more, much turns upon the nature of the comparative data available. Wright's chief contemporary critic was making use of tables of stature *versus* age which perforce, had been compiled from data collected in the late nineteenth and early twentieth century, but recent studies would not render the claimed physical stature exceptionally great for the ages required. Furthermore, gender becomes important here for if the children are girls and the height-estimates are valid then they could be younger still.[103] The question of the possible influence of such factors as sex, social class, nutrition, public health and childhood illness upon the height that mediaeval children attained at various ages is too broad to be examined in depth here.[104] Some general statements are possible, however:– that in England during the final quarter of the fifteenth century the traditional scourges were on the wane or, at least, quiescent (leprosy, plague, famine) whereas the new afflictions had yet to become established (syphilis, typhus, rickets) and that life, generally, was a vast improvement over the previous century (with its erratic grain harvests and pestilence) or the sixteenth century and its deterioration in climatic conditions.[105] If, moreover, membership of the nobility conferred an advantage where optimum physical stature was concerned, whether for genetic reasons or because of ready access to the best degree of nutrition available at the time, it is all the more surprising that Lady Anne Mowbray appears so tiny for her age, by modern standards that is.

It was remarked earlier that in the years since Wright's investigation copious anthropometric studies have been carried out on juvenile skeletons from archaeological excavations. These have monitored the growth of children in antiquity by means of measurements made upon the long bones in children of known 'dental age'. It is clear, moreover, that the results of such studies ought to be applicable to child skeletons potentially of fifteenth century date because the standards that they set fit the data obtained for Anne Mowbray's bones better than do the modern values. Such remarks apply to the two children under consideration here and reference to the graph reproduced shows clearly that they were not too tall to have died at the ages alleged. What is of interest in these comparisons is that, as with the studies on isolated bone-lengths, the difference in age between the two children involved could be smaller, (between one and one-and-three-quarter years), than the three-year age-gap required by Tanner.

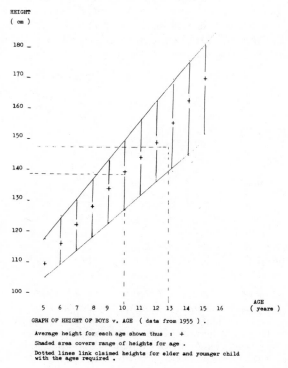

GRAPH OF HEIGHT OF BOYS v. AGE (data from 1955) .

Average height for each age shown thus : +
Shaded area covers range of heights for age .
Dotted lines link claimed heights for elder and younger child
with the ages required .

A potentially useful modern approach which might with profit be brought to bear upon the problem of height of the 'Princes' is the claimed ability to predict ultimate adult stature, calculated from the actual height at a known age during childhood, employing a mathematical formula which involves making an adjustment for 'skeletal age'. Therefore, using Wright's age- estimates but substituting also into the formula the 'skeletal age' figures deduced from the lengths of the diaphyses (*viz.* ten and eight years of age, respectively for the two skeletons, above), and employing the parameters recommended[106] the projected adult heights arrived at for the two children concerned are:–

<blockquote>
elder: 5'11"   (or 5'5", if *female*)
younger: 5'10½"   (or 5'3", if *female*)
</blockquote>

If the further assumption is made that 'skeletal age' for the remains is identical to the 'dental age' quoted by Wright then the heights are calculable as follows:–

<blockquote>
elder child: 6'0"   (or 5'3" if *female*)
younger child: 5'10"   (of 5'5" if *female*)
</blockquote>

Now, although there is no skeletal evidence to support the apparently widespread view that English people in the past were shorter, on average, than in modern times[107] the above figures are high in comparison with the average for either mediaeval or modern males. Dated skeletons which provide information about adult height during the fifteenth century are rather too sparse for average figures for the population to be quoted. Certain comparisons are possible however as seen from table 3.

Identity	Date	Height (ft. in.) quoted	modern estimate
Edmund of Langley, Duke of York	1402	5'11"	
William Lyndewode, Bishop of St Davids	1446	5'8"	
John Talbot, 1st Earl of Shrewsbury	1453	—	5'8"
Robert, Lord Hungerford	1459	5'5"	
King Henry VI	1471	5'9½"	
George, Duke of Clarence	1478	5'5"	
King Edward IV	1483	6'3"	6'2"
Sir John Cheney	1499	6'9"	6'5"
Anne Mortimer, wife of Richard of Cambridge	1415	—	5'6"
Queen Katherine of Valois	1437	5'6½"	5'4"
Isabella Despencer, Countess of Warwick	1440	5'4"	
Mary of Burgundy	1481	5'3"	
Margaret Daubeney	1520	5'4"	

Table 3: Physical Stature of Exhumed Persons of the Fifteenth Century.[108]

Comparison with the calculated heights for the two children and adults is of interest (subject to the assumptions made above). Any further discoveries will increase the size of the sample, and enable an average height for the century to be determined. This will act as a check on the heights obtained from Wright's data, which appears at present to fit the results better if the remains in the urn are female rather than male.

Professor Wright siezed upon two features in the two skeletons which he claimed showed that they were closely related: the discontinuous trait of hypodontia (certain teeth missing congenitally) and of wormian bones (extra bones in the cranial sutures of the back of the head). These will be considered in turn.

The anomalies of the teeth have attracted the greatest attention. Wright juxtaposed the observed 'absence of the second premolar in the upper jaw and of the third molar in the lower jaw' in the elder child with, in the presumptive sibling, the alleged absence of the second deciduous molar and the presumed third molar (wisdom tooth) absence in the lower jaw. Only the right half of this survived. Now, the failure of the second milk molar to develop is extremely rare and the example given here has not received general acceptance. Indeed Wright, himself, admitted that the tooth could have been shed or knocked out at a very early age and Rushton confirmed that this was the most likely explanation for in his examination of the teeth of Anne Mowbray he had noted that one of her milk molars had been lost abnormally early in her life.[109] As for the third molar, modern studies of hypodontia normally exclude this type of tooth because it is the category of tooth most often absent congenitally. As with the less common forms of hypodontia it is absent more frequently in females than in males.[110] This appears to have been the case in mediaeval times also. Moreover, the simultaneous absence of second premolar and third molar (as observed in the elder child), was and is the most common combination of missing teeth.[111] These considerations must be borne in mind when considering the possible family link with Anne Mowbray, to whom the Princes were related by descent from mutual ancestors, Ralph, Earl of Westmorland (who died in 1425) and Edward III (d. 1377).[112] An observed absence of second molars in the jaws of Anne Mowbray represents a genuine rarity and has been advanced as supporting evidence for the traditional identity of the 'Princes' bones because of a possible family tendency to missing teeth. Just how far the congenital absence of different categories is evidence of close family relationship remains largely unexplored, however, and much more research is required in this region. Evidence is hard to come by in this controversial area and Professor Bradford, for one, did not give it much credence.[113]

Turning to England generally during the fifteenth century dental information is rather sparse. Although a number of skeletons of this date have been disinterred only rarely has the condition of the teeth been recorded. Anne Mowbray is an honourable exception and, as luck would have it, teeth have a major part to play also in the story of her maternal grandfather John Talbot, first Earl of Shrewsbury. John Talbot died at the siege of Chastillon in 1453 and his herald identified the body on the battlefield two days later by checking for teeth that he knew to be absent from the left side of the jaws of his master.[114] These meagre remains may be supplemented by the consideration of the contemporary situation in Flanders, i.e. the teeth of Charles the Rash, Duke of Burgundy, and Mary, his daughter by his first wife. The skeleton of Mary of Burgundy has been discovered recently and was shown to have had the astonishing total of *eleven* teeth missing congenitally.[115] Her father had been killed at Nancy in 1477 and his body needed to be identified on the battlefield, again by a known pattern of missing teeth.[116] It is not clear in this instance, however, whether the absence of certain teeth was familial in origin or had occurred during life, for the same chronicle stresses the importance of his ancient battle wounds in identifying the recently mutilated corpse.[117] What emerges from a study of the scant fifteenth century jaws known is the curiously high proportion of missing teeth during the period.

The examination of the two Abbey skulls in 1933 revealed further that they shared the trait of large wormian bones upon the lambdoid suture.[118] Professor Wright used their presence as support for his assessment that the two were closely related. However, it is now known that wormian bones are not necessarily indicators of close kinship and that their incidence varies with the population concerned. In the view of a modern anthropologist 'common anomalies such as wormian bones [are] slender evidence'.[119] Wormian bones appear to have been far more common in ancient skeletons than in modern Europe (hence, probably misleading Wright). The over all prevalence in England in the middle ages is not certainly known but would appear to be around 50% of skulls.[120] That two associated ancient skeletons should both show this anomaly is not necessarily significant therefore, for it is as expected from chance occurrence (such as a coin being tossed and turning up 'heads' twice in succession).

Conversely, if the phenomenon of 'bilateral large wormian bones' is of value of elucidating the family relationship and hence identity of the skeletal remains attributed to the 'Princes' then this feature ought, too, to be observable in their known close relatives. Such remains are woefully thin on the ground, as has been remarked. In Tewkesbury Abbey there is, of course, a skull said to be that of George, Duke of Clarence, the Princes' uncle. This skull exhibits no wormian bones but there remains doubts concerning its ascription to Clarence.[121] However, since the skull of Anne Mowbray has been introduced in order to explore possible close relationships to the 'Princes' bones it is of considerable interest that it fails to possess bilateral large wormian bones.

Professor Wright diagnosed osteitis, (an inflammation of the bone), in the lower jaw of the elder child. Somewhat tortuously he attempted to link this chronic infection with ex-king Edward V, remarking that: 'It may well have accounted, in part at least, for the depression from which he is said to have suffered, for the relief of which his mother is said to have agreed to part with her younger son.'[122] This diagnosis of ill-health was used by Kendall (who accepted the Abbey bones as the remains of the Princes), to explain Dr John Argentine's observation that 'the young king, like a victim prepared for sacrifice, sought remission for his sins by daily confession and penance, because he believed that death was facing him . . .'[123] This interpretation of Mancini is a most unfortunate one, Edward's state of mind (inevitably influenced by uncertainties concerning his own future), can have had no bearing upon a specific illness such as osteitis.

Wright had first apparently diagnosed serious illness in the elder child then had cast about for documentary support. The evidence that he claimed to have found was slim, though apparently persuasive enough for others to follow in his footsteps.[124] As has been seen, however, there were many posssible reasons for young Edward's reported psychological distress: it is not necessary that a debilitating systemic illness be invoked. Indeed, ironically, it is a chronic illness of the younger prince that is better documented. This, too, is derived from Sir Thomas More. It is to be found in Elizabeth Woodville's curious obsession with the recent sickness of her younger son, with her in sanctuary, rather than with the state of health of the absent elder brother. This fact was first noticed by Gairdner, fifty years earlier, and though Tanner used Gairdner's *History* he skirted around this intriguing and, it would seem, contentious area.[125]

The use of X-rays in the examination is a very early one. It is unfortunate, however, that Wright did not go beyond the simple detection of unerupted teeth and use radiography more extensively: i.e. to confirm the jaw disease of the elder child, and detect lines of arrested growth in certain of the long bones of both children.[126] The latter technique had first been described in 1930 and was, therefore, available to Wright as a means of discovering any episodes of serious illness undergone by a child and a matter of consuming interest where the remains attributed to the Princes are concerned.[127]

A further claim was made that a stain 'of fluid origin' was visible on the bones of the face of the older of the two individuals represented in the urn, extending 'from just below the orbits to the angles of the lower jaw . . . of a distinctly blood-red colour above, or a dirty brown colour below . . . together with the complete separation of the facial skeleton . . .' and that this supports the traditional account of the murder of the Princes by being suffocated 'under a feather bed and pillows kept down by force hard unto their mouths.'[128] Now the detachment of the bones of the face from the cranium is unremarkable, given that the skull of a child is not a unity but a combination of twenty or so bones which only slowly unite during the growing period. Juvenile skulls are not well-knit and any rough handling of the dry bones after death – such as the exhumation, casting on to a rubbish heap, re-burial and further disinterment that was the fate of the 'Princes' bones – would have led readily to the sort of damage observed here.

The alleged blood-staining of the larger of the two skulls as the result of death by smothering is more problematical for there are no known exact precedents in the field of forensic medicine. This is because most homicide investigations involve the intact corpse and that where death is the result of any form of asphyxia (throttling, smothering, hanging, etc.) its manifestations are obvious. However, where only the skeletal remains are available the bones themselves are dubious testimony to the cause of death for only rarely do skeletons reveal the means of demise.[129] The deduction of death by smothering is entirely dependent upon the associated evidence. If, indeed, these remains are those of the Princes how unfortunate that they had not been embalmed for display, (as were Edward II, Richard II, Henry VI, the Earl of

Warwick and, apparently, the Prince's own father), for this would have allowed the persistence of the known signs of smothering: tiny haemorrhages visible in the skin of the face and neck.[130] Professor Wright was aware of the problem of connecting the apparent staining of human skulls and alleged murder by suffocation. To support his case he quoted extensively from William Shakespeare (not universally regarded as a forensic expert), upon the smothering of Humphrey, Duke of Gloucester: 'But see his face is black and full of blood . . .'.[131] Duke Humphrey (d. 1447) is an unfortunate choice of example, however, for his well-preserved body has been found in St Albans Abbey and it showed none of the stigmata of suffocation.[132]

The best examples of apparent blood-staining of bones comes from the field of Egyptology,[133] i.e. a series of skeletons of Nubians hanged by the Roman army of occupation and in whom the excessively violent method of execution had torn open the base of the skull with the result that it and the rear of the cranium were stained bright red.[134] If, as appears likely, the latter constitute genuine specimens of blood-stained bones then they do not necessarily set the precedent for skeletal victims of smothering since the manner of death is almost unique and so very different from that proposed by Wright. Recent medical opinion generally is dismissive of his evidence for murder by smothering for this is 'not borne out by experience'.[135] Instead, Philip Lindsay drew attention to the presence of several rusty nails, found amid the extraneous matter in the urn at the time of its being opened and which may have resulted in the discoloration of the skull by oxide of iron, thus mimicking blood stains.[136] Wilton Krogman, author of the standard work on the forensic possibilities of human skeletal remains, gave Kendall his opinion upon this controversial matter, 'The so-called staining of the facial bones, attributable to the suffusion of suffocation, is not borne out be experience. Unless there were a rupturing of vessels, the suffusion would be limited to facial tissue and would not register itself upon the bones.' This view finds support with Dr Lyne-Pirkis and, most notably the late Professor Keith Simpson, Britain's foremost forensic medical expert.[137]

Professor Wright had no doubts that the stains were caused by blood but he could not prove it. Here, with the cause of death (as with his curious juggling with the bones in order to fit them spatially within the supposed coffin) Wright far exceeded the bounds of what was permissible. Possibly he had been influenced by St John Hope's excesses, twenty-three years earlier, in the disinterment of Henry VI, whose hair, it will be remembered, was described as matted with blood.[138] It remains the case that valid tests for blood, whether human or no, have been carried out neither on the remains of Henry VI nor on those attributed to the Princes.

From the foregoing it is obvious that, in the present state of the art (and, even more so, in that prevailing at the time when Tanner and Wright performed their investigation), it would be folly to attempt to identify the remains in the urn based upon the slim evidence adduced thus far. Such an identification remains yet to be proved. The provision of further information

is long overdue and ought to be sought. Scientific techniques of great power
and sophistication that have become available since the investigation of 1933,
and together with techniques outlined above are capable of remedying the
major deficiencies in Wright's work. There are now many techniques known
for dating archaeological specimens (both relatively and absolutely). That the
bones under consideration are ancient is not in serious dispute, for the
greatest sceptic is likely to concede that they are at least three hundred and six
years old (dating from the time of their being deposited in Westminster
Abbey). Thus, simple techinques for testing whether or not the bones
involved are 'modern' (in the sense of being not greater than one hundred
years old) are inappropriate here.[139]

The best developed (and as yet most reliable), method for the dating of
bones is by radiocarbon assay.[140] Briefly it makes use of the natural
phenomenon that all living things absorb radioactive carbon (carbon-14) from
the atmosphere of the Earth. Upon the death of the organism the continuous
absorption ceases and the carbon-14 present undergoes radioactive decay at a
constant rate that is known. Hence the measurement of radioactivity present
in a sample of bone provides a measure of time that has elapsed since
death.[141] This scientific technique has been employed since about 1950 in the
elucidation of archaeological problems. Recent refinements have overcome
teething troubles so as to allow potentially greater precision and the use of
very small samples of bone. The amount that must be destroyed now need
only be a few milligrams (a vanishingly small amount), thus obviating a major
disadvantage of carbon-14 dating, which was formerly very destructive of
material.[142] Work on the sister discipline of dendrochronology (tree ring
dating), has permitted an increase in accuracy by cross calibration between
these two methods of absolute (i.e. not comparative), dating.[143]

In principle, therefore, carbon dating ought to be capable of deciding
whether the bones in the urn may be assigned to the fifteenth century or not.
However, even where genuine material of the fifteenth century is concerned
the statistical uncertainties in radioactive decay require that the error in the
date calculated may be as much as sixteen years from the true date.[144] It is
only with very recent samples, investigated for other purposes (viz. suspected
modern forgeries of works of art), that greater certainly prevails and that one
may see radiocarbon dates quoted 'plus or minus three years.'[145] Of course,
even this degree of accuracy would still be too imprecise to settle the question
of whether the 'Princes' met their deaths during the reign of Richard III or
under his successor.[146]

Other methods for determining the absolute age of bone give as yet best
results when the time that has elapsed since death is of the order of thousands
of years, where a degree of error referred to as 'plus of minus a few years' is
considered negligible.[147] Future refinements here may multiply the number of
techniques pertinent to our purposes. It is unfortunate that no portions have
survived of the 'chest' in which, according to a single account, the bones of
the 'Princes' were contained in 1674. In fact, a solitary fragment of 'peat-

stained wood' was all that was found when the urn was opened in 1933 and this, (together with the extraneous animal bones), was discarded subsequently. Had any larger pieces of wood been preserved it ought to have been possible to have arrived at a date at which the tree was cut down, (via dendrochronology, above), and hence provide independent evidence for the dating of the bones.

Mention of tree-ring dating is a timely reminder that Tanner and Wright had no independent means of calculating the date at which their 'Princes' died and that date of death and identity presumed were linked inextricably in a circular fashion. Thus, everything was left to hang upon the assessment of age at death and this is a major criticism of the earlier investigation. What appears to be required is some periodic aspect of human development that may be akin to the annual growth rings observed in the trunks of trees, and recent research, has revealed that certain aspects of the development of human bones and teeth are subject to just such an order of periodicity. There are thus now a variety of techniques of age-assessment that depend upon the change in appearance under a microscope of a cross-section of bone or tooth that is characteristic of a human being's age at death. As has been observed, the scope of age-diagnosis based upon the teeth of the 'Princes' is severely limited by the small number that survives in the urn.[148] In any case the microscopic method for age-determination promises better results for juveniles if bones rather than teeth are employed because remodelling of the former occurs at an earlier age.[149] The assessment of the changing pattern of the bone cortex as viewed microscopically has, as yet, a claimed accuracy of plus or minus six years.[150] It is hoped that this margin for error will be reduced to a much lower level.

The other major deficiency in the scientific knowledge of the bones in the urn is also within sight of resolution. Parallel to the greater confidence felt in diagnosing gender in juvenile skeletons by simple inspection, an analytical chemical means to establish the sex of human skeletal remains has been devised. It depends upon the fact that the bones of human females have a consistently higher content of citrate salt than do those of males,[151] so that the determination of citrate in human bones permits an assignment of sex to be made.[152] This work has been extended by the investigation of pre-pubertal remains, wherein an accuracy of one hundred per cent in the establishment of gender has been claimed.[153] Work in this field is continuing and has an obvious bearing upon the hitherto sexless bones in the urn.

The significance of Professor Wright's criteria for establishing close family relationship in human skeletal remains has been challenged, but there are now scientific techniques available which would allow the exploration of possible consanguinity by the determination of the blood group in these remains.[154] Indeed, at the very time that Wright was examining the skeletons attributed to the 'Princes' pioneering work in serology (the determination of blood groups) was being performed on ancient human remains. Initially the method was used to determine the ABO blood-groups in mummified bodies but, subsequently, it was applied to skeletal remains and made to incorporate the rarer blood types.[155] The great versatility of the method is to be seen in its widespread application in the field of anthropology for demographic studies on entire populations, in Egyptology, for the diagnosis of close family relationship, in forensic science, for the positive identification of the deceased and as a preliminary to the type of investigation proposed here, the demonstration that Mary of Burgundy had blood group 'A'.[156] Thus, it ought now to be possible to establish that the bones in the ossuary are of two children who were very closely related or, conversely, to exclude any such close kinship should their blood groups prove incompatible.

Although one may continue to point out the shortcomings of the paper of Tanner and Wright, and its disservice both to science and to history, this is not productive. The important point is that Wright had been influenced profoundly by the presumed circumstances under which these otherwise unprovenanced bones were found, the alleged locality of the find being taken as evocative of one of the tales of the disposal of the remains of the Princes, as told by More. Thus persuaded, he made categorial statements concerning the identity of the skeletal remains, whereas investigators schooled in the modern climate of scientific caution would stress the underlying uncertainties in the elucidation of age, sex, status, family relationship, pathology and cause of death. Certainly the pre-judged investigation cannot be held to have solved the problem of the missing sons of Edward IV. There remains little hard fact and doubts have increased with time and exposure. A new investigation would provide a firm scientific background against which the controversial bones could be discussed, and would provide concrete information upon crucial aspects, notably the sex and date of the bones (the most severe deficiencies of the 1933 study). Radiocarbon dating, with its capacity for consigning the bones to the requisite century, needs to be carried out as the minimum requirement in a fresh investigation. Even should carbon-14 assay place the skeletons within the framework of the late fifteenth century then this would provide at least a genuine (rather than a notional) starting point for the enquiry and a firmer justification for a serious discussion of the fates of the Princes than has been the case with the prejudiced study some fifty years ago. Conversely, the dating evidence has the potential ability to exclude the notorious Bones from consideration as relics of the Princes. Professor Ross says in his Appendix that since the medical evidence is inconclusive the onus of 'proof' is upon the historian.[157] However, it is clear that historical proof that any bones found in the Tower belong to the sons of Edward IV is based upon very shaky foundations. Many fields of science have yet to be brought to bear upon the question of the bones of the 'Princes' and science, alone, has the power to confirm or disprove their shaky identification.

Notes

1. See Chronology of Events in *Coronation of Richard III* ed. Anne F. Sutton and P.W. Hammond (Gloucester 1983), pp. 18, 19–20, 22, 25.

2. *The Usurpation of Richard III*, ed. C.A.J. Armstrong (Oxford 1969), pp. 4–5.

3. Armstrong, *op. cit.*, pp. 16, 18–20. For a brief survey of the career of John Argentine, C.H. Talbot and E.A. Hammond, *Medical Practitioners in Medieval England* (London 1965), pp. 112–115.

4. Armstrong, *op. cit.*, pp. 93. The date of withdrawal to the inner apartments cannot be before 16 June when Richard joined Edward. The removal of the young Edward's attendants, except for Argentine (and consequent payment of wages due), may be shown by payments to a number of men for services to Edward IV and 'Edward Bastard late called king Edward Vth', *British Library Harleian Manuscript 433*, ed. Rosemary Horrox and P.W. Hammond, vol. 2 (London 1980) p. 2. This was first suggested by P.M. Kendall, *Richard III* (London 1955) p. 395.

5. *Great Chronicle of London* ed. A.H. Thomas and I.D. Thornley (London 1938), p. 234. The chronology of the *Great Chronicle* is very confused, since it dates Shaa's mayoralty to 1483–84, and generally misdates all events late by one year. Lindsay suggests that the confusion could lie in the names of the Mayors, not the dates, and that Edward and Richard may have been last seen in 1484. (*On Some Bones in Westminster Abbey* (1934), pp. 14–15.) This would not fit with the chronology of events given by the *Great Chronicle* however, and there is little doubt that the reported sightings of the Princes should be dated in 1483. It is interesting to note though that Anne Neville is said by the *Great Chronicle* to have died after Easter 1484 (p. 234), instead of 1485, and if one event can be misdated by one year it is conceivable (if unlikely), that the sightings of the Princes are similarly misdated. For the 'Gardyn of the Towyr' see further, note 74.

6. Horrox and Hammond, *op. cit.*, vol. 2 (1980) p. 211; vol. 3 (1982) p. 114.

7. Clements Markham, *Richard III, His Life and Character* (1906) pp. 126, 236–237. For a recent and less positive, restatement of the argument see Audrey Williamson, *The Mystery of the Princes* (Gloucester 1978) pp. 121–122.

8. P.W. Hammond, 'John of Gloucester', *The Ricardian* vol. 5 (1981) p. 319.

9. Polydore Vergil *Anglica Historia*, ed. Denis Hay Camden Society (1950) pp. 2, 3. These points are also discussed by Kendall, *op. cit.*, pp. 407–408. Vergil, an Italian humanist scholar, was writing c. 1512

10. G.E.C. *Complete Peerage*, vol. 12, Part 2 (1959) p. 912.

11. Barrie Williams, 'Lambert Simnel's Rebellion: how reliable is Polydore Vergil?', *The Ricardian*, vol. 6 (1982) p. 120. It is also put forward here that uncertainty as to when Henry VII confined Edward of Warwick in the Tower could mean that Vergil's remark 'it was popularly rumoured that Edward had been murdered in that place' in 1486/7 (Vergil, ed. Hay, p. 13) could mean that Edward of York was murdered there at that time (pp. 120–122).

12. Robert Ricart, *The Maire of Bristowe is Kalendar*, ed. Lucy Toulmin Smith, Camden Society, New Series, vol. 5 (1872) p. 46. It is possible that the rumours

were those apparently current at Easter 1484, see below, and note 25. We would like to thank Anne Crawford for useful comments on the dating of events by Ricart.

13. Jack Leslau, 'Did the Sons of Edward IV outlive Henry VII' *The Ricardian* vol. 4 No. 62 (1978) pp. 2–14. Further discussion and criticism are found in 'Did the Sons of Edward IV outlive Henry VII: a Postscript', and 'Did the Sons etc: an Answer and a Rejoinder', *The Ricardian*, vol. 5 (1979) pp. 24–26, and pp. 55–60.

14. The question of whether or not any of the pretenders were in fact either of the sons of Edward IV, notably of course Perkin Warbeck, is too large to be discussed here. A full scale study of these pretenders is long overdue.

15. Kendall, *op. cit.*, p. 140.

16. C.A.J. Armstrong, 'Astrology at the Court of Henry VII', *Italian Renaissance Studies* (Oxford 1960) p. 450 (reprinted in *England France and Burgundy in the Fifteenth Century* (London 1983) pp. 157–178); Polydore Vergil, *Anglica Historia*, p. 64 (see also J. Gairdner *History of the Life and Reign of Richard III* (Oxford 1898) p. 118); Thomas More, *History of Richard III*, ed. R.S. Sylvester (Yale 1967) p. 82.

17. Richard Firth Green, 'Historical Notes of a London Citizen 1483–1488', EHR. vol. 96 (1981) pp. 585–586. The 'Notes' say they were 'put to deyth in the Towur of London be the vise of the duke of Buckingham', interestingly paralleled by the 'Lloyd' notes, see below, note 37.

18. Modernised spelling, from the text in *The Cely Letters 1472–1488*, ed. Alison Hanham, Early English Text Society, vol. 273 (1975) pp. 184–185.

19. Hanham, *op. cit.*, p. 285.

20. H. Hutchinson, *The Hollow Crown, a Life of Richard II* (London 1961) pp. 235–237; J.G. Bellamy, *The Law of Treason in England in the Later Middle Ages* (Cambridge 1970) pp. 120, 164; Polydore Vergil *Anglica Historia* p. 12; Armstrong, *op. cit.* p. 450; Rawdon Brown, *Calendar of State Papers and Manuscripts relating to English Affairs, existing in . . . Venice*, vol. 1 1202–1507, p. 156. These later rumours concerning Richard III were of course circulating on the Continent. The apparent attempt to start a rumour that Edward Prince of Wales was (in 1475), soon to die, may also be noted, Bellamy *op. cit.*, p. 127.

21. Charles Ross, 'Rumour, Propaganda, and Popular Opinion During the Wars of the Roses', in *Patronage, the Crown and the Provinces*, ed. Ralph Griffiths (Gloucester 1981) pp. 16, 17–18, 19. The rumours might be expected to spread the more quickly if recent arguments concerning fifteenth century attitudes to children are accepted, Lorraine Attreed, 'From *Pearl* Maiden to Tower Princes', *J.Med.Hist.* (1983) vol. 9, pp. 43–58.

22. Polydore Vergil, *Three Books of Polydore Vergil's English History*, ed. Henry Ellis, Camden Society, vol. 29 (1844) p. 189.

23. *Croylandensis Historia*, in *Rerum Anglicarum Scriptorum Veterum*, vol. 1 (1684) p. 568, '*vulgatum est, dictos regis Edwardi pueros, quo genere violenti interitus ignoratur, decessisse in fata*'. See translation and note by Alison Hanham, *Richard III and his early historians 1483–1535* (Oxford 1975) p. 14 note 4. For the most recent discussion of the date of this part of the Croyland

Chronicle, see Antonia Gransden, *Historical Writing in England*, vol. 2, *c. 1307 to the early sixteenth century* (London 1982) pp. 491–492.

24. *Rotuli Parliamentorum*, vol. 5, p. 348.

25. *Great Chronicle*, p. 234. This is the Easter when the *Great Chronicle* says Anne Neville died, see note 5 above, so that Easter 1485 may be meant. See also *Ricart's Kalendar* above.

26. Pamela Tudor-Craig, *Richard III*, National Portrait Gallery (1973), p. 52. Quotation from Richard's letter to York refuting rumours, *Extracts from the Municipal Records of the City of York*, ed. Robert Davies (1843) p. 209. Richard III had previously complained, in a letter to the Mayor of Windsor, of false reports being circulated in December 1848, Gairdner, *op. cit.*, pp. 193– 194.

27. Armstrong, pp. 22, 23–24. De Rochefort's speech is given in *Journal des Etats-generaux de France tenus a Tours en 1484*, ed. J. Masselin (Paris, 1835), p. 38. The relevant passage: 'See, I pray you, what happened in that country after the death of Edward IV. Think of those children, grownup, noble, murdered with inpunity, and the crown given to their murderer by the favour of the commons', is given by Armstrong in the original Latin. Several authors, e.g. Kendall *op. cit.*, p. 395, and Markham, *op. cit.* p. 242, quote the modern French of Masselin.

28. Armstrong, *loc. cit.*

29. Landsdowne Roll 6, see C.L. Kingsford *English Historical Literature in the Fifteenth Century* (London 1913), p. 184.

30. C.L. Scofield, *The Life and Reign of Edward IV*, vol. 2 (London 1923), pp. 329, 343, 363; Horrox and Hammond, vol. 3 (1982) p. 1; *Materials for a History of the Reign of Henry VII*, ed. William Campbell, Rolls Series, vol. 2 pp. 85, 128, 377. This Thomas may possibly be the same as the Thomas Warde, chaplain of London who shared a grant of the goods and chattels of a citizen of London in February 1485, *(CCR 1476–1485* (1954) no. 1385), although probably not either the Thomas Warde, Rector of Bradley Derbyshire in 1483, or the Thomas Warde, surgeon of London who died in 1521 (Talbot and Hammond, *op. cit.*, pp. 358–359).

31. *Ingulph's Chronicle of the Abbey of Croyland*, ed. H.T. Riley (London 1893), pp. 490, 491.

32. *Rotuli Parliamentorum*, vol. 6, p. 276.

33. R.J. Mitchell, *John Tiptoft 1427–70* (London 1938), pp. 119–120, 142. The accusation made on the scaffold is from Vespasiano da Bisticci, *Vite di uomini illlustri del secolo XV*, written after 1480. See translation in *English Historical Documents 1327–1485*, ed. A.R. Myers (London 1969), p. 1131.

34. Polydore Vergil, *Anglica Historia*, pp. 68, 70.

35. Dafydd Llwyd's poem, one of the half political/half prophetic Welsh poems concerning Henry Tudor, was written 1485–86, Tudor-Craig, *op. cit.*, p. 95; Pietro Carmeliano's poem celebrating the birth of Prince Arthur was written in 1486. It says that Richard destroyed both his nephews (*geminosque nepotes sustulit*), *Memorials of Henry VII*, ed. J. Gairdner, Rolls Series (1858), p. lvii, 'The Murder of the Princes', P.W. Hammond, *The Ricardian*, 1977, vol. 4, No.

57, pp. 23–24, see also DNB; for Diego de Valera see below, and note 40; for the Croyland Chronicler see above, and note 23.

36. *Croylandensis Historia*, p. 575. *Opprimere* can mean destroy (or suffocate), in a physical sense, but would more reasonably be expected to mean to oppress or suppress, i.e. to destroy in a political sense. The same word is used by Mancini (p. 60). The first person to draw attention to the use of *opprimere* in the Croyland Chronicle was Jeremy Potter in *Good King Richard?* (London 1983), p. 76.

37. Bodleian Library, Ashmolean Library Ms. 1448, f.287 (the Lloyd Manuscript), '*eos* [Richard's nephews] *de lumine hujus seculi qualiter vel quomodo nequiter et homicide abstrahebat*'. (This manuscript was probably written in the fifteenth century, not late in the sixteenth, as implied by Firth-Green, *op. cit.* (note 17), p. 587); John Rous *Historia Regum Anglia*, ed. Thomas Hearne (1745), p. 215, '*Edwardum quintum . . . et infra circiter tres menses vel parum* [of the beginning of May] *cum fratre suo interfecit*, translation in Hanham, pp. 120–21; Bernard André, *De Vita atque Gestis Henrici Septimi* (in *Memorials of Henry VII*, ed. J. Gairdner, p. 24). André's *Life* was written c. 1500. In *Les Douze Triomphes de Henri VII*, written c. 1497, André merely says that Richard 'made away with' (*deffaire*) his two nephews (Gairner, *op. cit.*, p. 138).

38. British Library Vitellius A XVI (*Chronicles of London*, ed. C.L. Kingsford (London 1905), p. 191), written c. 1500; Richard Arnold, written c. 1502 (Hanham, *op. cit.*, p. 109); Tanner 2, written c. 1505 (*Six Town Chronicles of England*, ed. Ralph Flenley (Oxford 1911), p. 169); Robert Fabyan, *The New Chronicles of England and France*, written c. 1504 (ed. Henry Ellis (1811), pp. 669, 670); *A Chronicle of Lynn*, written c. 1540 (ed. Flenley,p. 185).

39. Philippe de Commynes, *Memoires*, ed. Joseph Calmette and Chanoine de Durville (Paris 1924–5), vol. 1, pp. 53–54, vol. 2, pp. 233, 304, 306. The remark of about the same date in the Milanese State Papers is predictably terse, saying the English abandoned King Richard 'because he put to death his nephews, to whom the kingdom belonged' (vol. 1 (London 1913), p. 299).

40. Anthony Goodman and Angus MacKay, 'A Castilian Report on English Affairs 1486', *EHR*, vol. 88 (1973), pp. 92, 94. For the full text of De Valera's report see Elizabeth Nokes and Geoffrey Wheeler, 'A Spanish Account of the Battle of Bosworth', *The Ricardian*, vol. 2 (1972), No. 36, pp. 1–3.

41. Maaike Lulofs, 'Richard III: Dutch Sources',· *The Ricardian*, vol. 3 (1974), No. 46, p. 13.

42. See the paper by Dr Macdougall in the present collection. There appears to be no other evidence that Buckingham was godfather to the young Prince.

43. Jean Molinet, *Chroniques*, ed. J.A. Buchon, vol. 2 (1828), pp. 402–403. It has been suggested that Molinet wrote his *Chroniques* more or less contemporaneously with the events described (see Noel Dupire, *Jean Molinet, la Vie – les Oevres* (Paris 1932), pp. 16, 28), but the elaborate details of the scenes concerning the Princes make it seem more likely that these passages at least were written about 1500, possibly during revision of the work.

44. *Memoires de Martin et Guillaume du Bellay*, vol. 1 (Paris 1908), p. 43. It may be noted that rumours apparently continued to develop in France. Calmette and

Durville's edition of Commynes contains two footnotes saying that Prince Edward died in the Tower on 7th August 1483 and Prince Richard on 15th August (vol. 2, p. 232, notes 1 and 2). The edition of the *Memoires* by De Mandrot says between 7th and 15th August for both Princes, again no source is given (vol. 1 (Paris 1901), p. 456).

45.   *Great Chronicle of London*, pp. 236–237.

46.   Polydore Vergil, *English History*, p. 188.

47.   Thomas More, *The History of King Richard III*, ed. R.S. Sylvester (New Haven 1963), pp. lxxvi–lxxvii, 83–86.

48.   Thomas More, *op. cit.*, p. 83; Gransden, *op. cit.*, p. 452.

49.   Thomas More, *op. cit.*, p. 86; Susan E. Leas, 'As the King Gave Out', *The Ricardian*, vol. 4 (1977), No. 56, pp. 2–4; *Rotuli Parliamentorum*, vol. 6, pp. 545–546.

50.   Alison Hanham, *op. cit.*, pp. 152–190, particularly pp. 185–187. It is unfortunate that More is still treated seriously in this matter: see for example Desmond Seward, *Richard III: England's Black Legend* (London 1983), pp. 122–127.

51.   Thomas More, *op. cit.*, pp. 85, 86.

52.   See also Kendall, *op. cit.*, pp. 495–496. The development of rumours was not stopped by the publication of More's work nor by Tyrell's 'confession'. John Rastell's *Pastime of People* has some magnificent stories, including one where the royal brothers are lured into a chest by a cry of 'treason', the chest being later thrown into the 'Black Deeps', see Hanham, *op. cit.*, p. 104.

53.   Inscription upon the sarcophagus in Westminster Abbey.

54.   Sir George Buck, *The History of King Richard the Third*, edited with an introduction by A.N. Kincaid, (Gloucester 1979), p. 140. A contemporary of Buck gives a rather different version of an early seventeenth century find, saying that the Princes had been 'murdered in the Tower of London, which place ever since hath been mured up, and not known until of late, when as their dead carcases were there found, under a heape of stones and rubbish.' Ralph Brooke, *Catalogue of the Kings of England, etc*, (London 1619), p. 33. Miss Linda M. Gowans suggests that this is a modified form of the discovery recounted by Buck, since the material is inconsistent: it being stated of the younger of the two Princes that his 'place of buriall was never known certainly to this day.' *ibid.*, p. 378. There is no doubt that Brooke, York Herald, knew Buck and, therefore, there is the possibility that his account is merely a confused reworking of the latter's account, embellished with the tale of the 'Heape of stones' from the Tudor tradition. We are grateful to Miss Gowans for drawing our attention to this source.

55.   A. De Maurier, *Mémoires pour servir à l'histoire de Hollande*, (Brussels 1740), pp. 258–259, (cf. Paris edition, 1680), quoted in J. Robinson, 'Skeletons of the Murdered Princes', *Notes and Queries*, 7th series, vol. 8 (1889), pp. 361–362. See also Doreen Court's review of J.M. Rey, *Essais Historiques et Critique sur Richard III Roi D'Angleterre*, (Paris, 1818), in *The Ricardian*, vol. 5, no. 72, p. 325. Neither the Brooke nor De Maurier

accounts are mentioned by Lawrence Tanner. There remains the possibility that their two stories concern the same discovery rather than two separate finds.

56. E. Daniel, 'Skeletons of the Two Murdered Princes', *Notes and Queries*, 7th series, vol. 8 (1889), p. 497. This story ought to be dated to no later than 1614 – the date of the death of Lord Grey – hence there is the possibility that Brooke and Webb were dealing with identical skeletal finds. Tanner was able to trace the ownership of the manuscript down through Webb's descendants and he reproduced plans of the White Tower and its outbuildings for the period and sites concerned, L.E. Tanner and W. Wright, 'Recent Investigations Regarding the Fate of the Princes in the Tower', *Archaeologia*, vol. 34, (1934), pp. 9, 26.

57. S.B. Chrimes, 'The Fifteenth Century' (book review), *History*, vol. 48, no. 162, (1963), p. 23; A.R. Myers in W.S. Churchill's *History of the English-Speaking Peoples*, Part 30 (1970), p. 965.

58. C.D. Ross, *Richard III*, (London 1981), p. 97.

59. *Ibid.*, p. 98. Here he concurs with Professor Charles Wood, who had been persuaded of the authenticity of the 1678/1933 Bones because 'no other pair of children of roughly these ages, male of female, remains unaccounted for in the Tower from its construction under William the Conqueror to the discovery of 1674.' C.T. Wood, 'Who Killed the Little Princes in the Tower?' *Harvard Magazine*, vol. 80, (1978), pp. 35–40.

60. For Henry Pole see, see M.L. Bush, 'The Tudors and the Royal Race', *History*, vol. 55, no. 183 (1970), pp. 37–48 (41) and GEC *Complete Peerage*, vol. 9, pp. 96–97.

61. Sir Thomas Butler, *Her Majesty's Tower of London*, (London 1950), p. 5. We are grateful to Miss Elizabeth M. Nokes for this information.

62. G. Parnell, 'Excavations at the Tower of London 1976–7', *The London Archaeologist*, vol. 3, (1977), p. 97; Justine Bayley, Department of the Enviroment, *Archaeological Report* (in press).

63. Philip Lindsay, *On Some Bones in Westminster Abbey*, (London 1934), p. 40; Audrey Williamson, *The Mystery of the Princes, an Investigation into a Supposed Murder*, (Gloucester 1978), pp. 196–197; Ross, *op. cit.* App. 1, pp. 233–234; W.J. White, 'The Examination of Skeletal Remains: Henry VI and the Princes', *The Ricardian*, vol. 6, no. 80 (1983), pp. 159–161, *idem.*, 'The Bones' as Roman Remains, *ibid.* no. 81 (1983), pp. 195–196.

64. Lost MS, quoted in Davey's *Tower of London*; cited by Tanner and Wright, *op. cit.*, pp. 9–10; F. Sandford, *Genealogical History, etc*, 2nd edn. (London 1707), p. 427. Knight is thus the sole source for the wooden chest.

65. Tanner and Wright, *op. cit.*, p. 8.

66. *P.R.O. Lord Chancellor's Warrants* LC5/141.

67. Wren's *Parentalia* . . ., quoted in Tanner and Wright, *op. cit.*, pp. 8–9.

68. Thomas More, *op. cit.*, p. 86.

69. Tanner & Wright, *op. cit.*, p. 6; Gairdner, *Life and Reign of Richard III*, (Cambridge 1898), p. 119.

70. Tanner & Wright, *op. cit.*, pp. 7 & 13.

71. *Ibid.*, p. 12 cf. Robinson, *op. cit.*, pp. 361–2, note 55. The notion of the Garden Tower as the place of residence of the Princes has found fairly wide support. For example archaeological investigations at the Tower in 1975 led to the identification of an area of green known as the 'Lower Garden', presumed to be the location in which the Princes were observed 'shottying and playing' during the mayoralty of Sir Edmund Shaa, Thomas & Thornley, *op. cit.*, p. 234; G. Parnell, 'Observations on Tower Green', *The London Archaeologist*, vol. 3, no. 10, (1979), pp. 320–326. The idea that the Princes 'vacated the Tower of London's royal apartments for the more modest and servantless accommodation in the Garden Tower' appears to be based upon Mancini's observations (above), which may refer instead to the replacement of the Princes' attendants by those loyal to Richard (cf. the guards set over the Queen Mother and her daughters in sanctuary), whereas the fact that they were no longer visible to the public may reflect merely the impregnability of the new quarters in which they found themselves, Lorraine Attreed, 'From *Pearl* Maiden to Tower Princes: Towards a New History of Mediaeval Childhood', *Journal of Mediaeval History*, vol. 9, (1983), pp. 43–58 (52); Williamson, *op. cit.*; p. 185.
For a plan of the Tower see B.K. Davison, 'Excavations at the Tower of London', *Chateau Gaillard*, vol. 2, (1967), pp. 40–43; R.A. Brown, 'Architectural History and Development to c.1547', in J. Charlton, (ed.), *The Tower of London: its Buildings and Institutions*, H.M.S.O. (1978) pp. 32 and 36.

72. Tanner & Wright, *op. cit.*, p. 15; Lindsay, *op. cit.*, pp. 29–30; Lamb, *The Betrayal of Richard III* (London, 1959), p. 103; G. White, (ed.) *The Complete Peerage*, vol. 12, (1959), *Appendix J*, pp. 37 & 39; Kendall, *op. cit.*, p. 398, footnote 6.

73. Tanner & Wright, *op. cit.*, pp. 11–12; White, *op. cit.*, (n.72), p. 36.

74. A.P. Stanley, *Historical Memorials of Westminster Abbey*, 2nd edition (London 1868) pp. xliii and 181.

75. Tanner & Wright, *op. cit.*, p. 25; L.E. Tanner, letter to the *Daily Telegraph*, (1934), quoted in R.J.A. Bunnett, 'The 1933 Examination of the Alleged Bones of the Princes in the Tower', *The Ricardian*, no. 28 (1970), pp. 13–14.

76. Bunnett, *op. cit.*, p. 14; L.E. Tanner, *Recollections of a Westminster Antiquary*, (London 1969), pp. 153–165.

77. M.A. Rushton, 'The Teeth of Anne Mowbray', *British Dental Journal*, vol. 119, (1965), pp. 355–359.

78. Information from Tanner & Wright, *op. cit.*, pp. 24–25; Kendall, *op. cit.*, pp. 497–8; Ross, *op. cit.*, p. 234.

79. The accuracy in age determination of *tooth development* over mere *eruption* ('gingival emergence') is stressed in many publications: A.B. Lewis and S.M. Garn, 'The Relationship Between Tooth Formation and Other maturational factors', *Angle Orthodont.*, vol. 30, (1960), pp. 70–77; R.I. Sundick, 'Age and Sex Determination of Sub-adult Skeletons', *Journal of Forensic Science*, vol. 22, (1977), pp. 141–144; F.A. Moorrees, *et al.*, 'Age Variation of Formations Stages for Ten Permanent Teeth', *Journal of Dental Research*, vol. 42, (1963),

pp. 1490–1502; A. Demirjian, *et al.*, 'A New System of Dental Age Assessment', *Human Biology*, vol. 45, (1973), pp. 211–227.

80. Difficulties with the evidence as presented by Professor Wright are mentioned by the orthodontist Dr Arthur Lewis and by the anatomist Professor R.G. Harrison, Kendall, *Richard the Third*, p. 497; A.R. Myers, 'The Character of Richard III', *History Today*, vol. 4 (1954), p. 518. For Dr Northcroft's analysis of tooth-root development in the remains attributed to the Princes see Tanner & Wright, *loc. cit.*, p. 14.

81. Demirjian, *et al.*, *op. cit.*, pp. 220–222; cf. Tanner & Wright, *op. cit.*, p. 18.

82. E.W. Bradford, quoted in C.D. Ross, *Richard III*, p. 234; Moorrees, *et al.*, pp. 1495–1496, figures 5 & 6.

83. Tanner & Wright p. 18, versus Demirjian *et al. op. cit.*, pp. 224–225.

84. F.C. Downer, *Dental Morphology, an Illustrated Guide*, (Bristol 1975), p. 62.

85. Tanner & Wright, *op. cit.*, p. 16.

86. In Kendall, *Richard the Third*, p. 498.

87. Quoted in the standard text by yet another of Kendall's experts: W.M. Krogman, *The Human Skeleton in Forensic Medicine*, (Springfield 1962), p. 52. The situation is as summarised in P.L. Williams and R. Warwick, (eds.), *Gray's Anatomy*, 36th edition, (Edinburgh 1980), p. 283.

88. Marion M. Maresh, 'Linear Growth of Long Bones of Extremities from Infancy Through Adolescence', *American Journal of Physical Anthropology (A.J.P.A.)*, vol. 89, (1955), pp. 725–742; *idem ibid.*, vol. 66, (1943), pp. 227–254; F.E. Johnson, 'Growth of the Long Bones in Infants and Children at Indian Knoll', *ibid.*, ns, vol. 20, (1962), pp. 249–254; Patricia S. Gindhart, 'Growth Standards for the Tibia and Radius in Children Aged One Month Through Eighteen Years', *ibid.*, vol. 39, (1973), pp. 41–48; J.M. Hoffman, 'Age Estimations from Diaphyseal Lengths: Two Months to Twelve Years', *Journal of Forensic Science*, vol. 24, (1979), pp. 461–469.

89. M. Stloukal and H. Hanovka, 'Die Länge der Längsknochen altslawischer Bevölkerungen – unter besonderer Berucksichtung vom Wachtumsfragen', *Homo*, vol. 29, pp. 228–249; Jean Dawes, in J.D. Dawes and J.R. Magilton, (eds.), *The Cemetery of St Helen-on-the-Walls, Aldwark*, (York 1980), p. 23.

90. We are grateful to Miss Rosemary Powers of the British Museum (Natural History) who measured the bones of Anne Mowbray at the time of the latter's disinterment and who graciously allowed us to view her notes made at the time of the discovery of the body. She is not to be held responsible for the views advanced here however.

91. Indeed, the elder child may have been as young as ten or eleven years of age, upon this basis; cf. Dawes, *op. cit.*, p. 62; Maresh, *op. cit.*, pp. 727 and 729 (the latter being based upon the bones of the lower limbs *including* epiphyses).

92. Hence one ought to include similar measurements upon such bones remaining to be measured such as the length of the fibula in the younger child, the lengths of the calcanei of both children, the iliac diameters of both and the dimensions of the lower jaw of the elder child: R.J. Sundick, 'Human Skeletal Growth and Age Determination', *Homo*, vol. 29, (1978), pp. 228–249; W.E. Tracy, B.S.

Savara, 'Norms and Size and Annual Increments of Five Anatomical Measures of the Mandible in Girls from Three to Sixteen Years of Age', *Archives of Oral Biology*, vol. II, (1966), pp. 587–589. See also n.90 above. The lack of a full range of anthropometric measurements emphasises the incomplete air that the report possesses despite Professor Wright being allowed six days for his investigation of the partial remains of two individuals from the urn, Tanner & Wright, *op. cit.*, p. 15. For comparison, a modern osteologist might seek to report fully upon as many as five complete skeletons during the course of a single working day.

93.   Anon, 'Any Questions?', *British Medical Journal (B.M.J.)*, vol. 2, (1979), p. 322; E. White, *The Use of X-Rays for Age Determination in Immigration Control*, House of Lords, (Westminster 1981), pp. 10–14; P.L. Graitcer, E.M. Gentry, 'Measuring Children – One Reference Standard for All', *The Lancet*, vol. 2, (1981), pp. 297–299; 'A Measure of Agreement on Growth Standards', *ibid.*, vol. 1, (1984), pp. 142–143.

94.   Lindsay, *op. cit.*, p. 30.

95.   *Ibid.*; Dr Juliet Rogers in Ross, *op. cit.*, p. 233.

96.   F.E. Camps, J.M. Cameron, *Practical Forensic Medicine*, (London 1971), pp. 118–119; cf. J.D. Boyd, J.C. Trevor, 'Race, Sex, Age and Stature from Skeletal Remains', in C.K. Simpson, (ed.), *Modern Trends in Forensic Medicine*, (London 1953), pp. 133–152 and Krogman, *loc. cit.*, (n.89), pp. 114 and 122–129. For work performed in this area prior to Wright's own study see H. Fehling, *Archiv Gynäkologie*, vol. 10, (1876), pp. 1–80 and A. Thomson, *Journal of Anatomy*, vol. 33, (1899), pp. 359–380, quoted in S. Genoves, 'Sex Determination in Earlier Man', in D.R. Brothwell & E. Higgs, (eds.) *Science in Archaeology*, 2nd edition, (London 1969), pp. 429–439. Furthermore, research carried out since Wright's investigations indicates that sexual differentiation of the bones of the pelvis occurs at a much earlier age than was thought at one time (*viz.* even before birth), E.L. Reynolds, 'The Bony Pelvic Girdle in Early Infancy, *A.J.P.A.*, vol. 3, (1945), pp. 321–354; *idem.*, 'The Bony Pelvis in Pre-Pubertal Childhood', vol. 5, (1947), pp. 165–200; Barbara J. Boucher, 'Sex Differences in the Foetal Sciatic Notch', *Journal of Forensic Medicine*, vol. 2, (1955), pp. 51–54; *idem.*, 'Sex Differences in the Foetal Pelvis', *A.P.J.A.*, vol. 15, (1957), pp. 581–600. J. Caffrey, *et al.*, 'A Study of the Normal Variation in Acetabular Angles at Successive Periods in Infancy', *Paediatrics*, vol. 17, (1956), pp. 532–541. Among these experts at least one (Barbara Boucher) has the enviable reputation for unerring accuracy in sexing the bones even of foetuses.

97.   cf. Tanner & Wright, *op. cit.*, p. 21. The routine positive determination of sex in juvenile skeletal remains is to be found in, (*inter alia*), Dawes, *op. cit.*, p. 23, F.R. Dutra, 'Identification of Person and Determination of Cause of Death from Skeletal Remains', *Archives of Pathology*, vol. 38, (1944), pp. 339–349 (342), J.A. Imrie, G.M. Wyburn, 'Assessment of Age, Sex and Height for Immature Human Bones', *B.M.J.*, vol. 1, (1958), pp. 128–131.

98.   The pre-auricular sulcus is a depression seen in the hip bones of human females, between the sciatic notch of the ilium and the joint that the ilium makes with the

sacrum, W.M. Bass, *Human Osteology: a Laboratory and Field Manual of the Human Skeleton*, 2nd edition (Columbia 1979), pp. 151 & 161; D.R. Brothwell, *Digging Up Bones: the Excavation, Treatment and Study of Human Skeletal Remains*, 3rd edition (HMSO 1981), p. 62; Camps and Cameron, *op. cit.*, p. 119.

99. E.E. Hunt, I. Gleiser, 'The Estimation of Age and Sex of Pre-Adolescent Children from Bones and Teeth', *A.J.P.A.*, vol. 13 (1955), pp. 479–487.

100. T.H. Black, 'Sexual Dimorphism in the Tooth-Crown Diameter of Deciduous Teeth', *ibid.*, vol. 48 (1978), pp. 77–82; G.W. Thompson, *et al.*, 'Sexual Dimorphism in Dentine Mineralisation', *Growth*, vol. 39 (1975), pp. 289–301.

101. D.H. Goose, 'Dental Measurement: an Assessment of its Value in Anthropological Studies', In D.R. Brothwell (ed.), *Dental Anthropology* (Oxford 1963), pp. 125–148; M.L. Moss, 'Analysis of Development Processes Possibly Related to Human Dental Sexual Dimorphism', in P.M. Butler and K.A. Joysey (eds.), *Development, Function and Evolution of Teeth* (London 1978), pp. 135–147; cf. D.L. Anderson, 'Estimation of Age, Sex and Body Size from a Mandible', *Ontario Dentist*, vol. 55 (1978), p. 9. Subsequently, in a lecture at Glaziers Hall, London, in June 1985, Theya Molleson said of the elder child that in her experience, 'with complete dental development [it was] less likely that unfused epiphyses should exist in a girl than a boy. If the younger mandible is from a girl, then the lower canine ought to have erupted'. The latter is a conclusion by default, and is less tenable because it arose after an age calculation that presumed the remains were male. If the same calculations were made assuming female gender the anomaly disappears.

102. Tanner & Wright, *op. cit.*, p. 24; cf. Williamson, *Mystery of the Princes*, p. 186 and Lindsay, *On Some Bones in Westminster Abbey*, p. 33. Lindsay, of course, had used tables of average heights of children at various ages and this infomation, in turn, had been obtained from studies carried out at a very much earlier date, *ibid.*, p. 32. The current position is that although 'used universally in the earlier part of the century these tables have fallen into disuse', Camps and Cameron, *op. cit.*, p. 126; Krogman, *op. cit.*, pp. 163–164; Dawes, *op. cit.*, p. 24. The last of these, however, ventures to estimate the heights of *adolescents*. The effect of this would seem to be to make the elder child taller still: 5'1½".

103. Maresh, op. cit., pp. 720–731; J.M. Buckler, *A Reference Manual for Growth and Development* (Oxford 1979), p. 12.

104. W.J. White, Human Skeletal Remains from the Newgate Street Site, 1975–78 (Level III Report deposited with the Museum of London 1983). See R.M. Acheson, *et al.*, 'Some Effects of Adverse Environmental Circumstances on Skeletal Development', *A.J.P.A.*, vol. 14 (1956), p. 375; S.G. Vandenberg, F. Falkner, 'Hereditary Factors in Human Growth', *Human Biology*, vol. 37 (1965), pp. 357–365; S.M. Garn, Christabel G. Rohmann, 'Interaction of Nutrition and Genetics in the Timing of Growth and Development', *Pediatric Clinics of North America*, vol. 13 (1966), pp. 353–379; J.M. Tanner, *Growth at Adolescence*, second edition (Oxford 1962), pp. 121–134.

105. The late fifteenth century in England was seen by some contemporaries as a

'time of rude plenty', C. Creighton, *A History of Epidemics in England* (Cambridge 1891), pp. 38 and 222–225 (quoting Comines, Molinet, etc). This appears to have been because of a temporary respite from the 'alternating periods of abundance and scarcity' to which the country had been prone in the previous century, the last great famine before Tudor times having been experienced during 1438–39, *ibid.*, p. 65; J.D. Chambers, *Population, Economy and Society in Pre-Industrial England* (Oxford 1972), pp. 17, 22–24 & 55–56, quoting Molinet, Comines and the second continuator of the *Croyland Chronicle*.

106. J.M. Tanner, *et al.*, *Assessment of Skeletal Maturity and Prediction of Adult Height (TW2 Method)* (London 1975), pp. 21–24.

107. Average heights obtained for various English archaeological sites are tabulated in J. Schofield and W.J. White, *The Cemetery of St Nicholas Shambles, London* (in press). Preliminary results for the crew of the *Mary Rose*, which sank in 1547 give an average height 5'7", Margaret Rule, 'Tudor warship Reveals Health Aspects of Renaissance Man', *The Practitioner*, vol. 229 (1985), p. 21. For comparison the average height for men in modern Britain is 5'8½" (women 5'3½"), Office of Population Census and Surveys, 'Adult Heights and Weights Survey', *O.P.C.S. Monitor* SS 81/1, H.M.S.O. (1981).

108. The sources are as follows 'Report of the Committee Appointed by the Council of the Society of Antiquaries to Investigate the Circumstances Attending the Recent Discovery of a Body in St Stephens Chapel, Westminster', *Archaeologia*, vol. 34 (1852), pp. 406–430 (407); A.P. Stanley, 'On the Deposition of the Remains of Katherine de Valois, Queen of Henry V, in Westminster Abbey', *ibid.*, vol. 46 (1881), pp. 281–296; J. Evans, 'Edmund of Langley and his Tomb', *ibid.*, vol. 46 (1881), pp. 297–328; W.H. St John Hope, 'The Discovery of the Remains of Henry VI in St Georges Chapel, Windsor Castle', *ibid.*, vol. 62 (1911), pp. 533–542; W.H. Egerton, 'Talbot's Tomb in the Parish Church of St Alkmund, Whitchurch, Shropshire', *Transactions of the Shropshire Archaeological and Natural History Society*, vol. 8 (1885), pp. 413–440; C. Stothard, *Monumental Effigies of Great Britain* (London 1832), p. 98; R.O.C. Cotton, 'Sir John Cheney', *The Ricardian*, vol. 3, no. 45 (1974), pp. 19–20; P.W. Hammond, 'How Tall was Clarence?', *ibid.*, vol. 4, no. 54 (1976), p. 30; P.A. Janssens, 'Pathology of Mary of Burgundy (1451–1481): a Reconstruction of her Death', in A. Cockburn (ed.), *Papers on Palaeopathology Presented at the Third European Members Meeting of the Palaeopathology Association* (Caen 1980), p. C 10; R. Poulton, *Excavations on the site of the Dominican Friary at Guildford in 1974 and 1978* (Guildford 1984), p. 52. Whenever possible for the data quoted in the above papers the height calculated was checked using the currently accepted formula: M. Trotter, G.C. Gleser, 'Estimation of Stature from Long Bones . . .', *A.J.P.A.*, vol. 10 (1952), pp. 463–514 & vol. 16 (1958), pp. 79–123. The re-calculated heights appear as the final column in Table 3. The recent re-investigation of the skeleton in Tewkesbury Abbey attributed to Clarence tends to confirm that these were the remains of a person below average height, *Bristol and Gloucestershire Archaeological Society Transactions* (in press).

109. M.A. Rushton, 'The Teeth of Anne Mowbray', p. 357.

110. J.S. Rose, 'A Survey of Congenitally Missing Teeth, Excluding Third Molars, in Six Thousand Orthodontic Patients', *Dental Practitioner and Dental Record*, vol. 17 (1966), pp. 107–114; A.H. Brook, 'Dental Anomalies of Number, Form and Size: their Prevalence in British Schoolchildren', *Journal of the International Association of Dentistry for Children*, vol. 5 (1974), pp. 37–53; *idem.*, 'Variables and Criteria in Prevalence Studies of Dental Anomalies of Number, Form and Size', *Community Dentistry and Oral Epidemiology*, vol. 3 (1973), pp. 288–293.

111. P.J. Brekhus, *et al.*, 'A Study of the Pattern and Combination of Congenitally Missing Teeth in Man', *Journal of Dental Research*, vol. 23 (1944), pp. 117–131; H. Grahnen, 'Hypodontia in the Permanent Dentition', *Odontologia Revy*, vol. 7 (1956), Supplement 3.

112. Rushton, *op. cit.* (n. 77), pp. 358–359. The question of the common ancestry of Anne Mowbray and the Princes is to be examined in detail in a forthcoming article in *The Ricardian* by Rowena Archer.

113. In Ross, *op. cit.* (n. 58), p. 234.

114. Matthieu d'Escouchy's account of the battle and its aftermath is given in Egerton, *op. cit.* (n. 108), p. 432. See also S.G. Elkington, R.G. Huntsman, 'The Talbot Finger: a Study of Symphalangism', *B.M.J.*, vol. 1 (1967), pp. 407–411; E.A. Barr, 'Forensic Dentistry', *British Dental Journal*, vol. 122 (1977), p. 84.

115. Janssens, *loc. cit.* (n. 108).

116. B.H. Humble, 'Identification by Means of Teeth', *British Dental Journal*, vol. 54 (1933), pp. 528–536.

117. M. Vale, *War and Chivalry: Warfare and Aristocratic Culture in England, France and Burgundy at the End of the Middle Ages* (London 1981), p. 119, using Comines, vol. i, p. 30.

118. Tanner & Wright, *op. cit.*, p. 18. Wormian bones are the extra isolated irregular small bones seen occasionally in the sutures which join the component bones of the cranium. It was this feature of the two skulls which convinced the royal physician, Lord Moynihan, of a strong family relationship between the two sets of skeletal remains that he handled in 1933, Bunnett, *op. cit.* (n. 75), p. 13.

119. Brothwell, *Digging Up Bones*, p. 109.

120. *Ibid.*, p. 92; cf. Dawes, *op. cit.* (n. 89), p. 59; Schofield and White, *op. cit.* (n. 107); Brenda M. Stoessiger, G.M. Morant, 'A Study of the Crania in the Vaulted Ambulatory of St Leonard's Church, Hythe, Kent', *Biometrika*, vol. 24 (1932), pp. 135–202.

121. These doubts are set out in Hammond, *op. cit.* (n. 108), p. 31, using W.S. Symonds, 'Historical Notes on Some of the Tombs in Tewkesbury Abbey', *Transactions of the Bristol and Gloucestershire Archaeological Society*, vol. 2 (1878), pp. 194–209; *ibid.*, vol. 25 (1902), p. 44.

122. Tanner & Wright, 'Recent Investigations Regarding the Fate of the Princes in the Tower', p. 18, cf. Thomas More, *loc. cit.*, p. 25.

123. Armstrong, *op. cit.* (n. 2, above), pp. 92–93 & 127; Kendall, *Richard the Third*, p. 394.

124. This is particularly true of certain of the commentators impressed by the tales from the continent which featured Edward V dying before the Duke of York (despite the logical inconsistencies inherent in basing this upon the elder child's illness evident in the Abbey bones), including, of course, Perkin Warbeck's tale of his own escape from the Tower, Williamson, *The Mystery of the Princes*, pp. 116–117. See also n. 43, above.

125. Thomas More, *op. cit.*, pp. 35–36 quoting Elizabeth Woodville; Gairdner, *op. cit.*, p. 77; Attreed, *op. cit.* (n. 71), p. 54. Can it be that Wright, seeking authority in More for a princely illness, siezed upon the wrong brother?

126. H.A. Harris, 'Lines of Arrested Growth in the Long Bones in Childhood: Correlation of Histological and Radiographic Appearances in Clinical and Experimental Conditions', *British Journal of Radiology*, vol. 4 (1931), pp. 561–588; C. Wells, 'A New Approach to Palaeopathology: Harris' Lines', in D.R. Brothwell, A.T. Sandison (eds.), *Diseases in Antiquity* (Springfield 1967), pp. 390–404.

127. Indeed, an identical pattern of 'Harris' Lines' observed in two juvenile skeletons, found in association, had been used to deduce that the deceased were closely enough related to have been siblings, Krogman, *op. cit.* (n. 87), pp. 50–51. Thus, had Wright promoted more comprehensive X-raying of the bones from the urn in Westminster Abbey it should have become possible to test his hypothesis of close family relationship. The X-ray examination of the skeletal remains for evidence of such consanguinity must await a fresh investigation.

128. Tanner & Wright, *op. cit.*, pp. 18–19.

129. Theya Molleson, 'What the Bones Tell Us', in S.C. Humphreys and Helen King (eds.) *Mortality and Immortality: the Archaeology and Anthropology of Death* (London 1981), pp. 15–31.

130. C.K. Simpson, *Forensic Medicine*, fifth edition, London (1964), pp. 83–88; F.E. Camps (ed.), *Gradwohl's Legal Medicine*, third edition (Bristol 1976), pp. 328 & 334; Camps & Cameron, *op. cit.*, p. 300.

131. W. Shakespeare, *Henry VI Part 2*, Act 3 Scene 2, quoted in Tanner & Wright, p. 19.

132. W.H. Bloxam, *A Glimpse of the Monumental Architecture of Great Britain* (London 1847) p. 62. See also David Garrick's soliloquy upon seeing Duke Humphrey at St Albans, *Comic and Curious Verse* (Harmandsworth 1964), p. 101.

133. Brothwell, *op. cit.* (n. 98), p. 126.

134. F. Wood Jones, 'The Post Mortem Staining of Bone Produced by the Ante Mortem Shedding of Blood', *B.M.J.*, vol. 1 (1908), pp. 734–736. We have examined some of these skulls, courtesy of Theya Molleson of the British Museum (Natural History).

135. Kendall, *Richard the Third*, pp. 497–498; Ross, *Richard III*, p. 234. A single dissenting voice was that of the palaeopathologist Dr Calvin Wells for whom Professor Wright's reconstruction of the death and burial of the 'Princes' struck

a sympathetically imaginative note, C. Wells, *Bones, Bodies and Disease* (London 1964), p. 185.

136. Lindsay, *On Some Bones in Westminster Abbey*, p. 33, cf. Tanner & Wright,*op. cit.*, pp. 15 & 20. A well respected osteologist warns of buried skeletal material that 'a very serious complicating factor is the fact that some soils and other deposits produce patches of darker staining of bone through heterogeneous concentration of ferruginous material', Brothwell, *Digging Up Bones*, p. 126. Elsewhere he speaks of the staining that is found upon skulls excavated from 'Waterlogged peat, peaty gravels and alluvial muds in Britain', *ibid.*, p. 7. The latter may be of significance in view of another intrusive object in contact with the bones in the urn: a peat-stained piece of wood, Tanner & Wright, p. 20.

137. We are grateful to Professor Simpson for permission to quote his opinion of the significance of Wright's observation.

138. W.H. St John Hope, *op. cit.* (n. 108), p. 540. Modern methods of analysis would not merely determine whether Professor Wright's stain was indeed blood but, if so, distinguish the species of animal responsible (and if human, possibly the sex), T.H. Loy, 'Prehistoric Blood Residues: Detection on Tool Surfaces and Identification of Species of origin', *Science*, vol. 200 (1983), pp. 1269–1271, C. Orrego, 'DNA and the Disappeared', *New Scientist* (15th November 1984), pp. 14–15.

139. B.H. Knight, I. Lander, 'Methods of Dating Skeletal Remains', *Human Biology*, vol. 41 (1969), pp. 322–341; B.H. Knight, *Medicine, Science and the Law*, vol. 9 (1969), pp. 247–252; idem., 'The Dating of Human Bones', *The Criminologist*, vol. 6 (1971), pp. 33–40.

140. E.H. Willis, 'Radiocarbon Dating', in Brothwell & Higgs, *op. cit.*, pp. 46–57; W.F. Libby, 'Dating by Radiocarbon', *Accounts of Chemical Research*, vol. 5 (1972), pp. 289–295; *idem.*, 'The Physical Science of Radiocarbon Dating', in R. Berger (ed.), *Scientific Methods in Mediaeval Archaeology* (Berkeley 1970), pp. 17–21; W. Horn, 'The Potential and Limitations of Radiocarbon Dating in the Middle Ages: the Art Historian's View', in Berger, *op. cit.*, pp. 23–87.

141. C.V. Haynes, 'Bone, Organic Matter and Radiocarbon Dating', in *Radioactive Dating and Methods in Low-Level Counting* (Vienna 1967), pp. 163–168; Knight, *op. cit.*, pp. 38–40; Potter *op. cit.*, p. 235.

142. M. Stuiver, 'A Comparison of Beta and Ion Counting', *Science*, vol. 202 (1978), pp. 881–883; L.V. Pavlish, E.B. Banning, 'Revolutionary Developments in Carbon-14 Dating', *American Antiquity*, vol. 45 (1980), pp. 290–297; 'Researchers Set a New Date With Radiocarbon', *New Scientist*, vol. 100 (1983), p. 79.

143. R.E.M. Hedges, 'Radioactive Clocks in Archaeology', *Nature*, vol. 281 (1979), pp. 19–24; R. Berger, 'The Potential and Limitations of Radiocarbon Dating in the Middle Ages: The Radiochronologist'a View', *idem*, op. cit., pp. 89–139; H.E. Suess, 'Climate and Radiocarbon During the Middle Ages', *ibid.*, pp. 159–165; C.W. Ferguson, 'Concepts and Techniques of Dendrochronology', *ibid.*, pp. 183–199; R.M. Clark, 'Calibration, Cross-

Validation and Carbon-14', *Journal of the Royal Statistical Society*, vol. 142 (1979), pp. 47–62.

144.   C.L. Bennet, *et al.*, 'Radiocarbon Dating With Electrostatic Generators: Dating of Milligram Samples', *Science*, vol. 201 (1978), pp. 345–347; J. Gribbin, 'Extending the Radiocarbon Calendar', *New Scientist*, vol. 83 (1979), pp. 98–100.

145.   B. Keish, Holly M. Miller, 'Recent Art Forgeries: Detection by Carbon-14 Measurements', *Nature*, vol. 240 (1972), pp. 491–492.

146.   White, *op. cit.* (n. 72), pp. 34–35.

147.   J.B. Bada, E. Kvenvolden, E. Peterson, 'Racemisation of Amino Acid in Bones', *Nature*, vol. 245 (1973), pp. 308–310; C. Christodoulides, J.H. Fremlin, 'Thermo-luminescence of Biological Materials', *Nature*, vol. 232 (1971), pp. 257–258.

148.   J.M. Cameron, B.G. Sims, *Forensic Dentistry* (Edinburgh 1974), pp. 23–40; K.R. Burns, W.R. Maples, 'Estimation of Age from Individual Adult Teeth', *Journal of Forensic Science*, vol. 21 (1976), pp. 343–356; K. Kawasaki, *et al.*, 'On the Daily Incremental Lines in Human Dentine', *Archives of Oral Biology*, vol. 24 (1980), pp. 939–943; A.E.W. Miles, 'Teeth As an Indicator of Age in Man', in Butler & Joysey, *op. cit.*, pp. 455–464; G. Gustafson, K. Simpson, 'Dental Data in Crime Investigations', in Simpson, *op. cit.* (n. 96), pp. 153–167; Camps & Cameron, *op. cit.*, p. 133; T.G. Bromage, M.C. Dean, 'Re-evaluation of the Age at Death of Immature Fossil Hominids', *Nature*, vol. 317 (1985), pp. 525–27.

149.   E.R. Kerley, 'The Microscopic Determination of Age in Human Bone', *AJPA*, vol. 23 (1965), pp. 149–163; *idem.*, 'Age Determination of Bone Fragments', *Journal of Forensic Science*, vol. 14 (1969), pp. 59–68.

150.   W.M. Bass 'Developments in the Identification of Human Skeletal Material (1968–1978)', *AJPA*, vol. 51 (1979), pp. 555–562; D.D. Thompson, 'The Core Technique in the Determination of Age at Death in Skeletons', *Journal of Forensic Science*, vol. 24 (1979), pp. 902–915; S.D. Stott, Sarah J. Gehlert, 'The Relative Accuracy and Reliability of Histological Aging Methods, *Forensic Science International*, vol. 15 (1980), pp. 181–190; J.L. Singh, D.L. Gunberg, 'Estimation of Age at Death in Human Males from Quantitative Histology of Bone Fragments', *AJPA*, vol. 33 (1970), pp. 373–382.

151.   T. Thunberg, 'The Citric Acid Content of Older, Especially Medieval and Praehistoric Bone Material', *Acta Physiologica Scandinavica*, vol. 14 (1947), pp. 245–247; I. Lengyel, 'Biochemical Aspects of Early Skeletons', in Brothwell (ed)., *The Skeletal Biology of Earlier Human Populations*, (Oxford 1968), pp. 271–288.

152.   I. Kiszely, 'On the Possibilities and Methods of the Chemical Determination of Sex from Bones', *Ossa*, vol. 1 (1974), pp. 51–72; J. Dennison, 'Citrate Estimation as a Means of Determining the Sex of Human Skeletal Material', *Archaeology and Physical Anthropology in Oceania*, vol. 14 (1979), pp. 136–143. We should like to thank Theya Molleson for these references.

153.   I. Lengyel, G. Farkas, 'Critical Evaluation of the Results of Morphological and Laboratory Analysis of Human Bone Remains of the Early Bronze Age of Mokrin', *Anthropologiai Közlemenyk*, vol. 16 (1972), pp. 51–71.

154. Brothwell, *op. cit.* (n. 98), p. 4; Simpson, *op. cit.* (n. 98), pp. 98–115; Krogman, *op. cit.*, pp. 234–235; Camps & Cameron, *op. cit.*, pp. 136–142.

155. W.C. Boyd, L.G. Boyd, 'Blood grouping by Means of Preserved Muscle', *Science*, vol. 78 (1933), p. 578; *idem.*, 'Blood Grouping in Forensic Medicine', *Journal of Immunology*, vol. 33 (1937), pp. 159–172; P.B. Candela, 'Blood Group Reactions in Ancient Human Skeletons', *American Journal of Physical Anthropology*, vol. 21 (1936), pp. 429–432; Madeleine Smith, 'Blood Groups of the Ancient Dead', *Science*, vol. 131 (1960), pp. 699–702; Lengyel, *op. cit.*, pp. 280–281.

156. R.G. Harrison, *et al.*, 'Kinship of Smenkhare and Tutankhamun Demonstrated by a Serological Technique', *Nature*, vol. 224 (1968), pp. 325–326; Smith, *op. cit.*, p. 702; *idem.*, 'Blood Grouping of the Remains of Swedenborg', *Nature*, vol. 184 (1959), pp. 867–868; A.E. Mourant, *Blood Relations: Blood Groups and Anthropology* (Oxford 1983).

157. Ross, *op. cit.*, p. 234.

RICHARD III AND JAMES III: CONTEMPORARY MONARCHS, PARALLEL MYTHOLOGIES

Norman Macdougall

'Thank God,' exclaimed Edward IV in a letter to Pope Sixtus IV, '. . . for the support received from our most loving brother, whose success is so proven that he alone would suffice to chastise the whole kingdom of Scotland.'[1] He was referring to the Scottish expedition of Richard, duke of Gloucester, in the summer of 1482, a remarkable episode which brought into confrontation for the first time two of the most maligned rulers of their own and later ages – the future Richard III and James III of Scotland. In the case of the former, efforts to understand his career and behaviour have frequently included attempts to see King Richard as a man of his times, no worse – and possibly a great deal better – in moral terms than contemporary European rulers. Recently, this argument has been summarised most succinctly by Professor Ross. 'No-one,' he suggests, 'familiar with the careers of King Louis XI of France, in Richard's own time, or Henry VIII of England, in his own country, would wish to cast any special slur on Richard, still less to select him as the exemplar of a tyrant.'[2] This is undoubtedly true; yet it has often struck me as remarkable that those concerned to draw parallels have almost totally ignored Richard's contemporary in Scotland, James III (1460–1488) a ruler whose career and subsequent reputation are in many ways strikingly similar to those of Richard III. In this paper I shall look briefly at this enigmatic ruler, at his role as King of Scotland, at his relationship with King Richard, and at the growth of sixteenth-century Scottish legends of James III which bear a remarkable resemblance to, let us say, Sir Thomas More's or Edward Hall's view of Richard III.

The reign itself is easily described. James III became king in 1460 at the age of 8, assumed full control of government shortly after his marriage to Margaret of Denmark in 1469, and faced serious rebellions against his rule in

1482 and 1488, being killed in the course of the latter year at the battle of Sauchieburn near Stirling, aged 36, and succeeded immediately by his 15-year-old son and heir, the nominal leader of the rebels, who became James IV and – eventually – one of the most successful of Scottish kings.[3] Comparisons between James III and his contemporary Richard III are easy to make. Both men were born in 1452; both drew the greater part of their support from the north of their respective realms, yet had to rule in the south; both suffered from worsening, and ultimately fatal, relationships with close relatives; both survived the deaths of their queens by less than two years; both dealt capably with one major rebellion but succumbed to a second; and both were killed in battle in their 'thirties, fighting against their own subjects. The northern supporters of both kings produced strikingly similar obituaries; thus the city of York's lament on the day after Bosworth 'that King Richard, late mercifully reigning over us, was . . . piteously slain and murdered, to the great heaviness of this city' is echoed four years later by the provost and burgesses of Aberdeen, who complained that 'no punishment had been imposed on the treasonable vile persons who put their hands violently on the king's [James IIIs] most noble person.'[4] Yet both kings suffered long after their deaths from the growth of legends about them which reached towering proportions by the end of the sixteenth century; and the tyrannous reign of Richard III – in the works of Vergil, More, and Hall – has its parallel in the condemnation of James III by the Scottish writers Abell, Lesley, Pitscottie, and Buchanan.[5]

However, comparisons must not be pushed too far, for in some respects the contrasts between the two men are equally striking. Richard III was a usurper who reigned for little more than two years before being defeated and killed by another usurper; James III succeeded peacefully, was king for 28 years, an adult ruler for 19 of these, and his death in battle did not produce a new dynasty but the immediate succession of his son and heir. These facts reflect not only the relative stability of the Stewart dynasty in Scotland compared with its English counterpart, but also a striking difference between the workings of royal government in fifteenth century Scotland and England. The functions of both monarchies were of course broadly the same – to exercise justice within the realm and provide leadership in war. But in the late fifteenth century the resources of a Scottish monarch were at best one-tenth that of the English crown; the king could not normally afford a contract army; there was no vast government machine, no sophisticated bureaucracy as in England, but rather, as Dr. Jenny Wormald has shown, a collection of 'somewhat ill-organised institutions at the centre, and local worthies in the localities whose position could depend on inheritance and local prestige rather than direct royal appointment.'[6] Yet the system, if we may call it that, worked; for in Scotland, in spite of the premature deaths of all the fifteenth-century kings and royal minorities which equalled periods of adult rule in length, the Stewart dynasty not only survived but reached such a position of preeminence that long before the end of the century, it was unchallenged, the succession passing swiftly from father to eldest son with remarkable consistency. England during the same century witnessed three dynasties and no less than six violent changes of ruler.

Such challenge as there was to the Stewart dynasty in late medieval Scotland consisted mainly of isolated attempts within the royal house, or by those closely related to it, to secure prominent roles in government for themselves during the minority, physical or mental infirmity, or enforced absence of the king. When, however, there was an adult Stewart on the throne, the challenge to his authority represented by powerful families close in blood to the crown seems to have existed first of all in the king's mind, rather than in any overt treason by the families concerned. Thus James I embarked on a wholesale elimination of Stewart earls for no other reason than that their name was Stewart;[7] and James II systematically undermined and then destroyed the other great magnate family, the Black Douglases, whose only treason, as Dr. Nicholson reminds us, was to defend themselves when attacked by the king.[8] The traditional picture of a frightened monarch continually menaced by rebellions and overmighty magnates is simply not tenable in fifteenth-century Scotland; for in the cases I have cited it was the monarch, quite unprovoked, protected by Scottish political conservatism and assisted by a majority amongst the peerage, who attacked and wrecked the great kin groups of Stewarts and Black Douglases. The collapse and forfeiture of the Black Douglases in 1455 left the Scottish crown, though still poor by English or continental standards, in an unassailable position within Scotland in terms of both resources and authority. Unlike their feeble predecessors, both James I and James II had taken risks, had stepped outside the law, and had acted with ruthlessness and duplicity to achieve this position, and one may ask why they were able to assail their greatest subjects and get away with it to the extent that they were eventually praised by the three estates for doing so. The answer, as Dr. J.M. Brown has pointed out,[9] lies in what the Scottish monarchy had to offer – political and social stability. Only the king could keep a balance of power in the state, and bring to an end too great a concentration of power in the hands of a single magnate family, Stewarts or Douglases.

These assaults form dramatic, memorable, tableaux; but much more typical of crown-magnate relations in fifteenth-century Scotland was a tacit understanding between king and nobility to cooperate in advancing each other's interests, an understanding which worked in practice because each side had something to gain from, and to offer, the other. The king could exercise considerable patronage, but his power was always restricted by his income, which was small and which could be augmented by taxation only very rarely. He could not afford a contract army; so in time of war he relied heavily on magnates whose supporters would form the backbone of any Scottish army, or who, if local rebellion threatened, might act on the crown's behalf by crushing the opposition themselves. In time of peace, the king needed magnate support even more, to exercise justice and maintain law and order in the localities; for in Scotland there was no question of the crown having the wealth to pay judges or lawyers, or even give proper remuneration to important officials such as wardens of the marches. The answer to this problem, generally accepted by the mid-fifteenth century, was delegation of authority to responsible magnates who alone could represent central government effectively in the localities.

For their part, the magnates had good reason to cooperate with the king. For most of them, success lay in enriching themselves by acquiring more land, which was most likely to be achieved as reward for service to the crown. Royal patronage, considerably increased in scale after the forfeiture of the Black Douglases in 1455, might also extend to grants of offices of state, or remissions of customs dues or feudal casualties of various kinds. Thus there were good practical reasons why most of the nobility wished to serve, rather than challenge, the crown.

It was therefore to a position of considerable power that James III succeeded in August 1460. Although he was only eight, he had the advantage of inheriting his father's able officers of state, some of whom – notably Chancellor Avandale and Colin Campbell, first earl of Argyll – were to serve him loyally for more than twenty years. His mother, Mary of Guelders, survived the first three years of the minority, and showed herself a determined and capable stateswoman. Above all, it was Scotland's great good fortune that exactly three weeks after the civil war between James II and the Black Douglases had ended in the fight at Arkinholm on May Day 1455, England's far greater struggle got under way in the first battle of St. Albans. Thus the traditional enemy was neutralised, and a judicious Scottish policy of playing off Lancaster against York in the next few years produced the surrender of Berwick to the Scots by the refugee Henry VI and Margaret of Anjou without a shot being fired. Thereafter the Scots' cynical abandonment of the Lancastrian cause in the early 1460s – because Henry VI had visibly lost – led to a rapid rapprochement with the Yorkists, culminating in the fifteen years' truce of 1464. Thus when James III married Margaret of Denmark and emerged from tutelage at the age of seventeen in 1469, his future, given loyalty at home and a relatively weak England abroad, looked bright.[10]

Yet he received an appalling press from all the chroniclers of the reign, and within a century of his death was being cited as the classic example of incompetent and tyrannical kingship in late medieval Scotland. He was widely portrayed as a recluse who could not or would not govern, who offended his brothers and his nobility by giving ear to low-born favourites, above all Cochrane the stone-mason, the man largely responsible for bringing about the ruin of one royal brother, the Duke of Albany, and the death of the other, the Earl of Mar. Acquisitive and lazy, James III was no leader in war, and was contrasted in this field to his disadvantage with his manly brothers Albany and Mar, whom he destroyed. This damning sixteenth-century indictment of the king was further embellished in the ensuing three centuries, and although it has recently been questioned, much of it is still current today.[11] It is difficult to erase this view of the king from peoples' minds, partly because it contains so many dramatic tableaux and entertaining clashes of powerful personalities; but even more important, I suspect, in ensuring the durability of the sixteenth-century chroniclers' estimates of James III is the fact that in spite of the remarkable differences of social status, political attitudes, and geographical location of all five writers, they tell essentially the same tale. Thus Adam Abell was an Observantine friar of Jedburgh who listened to local gossip; Bishop John Lesley was a co-editor of the first published edition of the Scottish parliamentary acts; Giovanni Ferreri was a Piedmontese monk who had taught for some years in the Cistercian monastery of Kinloss; Robert Lindsay of Pitscottie was a Fife laird who more or less admits in the preface to his chronicles that his evidence is all hearsay; and George Buchanan, the great humanist and tutor to James VI, was writing at the very end of his life to justify at length his own theory of popular sovereignty.[12] In spite of this diversity, all five narratives of the reign are remarkably similar, stressing the king's estrangement from brothers and nobility, the evil counsel of the favourites, the assault on both Albany and Mar, and King James's failure as a leader in war.

When I first embarked, quite a few years ago, on research into the reign of James III, I was disturbed by this remarkable unanimity. It was not even a simple case of one man borrowing from another, or even having access to the same written sources (though they may of course have encountered the same, or similar, oral traditions). None of the chroniclers was even remotely contemporary with the reign of James III, or indeed with each other, the earliest writer being Abell in the 1530s, the last Buchanan in the 1580s. In any case, why should John Lesley, a zealous Catholic and the foremost champion of Mary Queen of Scots in her exile, and George Buchanan, Protestant revolutionary and the queen's most vitriolic critic and fanatically committed enemy, write the history of an earlier reign in exactly the same way? The solution to the problem seemed to be to discover an oral or written tradition common to all five writers – on whose narratives, after all, almost all later historians relied in describing the reign of James III.

In fact, such a tradition is not difficult to find. Criticism of James III became apparent early in the reign of his son and successor, and of necessity, for James IV had acquired his throne through taking arms against his father, and the defeat and death of the latter at the battle of Sauchieburn in June 1488. Overnight rebels in arms were transformed into pillars of the new establishment, with the most committed of them, the border families of Hume and Hepburn, acquiring the lion's share of offices in state and household. But the death of a Scottish king in battle against his own subjects was quite unprecedented, and the new regime agonised throughout the first parliament of the reign of James IV in a lengthy debate on the cause of the late king's demise. This was necessary because the new king, James IV, although only fifteen, had given orders before the battle that no-one should lay violent hands on his father.[13] An acceptable formula was eventually found, namely that James III had brought about his own ruin by accepting evil counsel – the standard claptrap of all rebels – and that he had 'happened to be slain' at Sauchieburn. But rumblings continued for years as to the manner of his death, especially in the north – I have already cited the burgh council of Aberdeen – and many must have taken exception to the method by which the new government legitimised its recent rebellion against its sovereign – introducing an act invalidating all grants of land or offices made by James III in the last four months of the reign – in effect backdating the beginning of the new reign in order to justify the rebellion which brought it into existence.[14] Here is a striking parallel with Henry VIIs cynical device of backdating the start of *his* reign by one day to obscure the fact that his kingship was based on conquest.

Inevitably, however, the establishment won the day, for even the most committed supporters of James III could not bring the late king back to life; and within about four years of Sauchieburn, references to the manner of his death ceased to raise much public interest; the new king busied himself with his job as expected of him, performed extensive if belated penances for any part he might have had in his father's death, and both sides in the civil war of 1488 eventually settled down to a relatively peaceful co-existence, consigning James III and all his works to a convenient oblivion. So long as James IV reigned, there was no point in *praising* his predecessor, and indeed many practical reasons for playing down any virtues the late king might have had; but there was no obvious reason to assail his memory and portray him as a tyrant. It took James IVs unexpected death at Flodden in September 1513, leaving a son aged only 1 to succeed him, to produce an extension of the James III legend. For the Governor of the king and realm during much of the ensuing minority, exercising considerable influence over the young king James V and continuing to advise him frequently well into his adulthood, was John, duke of Albany, the son of James IIIs brother Alexander, duke of Albany, forfeited for treason in 1483. The importance of John, duke of Albany, throughout the generation following 1513 undoubtedly revived interest in the career of his father Alexander, whose reputation was now rescued, his English treasons forgotten, and his actions praised as those of a nobleman who consistently advocated Franco-Scottish friendship. This remarkable rescue operation is arguably the biggest single contribution to the James III legend, for praise of Albany inevitably involved condemnation of the king who had forfeited him; and so, almost two generations after James IIIs death, we see an obvious political motive for condemning his kingship.[15] Significantly, it is in the 1530s that the complaints about James's low-born counsellors – especially Cochrane the stone-mason – first begin to appear, and when the Observantine Friar Adam Abell produced the first thumbnail sketch of the reign of James III in the course of a general history of Scotland (1533– 37), his narrative was little more than a eulogy of Alexander, duke of Albany, without whose support King James was apparently a doomed man.[16] But Abell was writing forty-five years after the death of James III, and relying by his own admission on oral sources – that is on popular tales or ballads describing the dramatic events of the reign – the banishment of the 'good' Albany and the death of Mar, the Lauder crisis of 1482, and the king's death in 1488. In short, apart from the conventional complaint about King James's use of young or base-born counsellors, and awareness of a need to rescue the reputation of Alexander, duke of Albany, early sixteenth-century writers had little of substance to offer to explain coherently the dramatic events of James IIIs reign. Their sources were unreliable or obviously biased, and they were writing at about the same distance in time from the events which they describe as, for example, Sir Thomas More was from the reign of Richard III.

A generation later still, when the fourteen years between 1568 and 1582 produced a remarkable clutch of four full length histories by Lesley, Ferreri, Pitscottie, and Buchanan respectively, all four had absorbed the legend of James III established in the 1530s, and faced the hopeless task of trying to reconcile such 'official' sources as were available to them – for example, the first edition of the Scottish parliamentary acts – with oral tradition, which for more than a generation had emphasised James IIIs incapacity and the sterling qualities of his brother Albany. So the late sixteenth-century chroniclers simply embellish the existing legend, and in the case of one of them, George Buchanan, there was a political motive for blackening James IIIs character almost a century after his death. This was Buchanan's implacable hatred towards Mary Queen of Scots, who had been deposed in 1567; intellectual justification for this unprecedented act was necessary, and Buchanan found what could be interpreted as a precedent for Mary's deposition in the rebellion against James III in 1488. This event was not, of course, a deposition, but it could be made to appear in this light if James IIIs kingship and character were sufficiently condemned in the pages of Buchanan's *History*. Thus James III, accorded by earlier chroniclers at least the virtues of devoutness and mercy in spite of his many vices, in Buchanan's prose has an early fall from grace 'into every species of vice' – worst of all his supposed incestuous relationship with his younger sister Margaret – and takes on the character of a Scottish Caligula.[17]

Here, surely, is the Scottish equivalent of the so-called Tudor myth of Richard III, with a mixture of deliberate distortions to enhance the reputations of later political regimes, and popular oral tradition, combining to produce a wildly inaccurate picture of both king and reign. In some cases the chroniclers' borrowings are hilarious; thus John Bellenden, the translator of Hector Boece's *Scotorum Historiae* in the 1530s, seeking to explain the death of James IIIs brother the Earl of Mar, remarks that Mar 'was slane in the Cannongait, in ane baith fatt.'[18] Bellenden does not say who was responsible for this bizarre execution; but the 'baith fatt' in which he claims Mar died is a bathing vat similar to, or identical with, a brewer's or dyer's vat – so that we have here an obvious borrowing from the stories of the death of George, duke of Clarence, in a butt of Malmsey wine, retold by Dominic Mancini, hinted at by the Croyland Continuator, and enshrined in sixteenth-century English tradition.[19] Likewise the prophecy, recounted by both Pitscottie and Buchanan,[20] attributed to a witch who told James III that he should be slain by the nearest of his kin, bears a remarkable similarity to the popular story that Edward IV was alarmed by a prophecy that George should follow Edward. But we need not insist on an English parallel; for the Scottish chroniclers of the sixteenth century, whether or not they used English sources, invariably saw themselves mainly as continuators of Hector Boece; and in Pitscottie's account of James IIIs demise, the king, sitting on his horse watching the approach of his rebellious son and remembering the witch's prophecy, might almost be the Macbeth of Bellenden's translation of Boece, who seeing the approach of Malcolm's army, 'understude the prophecy was completit, that the wiche shewed to him; nochtheles, he arrayit his men.' Scarcely had the battle begun when Macbeth, like Pitscottie's James III, took flight and was killed in the pursuit.[21] In essence, Pitscottie is telling the Macbeth story all over again; a tyrant's death is predicted by a witch or witches, and his fears of the fulfilment of the prophecy turn him into a coward on the battlefield – or to stretch a point in the case of Richard III, on the night before the battle.

When the origins of such myths have been traced to their sources, however, there is no need to go on retailing them as facts. Thus I was delighted to discover that the low-born favourites of James III were largely the creation of writers of a later period; that Bishop Lesley's statement that King James was despised by his nobility in 1482 because he had neglected his queen, Margaret of Denmark, in the pursuit of a whore called Daisy, was no more than a case of mistaken identity; and that the sixteenth-century view of the king as a recluse who disliked war, and was contrasted to his disadvantage in this respect with his brothers, was contradicted by every piece of available contemporary evidence.[22] I decided, therefore, to concentrate on contemporary 'official' sources, meagre though they were, supplementing them with stories retailed by the later chroniclers only when these could be substantiated by drawing on reliable evidence from the reign itself. Applying this method, I soon found that it was possible to present an entirely different view of the king and reign. James III could be praised quite legitimately as the first late medieval Scottish ruler to appreciate that the Franco-Scottish alliance rarely, if ever, worked to Scotland's benefit, and that the sensible – indeed necessary – alternative was an end to the cold war with England based on a firm peace and royal marriage. He had the courage to carry through such an alliance in 1474, and three times in the 1480s would again press for peace with England.[23] This policy, unpopular in the Scotland of James IIIs day, would be widely praised when his successor James IV concluded the Treaty of 'Perpetual Peace' of 1502 with Henry VII, and married Henry's daughter Margaret Tudor in the following year. It seemed that James III was a statesman, a man born ahead of his time who had suffered unjustly from the contrived political myths of a later age.

My initial enthusiasm for this discovery was, however, rapidly tempered by doubts about the king's virtues; for it soon became apparent that the reputation of James III, like that of Richard III, was not entirely the creation of malicious gossips or government hacks of a later age. There exists a short chronicle, in the British Library, probably dating from 1482, which ambitiously attempts to cover the entire history of Scotland from its mythological beginnings down to 1482 in a mere ten folios.[24] The last two of these are devoted to the fifteenth century, becoming longer and more interesting the closer they come chronologically to the terminal date of 1482; and this last year, and the internal crisis associated with the invasion of southern Scotland by Gloucester and Albany, is treated at some length. It appears from this contemporary account that James III was seized at the Scottish muster point at Lauder by 'the lords of Scotland', that some of his household servants were killed in the process, and that the king was unpopular on three counts – first because of the war with England, which by 1482 had dragged on for more than two years, second because of the royal debasement of the coinage and production of the infamous 'black money', and lastly because the king had taken the counsel of his 'sympill' household rather than that of his nobility. Even if we discard this last complaint as a commonplace medieval fiction to discredit the royal council, the other two have more substance – and in addition the chronicler makes further serious criticisms of James III. Under the date 1479, he describes the banishment of James's brother, Alexander, duke of Albany, who fled to France, where he was married, and subsequently to England; and in the same year, he claims that the other royal brother, John, earl of Mar, was slain because he had associated with witches and warlocks, all of whom were burnt on 'Crag Gate', which may possibly be identified with Cragingalt, the name given to the Calton Hill in Edinburgh at this period.[25] The chronicler is not clear that the king was directly associated with Mar's death, taking refuge in statements like 'some judge' and 'they said'; and he cannot have known much, if anything, about the manner of Mar's death, though the earl's supposed association with witches and warlocks strikingly recalls the execution at Tyburn in 1477 of Thomas Burdett and John Stacey for conspiring, in league with the Duke of Clarence, to bring about the death of Edward IV and his son and heir through use of the magic arts.[26] No doubt this story of Clarence's conspiracy with necromancers spread rapidly to Scotland;[27] and the chronicler of 1482 utilised it to explain the inexplicable, the death of the Earl of Mar, about which no-one had any precise information. Borrowings of this kind inevitably raise doubts as to the value of the short chronicle of 1482 as a source; but it must be admitted that much of the writer's information is specific and accurate, for example in his description of the dramatic rise in grain prices due to the war with England and the royal debasement of the coinage, and the exact period of time that James III spent as a prisoner in Edinburgh castle during the crisis of 1482.

Yet whether we accept the statements of the chronicler of 1482 as gospel or reject them out of hand as fiction does not remove the problem of explaining satisfactorily what happened in the crisis of that year. A Stewart king, in the thirteenth year of his adult rule, was seized by some of his subjects, imprisoned and in fear of his life for months – and seized, moreover, at the muster point of Lauder when preparing to resist an English invading army, the commander of which, Richard, duke of Gloucester, was charged with the task of deposing King James and replacing him with his brother Albany. These are unprecedented events in Scottish political history. Why did Albany imagine that in Scotland, with its remarkably conservative political community, he had any chance of success of taking the place of his brother James III, who had three male children to succeed him? More important, why did Edward IV and Gloucester – the latter a man of extensive experience in the north – believe that Albany was worth supporting with a huge English army? The answer to both questions lies, I believe, in the personality of James III, and in the fear and loathing with which many of his most influential magnates regarded him.

The personality of a medieval monarch is firmly linked in the popular mind with the policies he pursues; and in this respect, James III hardly inspired confidence with his failure to ride out on justice ayres; with his efforts to centralise royal administration in Edinburgh rather than making himself personally known to his subjects; and with his wild efforts in the early 1470s to raise money for invasion schemes on the Continent embracing Brittany, Guelders and Saintonge. This effort to introduce taxation on a much more regular basis than it had ever been known before called forth indignant protests from the parliament of July 1473, and demands that the king should stay at home and do his job.[28] King James seems to have taken little account of parliamentary criticism, for it continued unabated throughout the 'seventies and into the 'eighties; and alarm at the king's actions was further fuelled by the alliance which he made with Edward IV in the autumn of 1474, based on a promise of marriage between his son and heir James, and Edward's daughter Cecily, when both should reach marriageable age. In the meantime, James III would receive instalments of Cecily's dowry, paid at an annual rate of 2,000 marks sterling from February 1475.[29] This Anglo-Scottish treaty involved an immediate rejection of Louis XIs overtures for a renewal of the ancient Franco-Scottish alliance; and allowing a rapprochement between James III and the Yorkists was incidentally a considerable diplomatic blunder on the part of the French king, faced as he was with the imminent prospect of Anglo-Burgundian invasion. But the new alliance was extremely unpopular in southern Scotland, partly because England had been the traditional enemy – and France the traditional ally – for two centuries, and partly because Scottish magnates in the south, including James's brother Albany, and the young and powerful Archibald, 5th Earl of Angus, thrived on border warfare and appear to have resented the prospect of increased royal interference on the borders. In view of his later conduct, it is ironic to find Albany, as March Warden, mustering troops at Lauder in the spring of 1474 to resist a projected raid on the West and Middle Marches by Richard, duke of Gloucester;[30] while Angus was the first, when peace eventually broke down in 1480, to cross the border and lay waste parts of Northumberland.[31] The attitude of both men to the English alliance was probably that of the poet

Blind Harry, who condemned peace with England at the outset of his epic vernacular poem 'The Wallace' (completed 1476–78) with the dismissive words: 'Till honour Ennymyis is our haile entent.' (To honour enemies is our chief preoccupation).[32] To make the English peace work in southern Scotland, where after all he chose to live and reign, James III had to pay the price of its unpopularity – conciliation of the southern nobility and an even-handed distribution of rewards for his friends in the north and elsewhere. A generation later James IV would enter upon an English alliance in exactly this way, using patronage to win support. It was the failure of James III even to recognise that he must conciliate and reward to ensure the success of his policies which was his most obvious, and ultimately fatal, flaw.

Time and again one comes back to King James's personality, strongly reflected in a series of arbitrary and, on occasions, illegal actions throughout the 1470s which gradually undermined his kingship. Thus he conferred on his Chancellor Andrew Stewart, Lord Avandale, the liferent of the earldom of Lennox, depriving the legal heir, Lord Darnley, in the process;[33] he fostered a local Perthshire feud by appointing members of two warring families, Drummonds and Murrays, to the same offices – those of Steward, Coroner, and Forester of the earldom of Strathearn – and then seized the offices and their revenues for himself.[34] Most important of all, as the 'seventies advanced King James came to rely more and more on one man – William Scheves, who became archbishop of St. Andrews in 1478 and whose promotion at court and elsewhere was based entirely on his intimacy with the king. However, in spite of his early functions at court – acting as physician, obtaining drugs from the Low Countries, and on at least one occasion sewing the king's shirts – Scheves was not a favourite in the conventional sixteenth-century sense, but rather a somewhat colourless civil servant who seems to have enjoyed the routine drudgery of royal administration, acting annually as an auditor of exchequer, as a frequent member of the Lords of Council, a prominent parliamentarian, and on two occasions a member of the parliamentary Committee of the Articles, to draft legislation for consideration by the three estates. But Scheves' unique influence with the king – remarkable in view of James IIIs aloofness and keen sense of the royal dignity – is reflected in the survival of nine privy seal and signet letters on a large variety of topics – relations with England, royal gifts and admonitions, and taxation – which bear Scheves' signature as well as that of the king.[35] At no other period of the reign does a royal letter, signed by King James, bear anyone else's signature; and Scheves held no official post on the council. He was never Chancellor, Privy Seal, nor even Clerk Register, the last named office having been held for a time by his father under James II. Not surprisingly, Scheves' pre-eminence and intimacy with James III was widely resented; and part, at least, of the great crisis of 1482 may be seen as a struggle to force him to resign his archbishopric in favour of one of the king's uncles.

Yet the real key to 1482 lies surely in King James's appalling relations with his close family. Of his two sisters, the elder, Mary, was imprisoned in 1471 on returning to Scotland seeking a pardon for her forfeited Boyd husband, Thomas, earl of Arran, with whom she had fled to Bruges. The king married her off to James, Lord Hamilton, in 1474; but in the crisis of 1482 she defied King James and reverted to her Boyd allegiance. Margaret, the younger sister, finally evaded her brother's English marriage schemes for her – including such shortlived prospects as the Duke of Clarence and Anthony, Lord Rivers – by having an affair with William, Lord Crichton, one of the rebels of 1482–3.[36] James IIIs younger brother, John, earl of Mar, about whose death so many bizarre stories were eventually to circulate, is a shadowy figure about whom little is known; he seems to have spent most of his time on his estates in the north, rarely coming to court or parliament.[37] All that the official records tell us is that Mar sat in the Edinburgh parliament of March 1479; thereafter his name vanishes until 14 July 1480, when he is described as dead and his earldom forfeited.[38] There is not even a hint as to the reasons for his imprisonment; and his attainder is not to be found in the parliamentary records. However, stories soon began to circulate about his conspiracy with necromancers and witches, and it seems likely that he was condemned for treason by a parliamentary assize meeting in the spring of 1480 – for which records do not survive – and either died in prison or was privately executed.[39] Not until fifty years later would his death be associated with the scheming of the royal favourites.

In some sense, however, the greatest mystery of all surrounds the relations between James III and his other brother, Alexander, duke of Albany. It is of course tempting to judge Albany by his later treasons, to regard him in Professor Ross's phrase as 'a kind of Scots Clarence',[40] shifty, untrustworthy, and with an eye to the main chance. But the truth is that remarkably little is known of his career before his indictment for treason in 1479. Like Mar, he was not a regular parliamentarian, nor is he to be found on the council or more than occasionally at court. Unlike Mar, however, Albany held the important offices of Admiral of Scotland and March Warden; he had taken part in at least one justice ayre during his youth; and his earldom of March was in the front line of defence in the event of English invasion such as that projected by Gloucester in 1474.[41] In the circumstances, the indictment for treason brought against Albany in the parliament of October 1479 makes unconvincing reading. There are two main charges – violating the peace with England by making raids across the border and thereby abusing his office of March Warden; and fortifying his castle of Dunbar against the king.[42] The first of these has some substance, though in essence it does little more than reflect the intense dislike of the English alliance of 1474 on the part of the southern nobility; while the latter charge, the fortifying of Dunbar, is an extremely dubious one, because there would have been no need to defend Dunbar unless James III had first attacked his brother. Albany's crime, like that of the Black Douglases a generation earlier, may well have been to defend himself when attacked. Significantly, the three estates in parliament were prepared to forfeit Albany's captain and the defenders of Dunbar

against the royal forces; but they would not go so far as to forfeit the duke
himself. The conclusion is inescapable that members of the estates believed
that the king had gone too far, and that Albany's traditionalist anti-English
stance was widely popular. Thus no sentence of forfeiture was passed against
Albany; and for the next two-and-a-half years, the summons calling on the
duke to appear to answer the charges of treason was continued again and
again, from one parliamentary session to the next. Significantly, this continuation was first made 'at the gret raquest, instance, and supplicacioune' of
the three estates in parliament,[43] and probably reflects a widespread belief
that the duke's offences were not treasonable and did not merit forfeiture,
together with a fear that if a royal duke was not safe from this unpopular king,
then no-one was.

In the course of the next three years, the foreign situation – and therefore
the internal Scottish political situation – changed dramatically. Albany had
already escaped to France before the fall of Dunbar castle in 1479, and he was
well received by Louis XI; in January 1480, he married Anne de la Tour,
daughter of the Count of Auvergne and Bouillon.[44] Meanwhile at home his
brother's Anglophile policy rapidly collapsed, largely because Edward IV had
little interest in maintaining the Scottish treaty of 1474 once the French war
was over and he had himself become Louis XIs pensioner. On the other hand
he was keenly interested in recovering the money he had been paying out to
the Scots since 1475, as instalments of Cecily's dowry. James III, pressing
ahead with a further scheme to marry his sister Margaret in England,
discovered not only a coolness on the part of Edward IV, but a decided
unwillingness on the part of the Scottish estates to pay the huge sum of twenty
thousand marks to meet the expenses which King James would incur in
sending the bride to England.[45] The scheme was abandoned; and about the
same time, Louis XI began to make approaches to the Scottish king, inviting
him to break his alliance with Edward IV and revert to the traditional policy
of close friendship with France.[46] It required only angry Anglo-Scottish
exchanges about breaches of the peace on the borders to smash the already
brittle Anglo-Scottish alliance of 1474; and Scotland would once again be
drawn into essentially a European conflict, in which the only function of her
king was to embarrass Edward IV in the interests of leaving Louis XI of
France a freer hand on the Continent.

This, then, was the situation in Scotland during the war with England in
1480–82; a king who had undermined his initial advantages by use of
unpopular counsellors like Scheves, by his attacks on his family and his
arbitrary and illegal land transactions, finally saw his innovatory policy of
friendship with Yorkist England collapse in ruins. His duty as king was now to
defend southern Scotland against English invasion, in the process leading into
battle men whom he had alienated by his initial enthusiasm for the alliance,
and by his more recent pursuit of Albany. He was thus peculiarly vulnerable
to internal revolt; and when it came, it would be led by yet another
dissatisfied branch of the royal Stewart family in the persons of James IIIs

three half-uncles (sons of James Is widow, Joan Beaufort, by her second marriage), John Stewart, earl of Atholl, James Stewart, earl of Buchan, and Andrew Stewart, bishop-elect of Moray. The most aggressive of these three men appears to have been Buchan, a shifty and ambitious magnate, and acutely aware that his earldom, bestowed as recently as 1469 by James III, was at risk if he were to offend the king. In the spring of 1482 there were signs that he had done so, for he and his brother Atholl were given a remission from the king – presumably in a belated effort to achieve some sort of unity at home in the face of English invasion – for having seized and held Edinburgh castle without royal licence at some point during King James's legal minority.[47] Such a remission was hardly reassuring in view of the recent fates of other members of the royal family; and Buchan probably reckoned that the best method of defence was attack. Seizure of the king would avert a military disaster, secure his position in the royal household, and give him, together with his Stewart brothers, a dominant role in government. It may be added that as Warden of the Middle Marches, Buchan was actually responsible for the defence of the Lauder area, where the Scottish host was to be mustered, and was therefore in a unique position to seize King James. Buchan's younger brother Andrew Stewart, bishop-elect of Moray, was drawn into the plot because of his designs on Scheves' archbishopric of St. Andrews. The advent of Albany, Gloucester, and an English invading force was therefore a godsend, in political terms, to the Stewart half-uncles, for it gave them an excuse to act while at the same time obscuring the extent of their treasons – seizing the monarch in the face of an advancing enemy – and these treasons could subsequently be presented as an effort to ensure efficient government in a time of national crisis.

It is the existence of this last faction – the Stewart half-uncles – which explains the relative failure of the great English invasion in the summer of 1482. I do not want to give a blow-by-blow account of this remarkable episode, as the ground has been very well covered over sixty years ago by Miss C.L. Scofield and – much more recently – by Professor Charles Ross.[48] But neither writer was able fully to take into account the complexity of the Scottish dimension – that is, that various political groups with widely differing objectives had already appeared north of the border – so that the difficulty remained of explaining why a huge English army, under arguably the ablest of all the Yorkist commanders, could not accomplish the task with which it was entrusted. Recent scholarly writing in Scotland has sought to explain away this problem by suggesting that there was never any real intention on Gloucester's part to depose James III and instal Albany as king in his place; the real objective of the English force, we are told, was to take Berwick, in Scottish hands since 1461.[49] But such a statement simply does not fit the facts. While it is true that Berwick was important to both sides as a matter of prestige – acquired by the Scots during the minority of James III as a reward for their very temporary sheltering of Henry VI and Margaret of Anjou – it was not regarded as anything more than an expensive deathtrap by many

Scots, who insisted that James III himself pay for the garrison of 500 troops required to defend it in 1482.[50] Likewise on the English side, although Edward IV was keen to recover Berwick, the surrender of which he demanded in an ultimatum to the Scots as early as 1480, he was at least as anxious at that time to obtain possession of the heir to the Scottish throne and an acknowledgement of his overlordship from James III.[51] In May of 1481, Edward, in a letter to Pope Sixtus IV, again raised the issue of his overlordship of Scotland and announced that it was over this issue that he intended to invade Scotland that summer. In the event, he did not do so; the following year the opportunity to press his Scottish claims must have been irresistible. Not only had he satisfactorily achieved a rapprochement with Louis XI of France and ensured the payment of his annual pension, but from France also had come Alexander, duke of Albany, arriving at Southampton in a Scottish carvel at the beginning of May 1482 'to serve . . . the King of England, as his liege subject, against his Scotch enemies and rebels.' At Edward IVs expense, Albany lodged in London between 2 and 4 May at a house called the 'Erber'; and only a week later, he had already been accepted as pretender to James IIIs throne, as on 10 May a royal proclamation ordered every man who had indented to go with the 'king of Scotland' to be ready to do so on fourteen days' notice.[52]

This activity served as a prelude to the remarkable Treaty of Fotheringhay of 10–11 June 1482. Albany, signing himself 'Alexander R' and styling himself King of Scotland, promised to do homage to Edward IV on obtaining the realm of Scotland for himself; and he would also break the Franco-Scottish alliance and surrender Berwick. For his part Edward IV, who came to Fotheringhay with Gloucester and still intended to invade Scotland in person, bound himself to assist Albany in obtaining the crown of Scotland, but demanded in return the cession of Berwick, Liddesdale, Eskdale, Ewesdale, Annandale, and Lochmaben castle, to England. The treaty also provided for Albany's marriage to Edward's daughter Cecily if the duke could obtain an annulment of his recent French marriage.[53]

Thus Edward IV, in the summer of 1482, was acting in a far more belligerent way than ever before; and however we interpret the Treaty of Fotheringhay, far more than the future of Berwick was at stake. Gone was the old policy of using the exiled Earl of Douglas or the Lord of the Isles as a fifth column to embarrass the Scottish government; in its place was commitment to the overthrow of the existing regime north of the border. As for Albany, it seems likely that he fell in with Yorkist schemes to make him king rather than initiating them himself; and he may have felt that he had no option but to do so. He was not going to receive any practical assistance from Louis XI of France; and the English king was clearly not interested in him as another Douglas, an alien hanger-on to be put on show on expeditions to the Scottish marches. So his choice lay between languishing in France or England, or risking a return to Scotland backed by English military strength. He may have reasoned that the risk was worth taking because he had not yet been forfeited in Scotland, and because he could not afford to delay much longer if his cause was to attract support there.

In fact, there was no delay at all on the English side; on 12 June, only a day after the making of the Fotheringhay treaty, Edward IV renewed Gloucester's commission as lieutenant-general in the north, and the conduct of the subsequent campaign was entirely in the duke's hands. It was well-planned, with wages raised for no less than 20,000 men for a four-week campaign, about mid-July to mid-August 1482. On the disbandment of this main army, 1,700 men were to be retained by Gloucester and paid for a further two weeks' service from 11 August.[54] The York contingent – one hundred archers – attached to the main army left the city about 14 July;[55] so Gloucester and Albany must have entered south-east Scotland via Berwick at the end of the third week of July, or the beginning of the fourth week at the latest. The town of Berwick was tamely surrendered, and with troops paid for four weeks, Gloucester had no intention of delaying his expedition by laying siege to the castle. He moved swiftly north; and James III, with his useless five hundred men left behind in Berwick and a further pitiful six hundred scattered throughout the Marches in puny numbers, arrived at the Scottish muster point at Lauder to attempt to resist the largest and best-led English army seen in Scotland for over eighty years.

If he had been allowed to do so, the result would almost inevitably have been military disaster, the Scottish king's death, Albany as an English puppet king, and a protracted civil war in Scotland over the royal succession. Instead, James III was saved from all this by his Stewart half-uncles, who on 22 July – and presumably in the nick of time – arrested him at Lauder, took him the 24 miles north to Edinburgh, and incarcerated him in the castle.[56] As we have seen, they bore King James no goodwill, and the palace revolution on which they embarked was designed to give them control of the government; but by their action at Lauder they not only saved the king, but also made the object of the English invasion – the deposition of James III – impossible to achieve. For the simple fact is that when Gloucester entered Edinburgh unopposed at the beginning of August, and his great army camped on the burgh muir,[57] he found no-one with whom he could negotiate in order to achieve Edward IVs aim of installing Albany in James IIIs place. The Stewart half-uncles – Atholl, Buchan, and the bishop-elect of Moray – had possession of the king and the royal seals in Edinburgh castle, and were prepared to withstand a siege if necessary. A well-defended Edinburgh castle was an extremely tough nut to crack, and Gloucester's army could only be paid for little more than a week, until 11 August; an attack by royalist forces loyal to James III during any English siege of the castle was likely, so that the overall risks were probably too great in proportion to the likely gains. Alternatively an attempt might have been made to secure the persons of the queen, Margaret of Denmark, and her sons, as bargaining counters to force an accommodation with the defenders of Edinburgh castle; but the queen and her offspring were thirty miles away in Stirling, a castle at least as defensible as Edinburgh; so this possibility, if it was considered at all, was presumably rated a non-starter. There was also the problem that Albany, having arrived in the Scottish capital to discover that his chances of acquiring the throne were slim, was very ready to enter into public negotiations to secure a restoration to all the lands and offices which he had held before his flight in 1479.

Almost by a process of elimination, therefore, Gloucester found himself dealing with the remaining two groups of prominent Scots – James IIIs displaced counsellors, Scheves, Avandale, and Argyll, and the provost and community of the city of Edinburgh, all of them sharing the desire to be rid of the English army as quickly as possible. Thus peace settlements were hurried through on three consecutive days, 2–4 August. On the 2nd, Scheves, Avandale, and Argyll, together with Bishop Livingston of Dunkeld, bound themselves to secure Albany's restoration to his lands and offices in a full parliament; at the same time the duke was to be pardoned for his 'aspiring and tending to the throne'.[58] It is however doubtful whether, with no access to the king, the Stewart half-uncles, or the royal seals, the James III loyalists were in any position to honour this agreement; and if Edward Hall is to be believed, the following day Albany secretly promised Gloucester to observe the terms of the treaty of Fotheringhay, in spite of any agreements made with Scots lords.[59] Finally, on 4 August, the city of Edinburgh paid the price – a high price – necessary to rid itself of the English. Walter Bertram, provost of the city, together with the merchants, burgesses and community of Edinburgh, promised, in the presence of Gloucester, Albany, the Earl of Northumberland, the Earl of Argyll, and Bishop Livingston of Dunkeld, that if the marriage between Prince James and Edward IVs daughter Cecily was not accomplished, all the money which the English king had paid towards his daughter's dowry would be refunded at the city's expense in annual instalments.[60] The public statement that the ubiquitous Cecily, already contracted to Albany in the Treaty of Fotheringhay, might no longer be available for Prince James, strongly suggests that Edward IV had not abandoned plans to instal Albany as a puppet king in Scotland; and by 27 October Edward was insisting on a refund of the dowry money.[61]

As the man on the spot, Gloucester was probably more realistic about what could and could not be achieved in Scotland; and his agreements of 2–4 August had in fact left open a large number of possibilities for future intervention. Shortly after 4 August, he moved south, dismissing his large army on the 11th, and retaining only 1,700 men to take Berwick castle. The siege which followed must have been short, as Edward IV in London was able to write to the pope, reporting the fall of Berwick, on 25 August.[62] No doubt Berwick's garrison of five hundred was reluctant to fight for an imprisoned James III, who was in no position to pay them and might not even survive the crisis.

In spite of Edward IVs effusions to the pope about his brother's military abilities, he may have been less than happy about the results of the summer campaign of 1482. The continuator of the Croyland Chronicle sounded a sour note when he remarked that huge sums of money, raised only with the greatest difficulty, had been squandered simply to recover a fortress which cost ten thousand marks a year to defend;[63] and demobbed soldiers returning to York complained about the boredom of a campaign during which they did nothing but wait on the ordnance and baggage-train.[64] It is difficult, however, to see what more Gloucester could have done. If the Scots were not prepared to consider Albany as king even after the Lauder crisis and the imprisonment of the unpopular James III, they were never likely to do so; and Albany had been restored to his estates with English aid, and might be expected to be heavily reliant on, and amenable to the wishes of, the English king. Gloucester could well argue that this, together with the capture of Berwick, was no mean achievement for the price of a six-week campaign in the north.

He reckoned without the guile of James III and the political ineptitude of Albany. There may have been little that the duke could do to salvage his own undermining of his credibility in Scotland by appearing in Edinburgh at the head of 20,000 English; but in his subsequent frenetic activity to secure his position, he tried to make deals with Queen Margaret, with the Stewart half-uncles, with the city of Edinburgh, and with James III himself. He coveted, but never in fact received, the office of lieutenant-general, and as traditional loyalty to James III began to reassert itself, he found himself with only one option left open to him – the renewal of his English treasons early in 1483.[65] Even in the pursuit of these he was not consistent, and by 19 March 1483, badly frightened, he temporarily abandoned Edward IV to make an indenture with his brother King James, who had not only survived the winter but summoned a parliament packed with his own supporters to Edinburgh in March. Duke Alexander's treasons being by this time widely publicised, the king was able to deny him even the prominent place in the state for which he had been prepared to settle the previous August.[66] In desperation, Albany turned again to Edward IV for assistance and admitted an English garrison into Dunbar castle.

His luck had finally run out, for Edward IV died on 9 April. From James IIIs point of view, this was an unexpected stroke of luck; Edward V was only thirteen, and the establishment of a regency in England was bound to mean not only a relaxation of the aggressive policy towards Scotland which Edward IV had pursued in his last years, but also the departure from the north of Richard, duke of Gloucester. This breathing space for James III, fast recovering from the traumas of the winter, was a disaster for Albany. His treasons were now known in Scotland, and the main prop for these treasons – Edward IV – was dead. Probably in April Albany abandoned Dunbar to an English garrison – it would not be recovered by the Scots until the spring of 1486 – and fled south to join the Scottish fifth column in England. James III had no further difficulty in securing his brother's forfeiture in parliament at Edinburgh on 8 July 1483;[67] but only two days before, the political situation in the south had altered dramatically with the coronation of Gloucester as Richard III.

The ensuing two years provide a succession of 'might-have-beens'. There is little doubt that Richard's initial inclination was to continue the war against Scotland – witness his coolness in responding to James IIIs overtures for a lasting peace – but he was never in a position to do so effectively, partly because of Buckingham's rebellion, partly because of the problem of raising sufficient money to equip an effective army, and no doubt also because relations with Scotland were peripheral to Richard's interests, whereas relations with Brittany, Burgundy, and above all France, were vital and if allowed to deteriorate could rapidly prove fatal. Thus the years 1483–5 show James III and Richard III treating each other with a kind of cold respect, and only slowly moving towards an alliance of sorts once other possibilities had been explored.

For the Scots king, these other possibilities included the recapture of Dunbar castle, the powerful sea-girt fortress which Albany had surrendered to the English; he was prepared to negotiate in the autumn of 1483 to see if he could recover Dunbar – not to mention Berwick – by peaceful means; but King Richard, in spite of the major threat to his throne presented by Buckingham's rebellion in the autumn of 1483, gave a cool response to the Scottish king's enthusiastic letters calling for peace.[68] Scots pressure therefore consisted partly of a prolonged siege of Dunbar, starting in the late spring of 1484, and much more effectively, a renewal of the Franco-Scottish alliance of 1448–9. With remarkable speed, on 13 March 1484, James III confirmed a pact of friendship between France and Scotland, an offensive and defensive treaty directed against England. This treaty was signed in the presence of Charles VIIIs ambassadors, the expatriate Scot Bernard Stewart, Lord of Aubigny, and Master Pierre Milet, and ratified by the French king less than three months later, on 9 July.[69]

Richard III was probably not unduly worried about the siege of Dunbar; but the Franco-Scottish treaty was another matter, for Henry Tudor, pretender to the English throne, was being harboured by Charles VIII from the late summer of 1484; and the prospect for King Richard of an imminent war on two fronts, against both France and Scotland, not to mention the inevitable rebellion at home which such a war would provoke, cannot have been an inviting one. Yet the English king could do little to retaliate except invite the disinherited Scots, Albany and Douglas, to attempt another invasion of southern Scotland. Richard can hardly have had hopes of their success; having accompanied Albany to Scotland in much more promising circumstances in 1482, he was probably extremely cynical about the Scottish duke's popularity anywhere north of the border; but Albany was proving an awkward guest. On 12 March 1484, one of his ships seized two Burgundian wine ships bound for the port of London, and robbed them of £375 worth of wine, goods, and merchandise. This was not the sort of act calculated to endear the exiled duke to Richard III, who had to make restitution to the wine merchant involved, Anthony Kele of Antwerp;[70] and he may have been glad to see the back of Albany whatever the outcome. As with Albany, so also with his ally, James, the forfeited 9th earl of Douglas, King Richard displayed a greater realism than his predecessor, cutting Douglas's annual pension from £500 to £200.[71] The man had after all been an exile from Scotland for almost thirty years, and a whole generation of new families had grown up to possess and enjoy the Black Douglas lands in southern Scotland since the forfeiture of the earldom in 1455.

Thus in the summer of 1484, Richard IIIs armed support for Albany and Douglas amounted to a few hundred men at most. He was wise not to involve himself in greater expense, for on 22 July Albany, his former steward Sir James Gifford of Sheriffhall, and Douglas, were routed at Lochmaben in Dumfriesshire by a small army of local lairds, Crichtons, Murrays, and Johnstones.[72] Douglas was captured and imprisoned at Lindores in Fife for the remaining four years of his life; Albany fled back to France, the country which had first received him as a fugitive, and a year later was killed in a tournament in Paris at the age of thirty-one.[73] Lochmaben had shown that both he and Douglas were men of the past; in country where they had formerly ruled virtually as kings, they had been defeated by a small gathering of local lairds. Arguably Albany's credibility with the Scottish political community had already collapsed following the English invasion of 1482, which must surely rank as his most serious single mistake.

Richard III was probably philosophical about the Lochmaben débâcle. In any event, he had recognised even before Lochmaben that he must negotiate for peace with James III; and once his mind was made up, he pushed ahead swiftly, issuing safe-conducts for eight Scottish ambassadors, and meeting them in person at Nottingham in September 1484. At the outset of the peace negotiations, Archibald Whitelaw, James IIIs secretary, former tutor, and humanist, embarked on a long oration in Latin to the English king. This purports to be a declamation in praise of peace; but it is liberally sprinkled with quotations from Virgil's *Aeneid* and – whether included in an ironic sense or not we cannot know – praises of Richard IIIs martial exploits. Eventually, however, rhetoric was abandoned in favour of hard bargaining, and a settlement was reached before the end of the month. Prevailing circumstances – the existence of the Franco-Scottish alliance and the problems of Dunbar and Berwick – made this Anglo-Scottish peace at Nottingham considerably less convincing than its predecessor of 1474. It was, after all, only a three-year truce, not a forty-five year peace; and although its terms included a marriage alliance between James IIIs son and heir and Anne de la Pole, Richard's niece, no sum was specified for Anne's dowry in spite of the fact that the marriage was supposed to be solemnised within three years.[74] The impression conveyed by the settlement is one of caution on both sides; and in spite of the provision, in the parliament of May 1485, of ambassadorial expenses for a Scots embassy to travel south to York to settle the details of the marriage,[75] nothing appears to have been done before August, when Bosworth rendered the entire scheme obsolete.

Evidence for Scottish support for Henry VII at Bosworth is slight, and most of it comes from sixteenth-century and later sources. James III did not of course assist Henry directly; but he had apparently sent a large number of mercenaries to France with Bernard Stewart following the French treaty of 1484,[76] and some, if not all, of these may have been associated with the Tudor enterprise. In the late 1570s, Robert Lindsay of Pitscottie, the most colourful and least credible of the sixteenth-century Scottish chroniclers, claimed that there was a Scots company with Henry Tudor at Bosworth, led by Sir Alexander Bruce of Earlshall; and it must be admitted that both Henry VII and James III subsequently showed conspicuous favour to this man.[77]

However, Pitscottie's most memorable story about the Scottish war effort at Bosworth has nothing to do with Bruce of Earlshall; it concerns a Highlander named Macgregor, a servant of the bishop of Dunkeld, who, the night before the battle, stole the English crown from King Richard's tent. On being seized and brought before the king, he was asked why he had attempted such a theft, to which he replied that his mother had prophesied many years before that he would be hanged, and he felt that if this were the case he should be hanged for something worthwhile. This explanation apparently caused considerable amusement amongst the royal party, and earned Macgregor an immediate pardon from the king.[78] On the following day, Richard III rode out of Pitscottie's mythical tale to the reality of his death; and less than three years later, his Scottish adversary James III, alike the victim of later legends and his own inability to inspire enough committed support when he most needed it, followed him to the grave.

Notes

1. *Calendar State Papers (Venice)*, vol. 1, (1864), pp. 145–6.
2. Ross, *Richard III*, (London, 1981) p. 228.
3. The reign of James III receives extensive treatment in Norman Macdougall, *James III: A Political Study* (Edinburgh, 1982).
4. *York Civic Records* (ed. A. Raine, 1939), vol. 1, p. 119; *Extracts from the Council Register of the Burgh of Aberdeen* (Spalding Club, 1844–8), p. 45.
5. For a recent analysis of the growth of the James III legend, *see* Macdougall, *op. cit.*, pp. 269–295.
6. Jenny Wormald, *Court, Kirk, and Community: Scotland 1470–1625* (London, 1981), p. 13.
7. J.M. Brown, 'Taming the Magnates?', in *The Scottish Nation* (ed. Gordon Menzies, 1972), pp. 51–2.
8. R.G. Nicholson, *Scotland: The Later Middle Ages* (Edinburgh, 1974), p. 371.
9. J.M. Brown, 'The Exercise of Power', in J.M. Brown (ed.), *Scottish Society in the Fifteenth Century* (London, 1977), p. 50.

10. For an analysis of the political events of James IIIs minority, *see* Macdougall, *op. cit.*, pp. 51–85.

11. For the traditional view, *see*, for example, Gordon Donaldson, *Scottish Kings* (London, 1967), chapter 6; for the 'revisionist' view, see Macdougall, *op. cit.*, pp. 269–298.

12. The sixteenth-century histories which include the reign of James III are Adam Abell, 'The Roit or Quheill of Tyme' (unpublished MS., NLS MS 1746); John Lesley, *The History of Scotland from the Death of King James I in the Year 1436 to the Year 1561* (Bannatyne Club, 1830); Appendix to Hector Boece's *Scotorum Historiae* (2nd. edn., Paris, 1574) by Giovanni Ferreri; Robert Lindesay of Pitscottie, *The Historie and Cronicles of Scotland* (ed. Aeneas Mackay, Scottish Text Society, 1899–1911); George Buchanan, *Rerum Scoticarum Historia,* book xii (Edinburgh, 1582).

13. *The Acts of the Parliaments of Scotland,* ed. T. Thomson and C. Innes, (Edinburgh, 1814–75, henceforth *APS*), vol. 2, p. 230; Ferreri *op. cit.* f. 400v.

14. *A.P.S.,* vol. 2, p. 211.

15. For a full discussion of the development of the James III legend during this period, *see* Macdougall, *op. cit.,* pp. 278– 283.

16. Adam Abell, 'The Roit or Quheill of Tyme', ff. 110v–112r; and Macdougall, *op. cit.,* pp. 280–282.

17. Buchanan, *History*, vol. 2, p. 152.

18. Hector Boece's *Chronicles of Scotland,* translated into Scots by John Bellenden (edn. Thomas Davidson, Edinburgh, n.d., but about 1536), book xii, f. lxxv (r–v).

19. Dominic Mancini, *The Usurpation of Richard III,* ed. and translated C.A.J. Armstrong (Oxford, 1969), p. 63; Croyland Chronicle: 'Historiae Croylandensis Continuatio' in *Rerum Anglicarum Scriptores Veterum*, ed. W. Fulman (Oxford, 1684), p. 562; Polydore Vergil, *Anglica Historia,* ed. and translated Denys Hay (R.H.S., 1950), p. 167; Sir Thomas More, *The History of King Richard III*, ed. R.S. Sylvester (1963), p. 7.

20. Pitscottie, *Historia,* vol. 1, p. 166; Buchanan, *History,* vol. 2, p. 140.

21. Bellenden, *Chronicles*, vol. 2, pp. 173–4.

22. See Macdougall, *op. cit.,* pp. 163–5 (for the favourites); pp. 199, 270–271, 284 (for the king's supposed estrangement from his wife); p. 308 (James as leader in war).

23. For James's Anglophile policy from 1474 to 1487, *see* N. Macdougall, 'Foreign Relations: England and France' in Brown, *Scottish Society in the Fifteenth Century*, esp. pp. 107–111.

24. B.L. Royal MS. 17 DXX, ff. 299–308.

25. *Ibid.,* f. 307v.

26. Ross, *Edward IV*, pp. 240–241.

27. The chronicler seems to have been quite well informed about events in Yorkist England, including the defeat and death of Warwick the Kingmaker at Barnet, the death of the 'saintly' Henry VI and the miracles which followed his demise; and it seems likely that he was also familiar with stories about the death of Clarence.

28. *A.P.S.*, vol. 2, 104.
29. *Cal. Docs. Scot.*, vol. 4, Nos. 1417, 1418, 1425.
30. *T.A.*, vol. 1, p. 49.
31. B.L. Royal MS. 17 DXX, f. 307v.
32. Harry's *Wallace*, ed. M.P. McDiarmid (Scottish Text Society, Edinburgh, 1968), vol. 1, p. 1.
33. Macdougall, *op. cit.*, pp. 101–2, 121.
34. *Ibid.*, pp. 108–9.
35. For the details of Scheves' life and remarkable preeminence during the period 1476–79, *see* J. Herkless and R.K. Hannay, *The Archbishops of St. Andrews* (Edinburgh, 1907), vol. 1, pp. 80–164; and Macdougall, *op. cit.*, pp. 102, 126–8.
36. For the career of Princess Mary, *see* Macdougall, *op. cit.*, pp. 75–6, pp. 81, 88, 89, 171–2; for Margaret, *ibid.*, pp. 91, 140–143.
37. *A.P.S.*, vol. 2, pp. 103, 120.
38. *R.M.S.*, vol. 2, No. 1446.
39. For a discussion of Mar's death in contemporary and later sources, see Macdougall, *op. cit.*, pp. 130–133.
40. Ross, *Edward IV*, p. 287.
41. Macdougall, *op. cit.*, pp. 128–9.
42. *A.P.S.*, vol. 2, p. 126.
43. *Ibid.*, p. 128.
44. *Scots Peerage*, vol. 1, pp. 153–4.
45. *A.P.S.*, vol. 2, pp. 120–1, 122.
46. Macdougall, *op. cit.*, p. 143.
47. *A.P.S.*, vol. 2, p. 138.
48. C.L. Scofield, *The Life and Reign of Edward IV* (London, 1923), vol. 2, pp. 334–350; Charles Ross, *Edward IV* (London, 1974), pp. 287–290.
49. See, for example, Jenny Wormald, *Court, Kirk and Community: Scotland 1470–1625*, p. 6.
50. Macdougall, *op. cit.*, pp. 149–150.
51. *Cal. Docs. Scot.*, vol. 4, App. i, No. 28 (mistakenly dated as February 1475–6).
52. *Cal. Patent Rolls 1476–85*, p. 320.
53. P.R.O. Scots Docs. E 39/92, 17 and 38; summaries in *Cal. Docs. Scot.*, vol. 4, Nos. 1475, 1476.
54. Frederick Devon, *Issues of the Exchequer*, (London, 1837), p. 501.
55. *York Civic Records* (ed. A. Raine, 1939), vol. 1, pp. 56, 59–60.
56. B.L. Royal MS. 17 DXX, f. 308r; and *see also* Macougall, *op. cit.*, pp. 165–8.
57. Robert Pitcairn, *Criminal Trials in Scotland*, 1488–1624 (Edinburgh, 1833), vol. 1, p. 16.
58. Rymer, *Foedera*, vol. 12, 160.
59. Hall, *Chronicle* (ed. Henry Ellis, 1809), p. 334. Hall's knowledge of events in 1482 is extensive but ill-informed. For example, he believed that James III had incarcerated *himself* in Edinburgh castle, 'perfectly trusting there to be out of all doubts and danger'. (p. 332) Elsewhere he simply repeats the sixteenth-

century legend of Cochrane as the royal favourite (p. 330) and claims that Mar –
'a wise pollitique counsailer' – was beheaded in Edinburgh. (p. 331).

60. Rymer, *Foedera*, vol. 12, p. 161; *Cal. Docs. Scot.,* vol. 4, No. 1480.
61. *Cal. Docs. Scot.,* vol. 4, Nos. 1481, 1482, 1483, 1484.
62. *Cal. State Papers (Venice)*, vol. 1, pp. 145–6. Both Hall (*Chronicle*, pp. 334–5)
     and Lesley (*History*, pp. 49–50) state that Berwick fell to Gloucester on 24
     August. Even allowing for Edward IVs remarkable courier system, by which the
     distribution of information was considerably speeded up, it would take at least
     three days for news to be brought from Berwick to London; so that the date of 24
     August is impossible if the evidence of Edward's letter is accepted. Alterna-
     tively, Edward may have been anticipating the fall of the castle, or confusing it
     with the surrender of the town the previous month.
63. *Croyland Chronicle*, p. 563.
64. *York Civic Records*, vol. 1, p. 67.
65. For a detailed discussion of those events, see Macdougall, *op. cit.*, pp. 170–180.
66. S.R.O. State Papers No. 19, printed in *A.P.S.*, vol. 12, pp. 31–3.
67. *A.P.S.*, vol. 2, pp. 151–2.
68. The correspondence between James III and Richard III consists of six letters,
     four of which are printed in Gairdner, *Letters and Papers of Richard III and
     Henry VII.* 2 vols. (1861–63) These are:
     James to Richard,   16 August 1483 (Gairdner, vol. 1. pp. 51–2);
                         21 July 1484 (Gairdner, vol. 1. pp. 59–61).
     Richard to James,   16 September 1483 (Gairdner, vol. 1, p. 53);
                         7 August 1484 (Gairdner, vol. 1, pp. 61–2).
     All these are from B.L. Harl. MS. 433. Note that Gairdner does *not* print two
     further letters. James III to Richard III, 6 November 1483 (*BL Harleian
     Manuscript 433,* ed. Rosemary Horrox and P.W. Hammond, vol. 3 (1982) pp.
     50–1) and Richard III to James III, 2 December 1483 (*op. cit.* p. 51).
69. S.R.O. MS. Treaties with France, Nos. 16–19; B.N. MS. francais 23,023, ff.
     244–251v.
70. P.R.O., E 404, 78/3/26.
71. *Cal. Docs. Scot.,* vol. 4, Nos. 1494, 1496, 1497.
72. For details of the fight at Lochmaben, *see* Macdougall, *op. cit.,* pp. 211–213.
73. *E.R.,* vol. 9, Preface, p. lvi.
74. The peace negotiations of 1484 are described in Macdougall, *op. cit.,* pp. 213–
     214.
75. *A.P.S.,* vol. 2, p. 170.
76. B.N. MS. francais 15,889, f. 435v.
77. Pitscottie, *Historie*, vol. 1, pp. 191, 195–6; P.R.O. DL 42, no. 21, f. 97v; *R.M.S.,*
     vol. 2, No. 1638; *Cal. Docs. Scot.,* vol. 4, No. 1518.
78. Pitscottie, *Historie*, vol. 1, pp. 196–199.

1485 AND ALL THAT, OR WHAT WAS GOING ON AT THE BATTLE OF BOSWORTH?

Colin Richmond

There is a distinction between what happens and what is going on. For instance, about 30 A.D. a troublesome Galilean peasant is crucified. That is what happens; but what is going on? The historian has to be longer sighted than Pilate. It is not a question of his being able to be: hindsight is not long sight. The Roman centurion at the execution of Jesus understood what was going on; centuries later Roman historians still had no idea. What happened at Bosworth is clear: Richard III was defeated by Henry Tudor. Yet how that happened and why is not clear; and what was going on at Bosworth on 22 August 1485 remains a mystery which I shall endeavour to explore if not explain in this paper.[1]

First, what happened at Bosworth? How did Richard's defeat come about? Bosworth is the worst documented battle in English history. We think we know more of a limited engagement between Englishmen and Danes at Maldon in 991.[2] There is a great poem 'on' the battle of Maldon. There are also poems 'on' the battle of Bosworth, but they appear to me to be just as untrustworthy as the 'Battle of Maldon' when we seek to use them to tell us about the course of the battle and about who was there.[3] 'The Ballad of Bosworth Feilde' is the most interesting of the Bosworth poems. Dr. Rosemary Horrox has stated: 'apparently [it] includes a contemporary list of those who fought at Bosworth'.[4] Both the published version of this poem[5] and a variant of it transcribed by Stow[6] contain what certainly amounts to a list of noblemen and knights who fought for Richard III. At first, even second sight the list appears authentic. The names look right, some are recognisably of men who might have been at Bosworth, others among the knights are of north country families whose members were active in the later fifteenth century, some of them on Richard III's behalf. Yet a closer study of the list in conjunction with record material discloses frailties: alongside men certainly there and others possibly even probably there, are the impossible.[7] It is not only that there have been mistakes made in the course of the poem's transmission so that some names are hard to identify, it is also that the poet's sources were not, I think, other than those we have at our disposal: the list of attainted in the *Rolls of Parliament* for both 1485 and 1487, a knowledge of the nobility and gentry of the time, and the awareness of Richard's dependence upon a narrow, largely northern group of supporters. This makes his list of names plausible, temptingly so because it coincides with what we might consider likely too, but no more than plausible, and that is not good enough. An authentic statement is surely what there has to be, an apparently authentic one will not do. The poet, I believe, was at no greater advantage than we are, dealing in probabilities not certainties. It may be that a more thorough examination of the 'Ballad of Bosworth Feilde' and north country family records than I have been able to give, will show that the poem should be granted more weight than I am prepared to allow it here; what such an examination will not do, I think, is reveal that the poet was using a contemporary list or had accurate contemporary knowledge of the lords and gentry who were at the battle of Bosworth in Richard III's army.[8]

The most evident impossibilities in the poem's list are among the nobility.[9] Were the earls of Kent and Nottingham, and lords Maltravers, Fitzhugh, Ogle, and Lumley there? Was not Lord Audley at Southampton?[10] Even if they were at Bosworth, or rather were in the vicinity of the battlefield (wherever that precisely was), did they fight in the battle? For it is clear that being 'at Bosworth' may have been one thing, fighting in the battle quite another. Whatever happened that day and wherever (in the neighbourhood of Redmoor) it did happen, one thing is certain; there were a good many soldiers thereabouts who did not fight. Even more certain is it that most of them did not fight for their king. Richard III was almost as wholly deserted in 1485 as Richard II had been in 1399. So lords Maltravers, Fitzhugh, Ogle, and Lumley, and the earls of Kent and Nottingham may have been 'at Bosworth', but if they were they evidently did nothing to help their king, which meant that they helped his enemies. What, therefore, principally happened at Bosworth was the desertion of king Richard.[11]

Out of forty noblemen upon whom the king could call for service in August 1485 I estimate that probably only six turned up and fought for him against Henry Tudor: Ferrers of Chartley, Lincoln,[12] Lovel, Norfolk, Surrey, Zouch. Possibly the earls of Westmorland and Shrewsbury, and lords Audley, Grey of Codnor, Scrope of Bolton, and Scrope of Masham, or some of them (Scrope of Masham and the earl of Shrewsbury[13]) were at Bosworth with Richard, and may have fought on his behalf. It seems to me possible but not likely.[14] The Earl of Northumberland we know was somewhere near at hand; he did not engage. Lord Stanley was also at hand. Despite the subsequent story of his decisive part in the battle, it still seems to me that while his brother, Sir William Stanley, did at some point intervene on Henry Tudor's behalf, Lord Stanley did not.[15] His son, Lord Strange, was also at Bosworth but inactive; he was with Richard as a hostage for his father's good behaviour, perhaps effectively.

The overwhelming majority of English noblemen, therefore, either did not go to Bosworth or, if they did go, did not fight for their king there: three-quarters, or more than three-quarters did not. Henry Tudor, as Henry VII two years later, was able to do better; at least ten and perhaps as many as fifteen[16] of the thirty-six noblemen upon whom he could call turned out and fought for him at the battle of Stoke in June 1487; so that it was only about two-thirds who did not respond to their king's need for support against the rebels.[17] The difference (between two-thirds and three-quarters) may not be significant statistically, indeed may simply not be significant. The indifference of a large part of the nobility to the fate of their kings, whoever the king was, we may take to be a feature of English politics in the 1480s. It was not new: in 1399, in 1327, even in 1265 (let alone 1215) the enthusiasm of English noblemen for their kings had not been great.

Yet, in 1485 Richard III did not give his nobility the best chance to demonstrate their support, or (put the other way) he offered them an excellent excuse not to turn out: insufficient time.[18] Henry Tudor landed at Milford Haven on 7 August; Richard wrote to Sir Henry Vernon of the landing from Bestwood near Nottingham on 11 August;[19] John Howard, duke of Norfolk wrote to John Paston (probably from London) to join up with him at Bury St. Edmunds on his way to Richard on 12, 13 or 14 August.[20] On the 16 August, or possibly a day or so later, Richard moved from Nottingham to Leicester. On 21 August he set out from Leicester.[21] The battle was fought the following day. The authorities at York were unable to mobilize an armed force within this fortnight. They had learnt of the landing of Henry Tudor by 16 August when they sent Sergeant Spooner to Richard to discover how many men he might require. A messenger, John Nicholson, arrived at York from Bestwood on 19 August and it was decided to send 80 men. That was too late for the contingent to reach the king; indeed it may never have left. On 23 August John Spooner returned with news of the battle. He must have ridden hard. No doubt he set off immediately the brief encounter had ended, for his report was not accurate.[22] We can assume, I think, that the York councillors wished to aid the king; as Duke of Gloucester and as king he had been a good lord to them; we know, nonetheless, that raising 80 men, seeing that they were properly equipped and appropriately uniformed, and agreeing to and raising the money for their wages was (even at a time of pressing need) neither an easy nor a speedy business.[23] In August 1485 with so few councillors in the city – plague had sent many of them out into the country[24] – they did not have enough time to get their soldiers to the decisive battle. Other towns, probably less enthusiastic than York, may not even have begun to prepare a force to send to Nottingham.

Evidently Richard was impatient: the issue, as C.A.J. Armstrong has written, needed to be settled:[25]

Since Harold fell at Hastings victory was the supreme authentication of a title; and on this account Richard III from 1483–5 so passionately desired the armed trial of strength.

Even so Henry Tudor's change of direction towards London on 18 August may have been what ultimately determined Richard's move out of Leicester to stop him on 21 August. That move made, Henry was no less ready for a decision than Richard. Battle was duly joined early the next day.

It was a short, probably sharp battle, not unlike the one at St. Albans thirty years before, which had been the beginning of that generation of troubles. It was also like it in that casualties were few, and for the same reason: once the principal was dead – the Duke of Somerset at St. Albans, Richard at Bosworth – fighting ceased. What fighting there had been that is, for at Bosworth there cannot have been much outside the 'battles' of the main contestants: Richard against Henry, the Duke of Norfolk against the Earl of Oxford. The dead were a handful. On Henry's side William Brandon, killed by Richard himself, was the only notable casualty,[26] while it is remarkable how few of Richard's closest supporters were killed; even John Kendal and William Catesby survived, the former to marry the widow of perhaps one of the unluckiest of the dead on Richard's side, Sir Richard Charlton,[27] the latter to be executed at Leicester three days after the battle.[28] Still others got safely away, Viscount Lovel, the Harrington brothers, Sir Thomas Pilkington, Sir Robert Middleton. At least they had been there. Many, as it turned out for their king too many, had not. Lack of time between summons and battle may have been one reason for that.

For those who did not want to be there the speed with which battle was joined was (so to speak) a godsend. Its result, of course, was a greater act of God which subsumed into itself the lesser; nevertheless had Richard won at Bosworth Sir Henry Vernon, John Paston and those twenty to thirty missing magnates would have had good excuse for their absence.[29] Or most of them would, those that is who had a distance to come. One wonders therefore, how Sir Henry Vernon would have justified his not having come the short distance from Haddon in Derbyshire, though, as he had disappointed the Duke of Clarence *and* the Earl of Warwick in 1471 (when there was more time to spare for a somewhat longer journey), he perhaps had his excuse well prepared.[30] John Paston, on the other hand, had to come a long way from East Anglia and if he had contemplated making the journey we can be sure it would have been to join John de Vere earl of Oxford not John Howard duke of Norfolk. He had in fact already fought for the Earl of Oxford against John Howard, at the battle of Barnet in April 1471 (and been wounded); he would fight for him again, and for Henry Tudor, at Stoke in June 1487 (and be knighted); but in August 1485 he followed the course most others followed, and fought for no one.

John Paston was much closer to the Earl of Oxford than he ever had been or was likely to be to John Howard. The Earl had been a notably active patron to the family during the Readeption, whereas there had been trouble between Howard and the Pastons, though most of it in the past by 1485. Nor as Duke of Norfolk had John Howard stepped straight into the place of the last Mowbray duke, and thus into the leadership of a group of clients, friends and well-wishers, which every great landed magnate could reasonably expect. After John Mowbray's sudden death in January 1476 it was the king's second son, Richard duke of York, who became Duke of Norfolk and who married the sole heiress Anne Mowbray. As both bride and bridegroom were children, the estates were controlled by the king; they remained in the king's hands, despite Anne's death in November 1481, until 1483 when Edward IV died and Richard duke of York, having been disinherited by his uncle, disappeared. John Howard was created Duke of Norfolk on 28 June 1483. In these circumstances there had been no chance of this elderly, erstwhile Suffolk gentleman – plain Sir John Howard of Tendering Hall, Stoke-by-Nayland he had been until 1470 – succeeding to what we might be allowed to call a ready-made Mowbray affinity. Besides, so far as John Paston was concerned in 1485, Howard was holding many of the properties the Earl of Oxford had forfeited by his attainder while the king himself was in possession of other estates which, as Duke of Gloucester, he had taken from the Earl's mother, Elizabeth.[31] The Pastons, moving nearer to the earls of Oxford as the 1460s succeeded the 1450s and the 1470s the 1460s,[32] had observed all this from near at hand. One way and another it does not seem that John Howard ought to have expected John Paston to turn up with a 'company of tall men' in August 1485, particularly as he had not done so with the 'six talle felaws in harnesse' whom Howard had asked him to bring less than two years before to help put down 'Buckingham's Rebellion'.[33] Yet Howard's letter reads sanguinely enough; perhaps it was written more in hope than anticipation and therefore its tone appears more cheerful than Howard felt.

There were many men in East Anglia (and in Surrey and Sussex) from whom Howard reasonably could have looked for more than he could from Paston. He had made a large promise to Richard III: 1000 men at his own cost were what he said he would provide.[34] The names of these (or many of them) were set down in his household books. There are the household servants (the core of any military contingent) and there are the tenants (the bulk of the troops). There are also just less than fifty men separately listed, who are to bring with them two or three others at Howard's cost; these are estate officers, councillors, and others: Roger Tymperly, the auditor John Knight, 'Bullock and his man', 'Wisman and a man', Richard Southwell, 'the Secretarye and hys man', James Hobart.[35] There is no list, however, of East Anglian gentlemen, no retainers or friends or associates of that sort feature.[36] John Paston's name, therefore, is not here. Yet we know he was written to in August 1485. Were these others, presumably considered entirely reliable (where Paston presumably was not), more bluntly even peremptorily called upon? How many of them came to Bosworth to fight alongside their lord who died so valiantly fighting for *his* lord? No poem was composed to commemorate this East Anglian 'menie's' stand beside their dead lord, going down one by one to heroic defeat. Over 600 years much had changed. It is not only that 'The Battle of Maldon' could not have been written in the second half of the fifteenth century, it is also that the action it celebrates could not have occurred: dying for one's lord was even a little old-fashioned in East Anglia about the year 1000, about the year 1500 it was thoroughly anachronistic. John Howard, we can be pretty sure, was dying on his own behalf when he perished at Bosworth; so certainly was Richard, whose whole career since spring 1483 had been determindly self-centred.[37] Nonetheless John Howard's fame, like that of Bryhtnoth and his followers, has persisted, for he, like them, went down fighting. Their names (albeit they are fictitious ones) are still spoken; not even one of those of Howard's 'affinity' has come down to us. If James Hobart (who had promised to get Howard as many men as he could)[38] is typical of them, then most of them, let alone dying alongside their patron, were not even at the battle.[39] And if Howard died a disappointed and disillusioned lord that August morning (because he had led a diminished following), so, I believe, did Richard III and for the same reason. His 'affinity' had let him down too.[40]

This may seem, superficially at least, too harsh a judgement on Richard's affinity as some of his retainers certainly were at Bosworth and died for their lord there, Sir Richard Ratcliff and Sir Robert Brackenbury for instance. Others were there but escaped, some of them to fight another day, Sir Robert and Sir James Harrington,[41] Sir Thomas Pilkington, Sir Robert Middleton for example. But were Sir Thomas Broughton or Sir John Hudleston there, or Ralph lord Greystoke or George lord Lumley?[42] It is here that 'The Ballad of Bosworth Feilde' is important, naming as it does so many of Richard's northern followers who responded to his summons and came to the battle. Or, should the poet be believed after all, and should we assume that though they were there they did nothing, thus escaping attainder, or any other punishment or setback to their careers?

There was certainly one way they could have been there but have done nothing. They might have been in the inactive 'battle' (or retinue we should perhaps call it) of the Earl of Northumberland, himself a member of Richard's retinue, probably the foremost member, certainly the most grand, and he (we know) did nothing.[43] There can be no doubt that Richard was let down by this particular retainer; no doubt too that he died aware of the fact.[44] Northumberland had his reasons (we presume) for not helping the king; they concerned his distaste for that increase in royal power in the north which had naturally followed on the Duke of Gloucester's usurpation of the throne, for as Duke of Gloucester Richard had established himself, and been established by his brother the king, as the dominant magnate in the West March and in Yorkshire, thus not simply rivalling the Earl of Northumberland but outstripping him in the north of England. Despite their agreement of July 1474 'on a carefully constructed co-operation in the north',[45] the usurpation upset whatever balance that had created; one of the parties now being king he had all the advantages, and the Earl can have had no confidence in old agreements. He therefore did in his own hesitant way what his great-great-grandfather had done in 1399: deserted the king who had become a threat to his power in the north.

But would he have been able to prevent other, less notable but (we must assume) more loyal northern retainers of Richard's, who were under his command, from fighting? Dr. Hicks has suggested that the Earl's inactivity was a compromise: 'it may have been his inability to commit his retainers against Richard and their inclinations that made him stand aside'.[46]

Here, it is to be assumed that in Northumberland's retinue at Bosworth there were retainers of Richard's; or, to put it more accurately, Northumberland commanded not only Richard's northern retainers as well as his own, but also men who were retainers of both of them. For the retinues of king and earl overlapped and interpenetrated one another, and were no more solid than they were separate, there having been constant movement of men between one and the other. I do not think we can know what the 'inclinations' of such a body of men were, if the body of men Northumberland led at Bosworth was composed after that fashion. Yet, *if* Richard's Cumbrian and Yorkshire retainers were there with Northumberland, can one imagine them *not* joining in?[47] Men who helped raise revolt in 1486 and 1487 after their lord had been killed would surely not have meekly stood by when he was fighting for his life a few fields away. He had certainly been a good enough lord to them since he had become king; land and office had flowed in their direction, much of it in the softer south where some of them had gone to live.[48] On that score they ought not to have held back. As, however, only one of Richard's northern affinity was attainted (the Lancashire Harringtons and Sir Thomas Pilkington apart)[49] – it is an oddity, not to my knowledge previously remarked on, that it is the Midland and southern supporters of Richard who fight (and die) for him and who in consequence are attainted[50] – we are forced to the conclusion either that they *did* hold back (or were held back by the Earl of Northumberland), or that they were not there at all.[51]

Thus we have either to follow *The Great Chronicle of London* and Dr. Hicks, or to ask ourselves where were the northerners on 22 August 1485. *The Great Chronicle of London* states that 'The Comons of the North' killed the Earl of Northumberland in 1489, 'They owyng unto hym dedly malyce ffor the dysapoyntyng of kyng Rychard at Bosworth ffeeld.'[52] Dr. Hicks comments that 'this was not, in fact, a strong motive in the rebellion of 1489 but it may have influenced the Percy retainers'.[53] He goes on to show how the Earl's retinue after 1485 was augmented by former retainers of Richard's; it was they particularly who deserted Northumberland in 1489, not only because they remembered August 1485, but also because since then 'by failing to exercise good lordship, the Earl had given them little cause to keep him alive.'[54] If we accept this explanation then we have to visualize the Earl's retinue at Bosworth, an expanded retinue for that day it also comprised Richard's retainers, as static, either because its inclinations were so diverse no one, below the commander himself perhaps, could decide on what to do – a sort of impotence through disunity – or because Richard's loyal retainers were in such a minority that they could not break out on their own to join the king. It does not seem at all acceptable that Northumberland could absolutely determine the retinue's policy; if it did not do what he wanted in 1489 it is not likely that it would have done so in August 1485; Dr. Hicks' description of the Earl's 'inability to commit his retainers *against* Richard' seems right here. Yet, need we accept an explanation which involves Richard's retainers being there with Northumberland? Can we not simply take it that they were not there at all. And if they were not, ask why not?

Insufficient time to get to Bosworth, as we have suggested above, may be one explanation. Another should also be considered. As (we are always being told) the ties between lord and retainer, patron and client, in the fifteenth century were so patently ones of self-interest,[55] a possible explanation may consist of Richard's northern followers deciding not to join him against his rival. They judged, in other words, either that he was going to lose or, whatever his previous goodlordship on their behalf, that he ought to. If the latter, which seems the more likely of the two, then their self-interest was of a peculiar kind, for it involved more than themselves. It took into account Richard's kingship not only, not at all perhaps, his lordship. Did these men (in other words) have a broad vision which took in, beyond personal and provincial interests, those of the kingdom? Or rather: were they viewing their interests (personal and provincial) as but part of, if not subordinate to the kingdom's? Richard may have been a good lord but was he not a bad king? If that was their attitude then we can say that Richard perished more by design than by accident.

But can we say it? After all, the northern affinity did not act as a group; this the events of 1485–1487 show. If we take only the Cumbrian affinity, that is those retainers who came from the area in which Richard when Duke of Gloucester and Warden of the West March had his greatest power and over much of which he was granted palatine authority in January 1483, then we discover, as we might anticipate, different men doing different things.[56] Of 29 Cumbrian gentry families, on my rough and provisional reckoning, eight only are actively 'Ricardian' in the years 1485–7; another nine are actively 'anti-Ricardian'; while twelve fall into neither category: most of these twelve are probably inactive, most probably the five or six who provide Percy retainers.[57] This is despite the fact that the 1487 invasion began at Furness, where Broughtons and Harringtons (but not Huddlestons) gave it their support. As the rebels moved into Yorkshire they picked up further aid in the North Riding, the other area of Richard's power centred on his favourite lordship of Middleham. It was insufficient. They were decisively beaten at Stoke.

In some respects, therefore, 1487 resembles Epiphany 1400: the rebellion of 1487, like the Epiphany plot of 1400, appears to be the king's 'party' attempting to do too late what it should have done in time: rally to its leader –

in 1487 indeed its lost leader. Certainly Richard II and his supporters had
been more surprised and thus more readily overcome than had been Richard
III and his supporters in 1485: the latter at least made a fight of it.

Yet on the crucial day Richard III did not get the sort of support he had (as
king) a right to expect. If the Cumbrian gentry failed him, as it seems and as I
believe they did, then the whole structure of authority as represented by lord
and retainer is called into question. Richard in Cumbria was, it has been
said,[58] the most over-mighty subject of them all: that was as Duke of
Gloucester in 1483. Can two years of kingship have undermined such
authority? The Cumbrians had gained as much from Richard's royal patronage as had his other northern retainers: good lordship is not what is at issue
here. So, if where he was apparently strong – at his strongest on most readings
of the way in which power 'worked' in the fifteenth century – he was weak, we
surely have to look again at Richard's kingship as well as at where power lay
(and how it worked) in the fifteenth century. The second is a task to be
deferred.[59] The former is more important to our immediate question (what
happened at Bosworth?), for as it took nearly twenty-five years of Henry VI's
execrable kingship for just enough men to give him up so that he lost the
crown (and it was still a close run thing at Towton), Richard III's mere two
years as king must be decisive for any assessment of Bosworth. By then, it
seems, he appeared a tyrant to many.[60] To many in the south at any rate.
Richard's rule was seen, and by the Croyland Chronicler described, as an
imposition of northerners upon the south. This was markedly true after the
rising of October 1483, which had been a southern affair. The tyrannical
aspects of Richard's government thereafter, as they would have struck
contemporaries (southern contemporaries at least) have been described by
Dr. Pollard and there is, therefore, no need to go into them here. Not, I
think, that the rising of October 1483 was a turning point; that rising was a
consequence of Richard's usurpation in June 1483, it was not independant of
it. Buckingham's part in it was certainly limited and probably late. The most
plausible explanation of his participation, it seems to me, is that which has
him becoming aware of Henry Tudor's involvement with the rebels sometime
in September and so, not wishing to be bypassed by one who had a less good
claim to the throne than himself, joining the conspiracy hastily and without
any following to speak of.[61] Given his important and presumably well-
informed position under Richard III he must have considered the rising had
every chance of success. We should hesitate before impugning his soundness
of judgement for he had backed, perhaps promoted, the unlikely winner of
June 1483, while the rising of October 1483, whatever his own part in it might
have been, had excellent prospects. It did not fulfill them, principally for lack
of coordination between its component parts which allowed its most important sector in Kent and Surrey to be overwhelmed by the Duke of Norfolk.[62]
The equally prompt and fierce response of Richard himself was also perhaps
not what the rebels – an heterogeneous group composed of men who six
months previously had not seen eye to eye[63] – had anticipated: until the end

at Bosworth Richard drew enormous advantage from his fellow politicians' consistent, though surprising, under-estimation of him. This is outstandingly true of his usurpation, which is where the rising of October 1483 really began. Bosworth too 'began' there.

It is clear that Richard's usurpation took everyone by surprise. The shock of it was great. The Duke of Clarence had been *a* bad brother, Richard is *the* wicked uncle. These Yorkists had not even the family loyalty of the Lancastrians let alone their dynastic sense. Even if Clarence's behaviour reminds one a little, but only a little, of Humphrey duke of Gloucester's, Richard's is as distant as is possible from that of John duke of Bedford. 1483 is in every way a contrast to 1422. The more the two are put together the greater grows one's admiration for the politicians of 1422. Those of 1483 were in disarray from the start.

Or not quite from the start perhaps.

Whatever the chroniclers say about the disharmony between the two groups headed on the one hand by the dowager queen Elizabeth and on the other by William lord Hastings,[64] there appears to have been agreement between them about the coronation of Edward V. They arranged this for 4 May, a fortnight after the funeral of Edward IV, and time enough for the young king to be brought from Ludlow. Henry V had been crowned within eight days of his father's body being taken to Canterbury, but, unlike Edward V, Henry V was in the capital.[65] There is no indication in April 1483 that an 'anti-Gloucester' manoeuvre was being mounted. Hence Richard was able to take Earl Rivers entirely by surprise when he seized him at Stony-Stratford on 30 April, the more so in that Rivers had, it seems, gone out of his way, in bringing Edward V to London, to meet him.[66] Anthony Woodvill's complete unpreparedness, like Lord Hastings' later, shows just how far Richard's audacity left these experienced politicians gasping. They were not tyros, yet for all their years 'inside' politics Richard's behaviour lay outside their terms of reference.

Although there may have been some excuse for Rivers' surprise in April – for that was Richard's first and unanticipated departure from the rules of the political game – Lord Hastings in June ought to have been warned and therefore forearmed. He was not. When Richard made his second decisive strike on 13 June 1483 Hastings was caught out. It is astonishing that he, of all people, was so easily disposed of. The idea that Richard might usurp the throne cannot have entered his head.[67]

It may be that like many elderly politicians he was unable to see the greater enemy because of a complacent preoccupation with lesser, familiar and predictable opponents. If Hastings could ignore (as straws in the wind) the arrest of Rivers and the dispersal of the other Woodvills at the end of April, and Richard's later attempt in Council to have them condemned for treason[68] – a blatant instance of the pot calling the kettle black – then perhaps it was because he was glad to see not only Earl Rivers depart, but also the Marquis of Dorset disappear, not so much from Westminster as from Leicestershire.[69]

And if he paid no close attention to what his man William Catesby was up to with the Protector, then possibly it was because he was intent on what was afoot between Catesby and Catesby's other lord, Henry Stafford, duke of Buckingham. For Hastings' dominance of the Midlands (from Sheffield to Bedford, from Lincoln to Warwick) had been threatened by the queen's son Thomas Grey at its very heart, in Leicestershire, and was also bound to be challenged by any revival of Stafford power.[70] Intent on local rivalries Hastings apparently forgot the elementary political fact (on which his own successful career had been based), that to be anybody in the provinces you had to be somebody at Westminster. This uncharacteristic lapse in getting his priorities right was fatal.

Nor did he only fail himself; he also let down the late king's affinity. The royal household – the above-stairs household – was the core of the king's affinity; it naturally looked to its official head, the Chamberlain William lord Hastings for leadership. In May 1483 he remained Chamberlain,[71] and even if Edward IV's household no longer existed as such, its 'political' members continued to consider Lord Hastings as, so to speak, their representative on the Council of the young king, to whom they now owed their principal loyalty. Whether after Edward IV's funeral Lord Hastings addressed the household as after Charles VII of France's funeral his Chamberlain had addressed that king's household we do not know: Charles' Chamberlain had said that he 'and all the other servants had lost their master, and that every man must think for himself, and each one should provide for himself'.[72] It is evident, however, that providing for themselves would have been on the minds of Edward IV's household men. How Edward V's household was to be composed was as burning an issue for them as what political role he was to play was for Lord Hastings. He appeared a protector to them, they may have seemed some kind of insurance to him. If they did, it was another of his miscalculations, another of his underestimations of the Duke of Gloucester, who here once again ignored conventions he, Lord Hastings, had lived by, but was going to die without. On 13 June Richard killed Lord Hastings, and thus alienated those members of the late king's household who had hitherto given him, as Protector of Edward V, their support. When he eliminated Lord Hastings, Richard destroyed the very heart of Yorkism – its political base, which since 1471 Edward IV, with Hastings' help, had created in his household. That would have been Edward V's strength, hence Richard's need to dispose of it by lopping off its head; but in so cutting his way clear to the throne he also disposed of the best support he had had as Protector – as king he would not have it and thus he would be weak, fatally weak from the start, from in fact 13 June. It was on that day that the minority government came to a halt and men began waiting for what they knew was coming.[73] All that remained was to get hold of the king's younger brother and to publish the propaganda which would give Richard's claim some semblance of respectability.[74] This was duly and speedily done between 16–22 June and all was complete by 26 June when Richard sat on the king's chair in Westminster

Hall. Yet it was the execution of Hastings on 13 June which had been decisive. Decisive and fatal, for Richard as well as Hastings.

That then seems to be the paradox: in getting to be king Richard virtually ensured his not remaining so. Why he should have exchanged the security he had as Protector for the insecurity, indeed the nightmare of his kingship is a mystery, frequently examined but never adequately explained. He does strike me as a 'driven' character, whose confusion of a small matter (sexual immorality) with a greater (political immorality) may have been real rather than feigned. He might justifiably murder Hastings but the Marquis of Dorset's affair with the divorced Jane Shore was a sordid crime, possibly even a sin.[75] Such a conjunction – of political extremism, even political terrorism with a publically avowed moral uprightness – has too many ancient and modern parallels. Richard, at any rate, only had himself to blame, though in the usual way of these things everyone else but himself he regarded as the cause of his troubles.[76] If, therefore, he appears a lonely figure, his world collapsing about him even before the end, it is because, from the moment he decided upon usurpation and because he did so, he isolated himself in a manner and with a style sharply at variance with his elder brother's more nonchalant, less calculated attitudes. There is no tragedy in Richard's self-imposed fate, but there is in his destruction of Yorkism. It deserved better.

For most Englishmen it cannot have been the scattering of the ultra-loyalist Yorkists of Edward IV's household on 13 June which marked the break with the recent past. For many politically aware Englishmen, which perhaps means more than we are usually led to believe, it may have done, but for others at a greater distance from Westminster what happened at Bosworth was tied more closely to what had happened to Edward V and the Duke of York. The disappearance of the king and his brother was what alienated such Englishmen from the man they held responsible for their removal. One should not underestimate the impact of this removal, and of the connected belief that he had murdered them. What mattered was not that such an action was a crime, but that it was a scandalous and shameful crime.[77] Thomas of Woodstock had done nothing of that sort;[78] indeed Thomas's nephew had survived to murder him. Unconventional as Richard's moves were in the usurpation, which was for that very reason successful as conventional politicians were swept aside in stunned disbelief, the culminating and most unconventional of the series had repercussions far beyond the political world in Westminster and the home counties. Although Richard, when he had put down the rising of October 1483, may have thought *that* world had been conquered, it was the wider one of English provincial politics which, so to speak, conquered him at Bosworth. Even the lukewarmness of his northerners, manifest at Bosworth, may have had its origin in what he had done or was held to have done to the Princes.[79]

English provincial politics may have contributed to what happened at Bosworth in other ways too. At the battle Stanleys may have been fighting Harringtons as much as (or certainly as well as) Richard was fighting Henry

Tudor. Moreover, the Earl of Northumberland may not have fought for
Richard because the 'local' issue of the north was uppermost in his mind. In
John Howard's, perhaps, it was the Earl of Oxford who was the principal
antagonist, and predominance in East Anglia which was the primary issue.[80]
In this fighting out of provincial rivalries Bosworth may be considered to
resemble the first battle of St. Albans,[81] – and indeed other battles of other
English civil wars: Boroughbridge and Radcot Bridge for example,[82] and the
war between Stephen and Matilda, which (it has been said) dissolved into
disputes between baronial families.[83] In other words, English central and
local politics were, and always had been closely bound together: England was
too small and English kingship too big for them to be otherwise. Nevertheless, what happened at the centre determined what happened in the provinces
and not the other way about.

It was a disputed succession, or the unsuitable character of the king which
gave rise to difficulties. Minorities posed far fewer problems, and until 1483
were safely negotiated – Henry III's, Richard II's, Henry VI's: 'Woe to thee,
O land, when thy king is a child' had not been shewn by English experience.
Nor in 1483 was it the suddenness of Edward IV's death which led to trouble;
Henry V's death had been as untimely. Yet Edward has been blamed for
contributing to the usurpation of his brother. Just as Edward I is supposed to
be partly responsible for the disaster of his son's reign, so Edward IV is held
to have prepared the way for the overthrow of his son by his brother.

It is not Scotland which concerns us here. Both Edwards left a Scottish war
to their successors; but Edward II's war was of an entirely different dimension
to Richard III's.[84] It is the domestic policies of Edward I and Edward IV
which are the issue: more precisely their family policies. Both kings in the
course of promoting the interests of their families are said to have created a
disaffected nobility with which their successors had to deal. They were, like
most kings, kind to their kin,[85] Edward IV to his brother Richard no less than
to his wife's brothers and sisters and her sons by her first mariage. Also, in the
ways they went about it, both wilfully abused their power.[86] We should,
however, bear in mind the advice of the late K.B. McFarlane; he is discussing
Edward I:[87]

> This royal partiality for sons and brothers is condemned as short-sighted and in
> particular as against the best long-term interests of the monarchy. It was a case
> of putting the family before the crown. Whether it did or not, we must at least
> try to grasp the fact that it was inevitable, that it was due as much to a sense of
> what was right as to indiscriminate affection, and most of all that contemporary
> opinion would have been outraged by anything less generous...For the more a
> king could do to exalt his family, the greater king he.

In Edward IV's case, as if to bear this out, we have also to remember his
use (or wilful abuse) of a compliant parliament to advance his family's landed
estate. As a result there probably were some angry noblemen (John Howard

and Ralph Nevill were possibly two of them),[88] as there had been in the later years of Edward I and early years of Edward II. Nonetheless as McFarlane says, 'to conclude that "the family settlement of Edward I explains the reign of Edward II" is to take no account of the major factor: the character of Edward II himself'.[89] Exactly. No more does Edward IV's family settlement explain the short reign of Edward V; the character of Richard duke of Gloucester does.

If any policy of Edward IV's laid up trouble for the future, it was not his family policy but his 'land policy'.[90] It is not therefore Edward I with whom he ought to be compared, but Henry I. The kind of 'territorial re-ordering' both these kings went in for, in an effort to make things 'sit still and be quiet', involved (could not help but involve) the exclusion of some families from local power. If Lord Stanley 'was made undoubted ruler of Lancashire', the Harringtons among others had to be cast aside; if Lord Hastings became the 'ruler of the north midlands from Rockingham to the Peak' the Staffords were 'not so accomodated'[91] – nor perhaps were others, lords Zouch and Grey of Codnor for instance. Henry I's harsh treatment of particular families, for whom he had no room in his territorial schemes, resulted in their disinheritance. The role of the 'disinherited' in Stephen's reign has been made clear; it was not an unimportant one.[92] It may be, therefore, that Edward IV's policy for governing the realm also had its 'disinherited', men disinherited from the power which they thought they had a right to exercise in the locality where their inheritance lay.

Some of course were disinherited in the strict sense: those who were attainted, the Earl of Oxford, Viscount Beaumont, Lord Roos, for example. For them there was no chance of their attainders being reversed, for in Edward's territorial planning they had no place;[93] their place (as they saw it) had been usurped: for Viscount Beaumont and Lord Roos Lord Hastings was the usurper,[94] for the Earl of Oxford it was Edward himself (through the council of his second son, Richard duke of York) as well as the Duke of Norfolk. To the attainted the death of Edward IV brought no relief, as the death of Henry I had brought none to those whom he had disinherited; for both groups it was the struggle which developed between the new king and his challenger that gave them their opportunity. For the 'disinherited' who had joined Henry Tudor Bosworth turned out to be a decisive victory, unlike Stephen's defeat at Lincoln: killing the usurper was more effective than capturing him.

In 1483, however, it was not the attainted who counted; they were either in exile or in prison. The death of Edward IV gave them no immediate hope. The Yorkist regime seemed tough enough to survive such a setback. It was. Until the Duke of Gloucester began to dismantle it. And, because Edward IV's 'land policy' had excluded certain men from the influence they considered they ought to have had, he may have had helpers, or one helper certainly: Henry Stafford, duke of Buckingham. Ambitious Protector and thwarted territorialist did not necessarily share the same opponents, save one:

the most important Yorkist of them all, William lord Hastings. The Duke of Buckingham may have coveted Lord Hastings' local power as much as the Duke of Gloucester needed to break his authority at the centre. Did they encourage each other to the action of 13 June?[95]

It may be therefore that a policy which had excluded a great nobleman from local power was disastrous for the peace of the realm and the survival of a dynasty, as disastrous as the policy of excluding another great nobleman from the exercise of power at the centre had been in the 1450s. It was, nonetheless, circumstance, accidental circumstance at that, which allowed these frustrations effective play: Henry VI's astounding incompetence on the one hand, Edward IV's sudden death on the other. Edward's 'land policy' worked so long as he was there (active and able) to work it. It was too delicately balanced to function without the fulcrum of his authority. He had to manage the touchy men upon whom the policy depended, whether their part in it was very great or not so great or not at all, and that was a matter of day to day application, for the policy was neither static nor the territorial scheme it comprised stable. Without king Edward it was bound to founder, and if, as it collapsed, it helped bring down his son, he cannot be blamed for that: he had not anticipated death at forty-one, nor could he, nor should he have.

Nor can he be blamed for his brother. Through loyal service Richard had earned his promotion to hereditary palatine power in the north west and had deserved to be a Protector with wider authority than Duke Humphrey had been allowed in 1422.[96] He turned out bad but in April 1483 that was not foreseeable. Ultimately, therefore, what happened at Bosworth was to do with character.

Was what was 'going on' at Bosworth – for that matter what 'went on' throughout the Wars of the Roses – also all to do with character? Was there something which helped to shape all the characters of the major protagonists of the wars? Something they had in common, something which, perforce, they shared? When, for example, the behaviour of Edward IV's brothers is contrasted with that of Henry V's – on the one hand service to the dynasty, on the other Clarence and Gloucester who were their dynasty's worst enemies – one ponders the possibility of foreign war making all the difference between them. Can the lack of a foreign war have helped shape the attitudes of the leaders of English society after 1453? Is it that which lies at the root of an explanation of the Wars of the Roses, which underlies Bosworth, which was what was 'going on' there: the absence of foreign war?

William Worcester might have said so. In his *Boke of Noblesse*,[97] which argues for the reopening of the war against the king of France, he did not. Nowhere in that short work does he make explicit the connection between civil disorder and foreign war, or rather the lack of it. The connection is implicit perhaps for a number of reasons, but certainly, I think, for one. Although the *Boke of Noblesse* was presented to Edward IV in June 1475 on the eve of his invasion of France, Worcester had written it more than twenty years previously, just after the loss of Normandy and Gascony in 1451. He had not brought it up to date, except in so far as to make it presentable to Edward IV rather than Henry VI. He had not rewritten it in the light of the lessons of the intervening years. He had probably been too busy. It is a pity, for his oft-quoted condemnation of young noble- and gentlemen who, instead of learning 'noblesse' (that is, the noble arts of war), study the law and so stop at home to oppress and stir up 'youre poore and simple comyns . . . that lust to lyve at rest' might have been extended (with copious illustration) out of his experience of the years 1453–1475.[98] As it is, from the vantage point of 1452, he is still able to point this conclusion:[99]

> And if the vaillaunt Romayns had suffred theire sonnes to mysspende theire tyme in suche singuler practik, using oppressing by colours of custom of the law, they had not conquered twyes Cartage ayenst alle the Affricans.

After the expeditionary force of 1475 had ignominiously returned home and before he died in 1482 or 1483 William may well have been tempted to comment: I told you so.

William Worcester's practical good sense has recently been described as 'enthusiasm for war . . . from a vanished past.'[100] Nonetheless that past was still present in 1474 when a speaker in the Commons commended the king's intention to invade France, explicitly arguing from the history of England the value of foreign war as a healer of social tensions:

> And be it well remembred how that it is nat wele possible, nor hath ben since the Conquest, that justice, peax, and prosperite hath contenued any while in this lande in any Kings dayes but in suche as have made werre outward. Example by Kyng Henry the First, Henry the Secunde, King Richard the First, Henry the Thirde for the tyme he werred oute, Edward the First, and Edward the Third, Henry the fifthe usurpour, and Henry the Sixth which also usurped. Which last Henry in his daies, notwithstandyng his simplenesse of witte, stode ever in glorie and honour while the werre was contynued by yonde; and, that left, successively all fell to decay.[101]

That speaker and William Worcester were right: 'werre outward' was a cohesive agent. It bound society together. It was particularly binding in a warrior society, and fifteenth-century England was still a warrior society. It would be many years, probably centuries hence, possibly as far away as 1919, before the noble and gentle leaders of English society were not warriors. War was central to their lives. If there was not war they were not fulfilled. Frustration and bitterness could (and did) result from that. No wonder Victorian England was so placid: its warriors were fighting one colonial war after another, often on the most feeble of pretexts.[102]

As for the fifteenth century, the contrast between its first and second halves is sharp: foreign war and national unity succeeded by civil conflict and a quite remarkable lack of enterprize abroad. The earlier fifteenth century has a

clarity which is all the sharper because of the opaqueness of what follows.
'Werre outward' simplifies things for historians too. How it made the
difference then is shewn readily enough by contrasting not only royal
brothers; contrast, for instance, the careers of the Beauchamp and Nevill
earls of Warwick. Both were complicated men, the first no 'better' than the
second, but how much more straightforward foreign war made the life of
Richard Beauchamp; Richard Nevill's route to Barnet, on the other hand,
could not have been more crooked. It was war not peace which made life
simpler for such men; war clarified such things as duty, service, obligation to
one's prince; without it the question of what a man might do, rather than
what he had to do, or ought to do, arose: he was stretched on the rack of
choice. And everything was second best.[103] For noble Englishmen it was
peace which sowed confusion; no wonder that after 1450 the times were out
of joint.

No wonder then that when at last it took place in 1475 the invasion of
France was so keenly supported; it promised some relief. That was a false
hope. Edward IV at Picquigny rejected a war policy. His decision put his
new 'land policy' under increasing strain. What turned out to be the later
years of his reign were tense (when they should have been relaxed) just
because war against France, part of the Yorkist programme from the outset
and in prospect since the mid-1460s, had been started only to be stopped
before it had been properly tried. It was not that at Picquigny Edward put
his own interest above that of the country – in such terms he would not have
thought – it was that he put his own interest before that of the dynasty. He
was no better, therefore, than his brothers. For one of the results of
choosing peace and not war in 1475 was that the nobles who went to France
that summer returned to their old muddled and muddied lives, most notable
among them (for muddle and muddiness) George duke of Clarence.
Moreover, Richard duke of Gloucester and the queen's sons might have
discovered their talents and displayed them in a war in France.[104] We
cannot say, of course, that Picquigny led directly to the Tower for Clarence,
Hastings and the princes, and to Bosworth for Richard III, but surely there
is a connection between them which should be indicated. We could put this
another way: contrast the ten years after Agincourt with the ten years after
Picquigny. Indeed 1415 and 1475 themselves cry out to be compared.

Some comparisons have recently been made by Professor Lander. He tells
us, for example, that the 1475 expedition was poorly supported by the
nobility, only 23 peers accompanying the king, whereas half the nobility
went on the Agincourt campaign.[105] Yet the number of English noblemen in
1475 was 46; in that year therefore the peers were no lesser reluctant to fight
than their predecessors had been sixty years previously, in fact perhaps less
reluctant, as Professor Lander does not include in his figure of 23 Lord
Audley who (with the Gascon Lord Duras) commanded the force sent to
Brittany, and Lord Dinham who commanded the naval squadron which
protected the army's Channel crossing.

As further evidence of declining enthusiasm for the French war Professor Lander discusses the slowness with which parliamentary taxes (reluctantly granted) came in.[107] Yet, there had been, as he himself points out, some disgruntlement expressed at a Great Council meeting in 1414 at the thought of the money which would have to be raised for a renewal of the war against France.[108] Both Edward IV and Henry V, nonetheless, got about the same in taxation over a similar period of time.[109] If there was little difference in the way English taxpayers responded to the government's requests for money in 1414 and 1474 that is not, and was not by the government, unexpected. It was what was done with their money which makes the difference. K.B. McFarlane explains:[110]

A successor to Crecy and Poitiers was needed to make the English enthusiastic for war and willing to pay for the cost of its early stages and to demoralize the already divided French. Then conquest might be attempted. But the purpose of the carefully prepared expedition of 1415 was not conquest but a victorious battle. It was achieved by taking enormous risks.

Henry V took those risks and won his battle at Agincourt. English enthusiasm was handsomely demonstrated in subsequent parliaments: in the following four years Henry got six tenths and fifteenths and in November 1415 was granted the wool-subsidy and tunnage and poundage for life.[111] He duly conquered Normandy.

Edward IV took no risks, won no battle, made no conquest. He came back to England undefeated but untriumphant, though everyone knew, as Edward soon enough came to know, that it was Louis XI who had had the victory. In the twentieth century it may be as Alexander Solzhenitsyn has written that 'governments need victories and people need defeats',[112] but in fifteenth-century England the interests of government and people were not in opposition. Edward's defeat in 1475 (as defeat it turned out to be) was also that of his subjects. Particularly was this the case where government and people tended most readily to fall out, namely over taxation. Professor Lander has long ago drawn our attention to the fact that in the second half of the fifteenth century taxation became, if one may phrase it, 'a hot potato' which neither government nor people desired to handle.[113] Avoiding war was how Edward IV and Henry VII evaded the issue of taxation. They took other, unsatisfactory, courses to pay their peacetime way, but these were not only unsatisfactory in themselves – an aggravation to the people in another fashion than parliamentary taxation was – they could never do the job in wartime. Nor could war be avoided for ever. Indeed by some, the young Henry VIII for instance, it would be relished. In other words Edward IV and Henry VII ducked the biggest problem of all; the breakdown of the 'system' of taxation which had come into being in the reign of Edward III, had worked perfectly in the reign of Henry V, but, because mutual confidence was what made it work, had collapsed after 1437 when parliament became reluctant to grant money to

a government which did not know how to spend it. A return to dependance
on parliamentary taxation, therefore, would have been a sign of strength, for
it would have marked a revival of mutual confidence between government
and people.[114]

Such a return never did take place. The twists and turns sixteenth and
seventeenth century monarchs were forced to in order to raise money,
because those of the second half of the fifteenth century did not make that
'comeback' when it would have been easiest to accomplish, are, it seems to
me, part, perhaps a large part of the story of how confidence between
government and people came to breaking point in 1642, over, needless to say,
taxation to finance a war. One of those twists had been Henry VIII's plunder
of Church property, seemingly popular but eventually, because of the
religious changes which accompanied it, divisive and not coheseive, and
divisivenss in religion put mutual confidence – for all queen Elizabeth and the
king of Spain's efforts – beyond recovery.

Perhaps it is going too far to hold Edward IV responsible for the English
Reformation *and* the English Civil War, as well as the battle of Bosworth. Yet
the 1475 expedition to France was the best opportunity there was for a return
to the medieval system of taxation and all that it embodied in terms of
harmony between government and people. It was the best opportunity
because Edward had given every indication (until he talked to Louis XI at
Picquigny) that such a return was precisely what he was about. The long
build-up to the expedition and the expectations it set up (hence William
Worcester's hurriedly dusted-off booklet), the careful and militarily up to
date preparations,[115] the size and scale of the enterprize,[116] the remarkably
well-organized naval operations to cover the invasion,[117] the expense (no
expense spared is one's impression), the engagement of the nobility and the
gentry, all this suggests that Edward was as committed to war as Henry V had
been in 1415.[118] After all that, Picquigny was a shock to Englishmen, even
perhaps a surprise to Edward himself. It certainly reduces his quality as a
king: he opted for the small rewards of peace and not the larger benefits
which war could have brought. He is the very antithesis of Henry V.
Moreover, he was shortly to discover that the rewards of peace did not
amount to anything: his diplomacy after 1475 was one long defeat; by 1480 he
was at war with Scotland; and had he lived he would probably have gone to
war with Louis XI after all.

Thus, 1475 was a turning point both in the long term and the short. It had
its importance for many years to come, but the ten years which immediately
followed were deeply (and sharply) moulded by it. The Wars of the Roses
could have ended in 1475: they had been caused by collapsing confidence in
government, they could have been ended by its renewal. As it was, twenty-
five years of tension and animosity were not eased, twenty-five years
experience of killing and counter-killing were not erased. In short, Edward
IV did not do what Henry V had done in 1415, turn England out of the recent
rut of its bad habits by the strength of his genius. Henry imposed himself on

history; Edward never made the attempt. After 1475 there were still more of the bad old days to come. The spectre of civil war was not laid as it had been in 1415. It reappeared in 1483. Two years later it was in full cry. What was going on at Bosworth in August 1485, therefore, was the fighting which ought to have taken place at Agincourt (or thereabouts) in August 1475.

Notes

1. My starting point here has been the two profound papers of Donald Nicholl, 'A Historian's Calling' and 'Historical Understanding' in the *Downside Review*, vol. 76 (1958) and vol. 97 (1979).

2. It may not have been limited: Eric John, 'War and Society in the Tenth Century: The Maldon Campaign', *TRHS*, Fifth Series, vol. 27 (1977).

3. For 'The Battle of Maldon' see N.F. Blake, 'The genesis of the Battle of Maldon', *Anglo-Saxon England*, vol. 7 (1978).

4. Note 120, p. xlv in *British Library Harleian Manuscript 433*, ed. Rosemary Horrox and P.W. Hammond, vol. 1 (Upminster/London 1979). Charles Ross, *Richard III* (London 1981), also decided that the poet, apparently a northerner writing before 1495, was to be trusted when he names those present with Richard at Bosworth: appendix II, pp. 235–·7. The authenticity of the poem is an important matter, for Professor Ross (as he said) placed 'much reliance' on it 'in the later chapters' of his book. For further comment see *History*, vol. 68 (1983), pp. 55–6.

5. *Bishop Percy's Folio Manuscript*, ed. J.W. Hales and F.J. Furnivall, vol. III (1868), p. 233 *et seq*. The Percy Manuscript is BL Add. Ms. 27879; the 'Ballad of Bosworth Feilde' is on f. 434 *et seq*. What was his source?

6. British Library, Harleian MS 542, folio 31 *et seq*. The manuscript belonged to Sir Henry Saville.

7. *All* the knights, it should be stressed, *are* knights. If these seventy members of the gentry, mainly from the North, are real, can they really all have been knights? Or has the poet made knights of esquires and gentlemen? If he has, it does not help us believe in him as an accurate reporter.

8. For more on 'The Ballad of Bosworth Feilde' see appendix I.

9. For the poem and the nobles at (or not at) Bosworth see appendix II.

10. He was said to have been there from 10 July to 21 August seeing to the needs of the naval squadron patrolling in the Channel: PRO E405/74.

11. This is hardly a novel conclusion. John Rous tells us Richard 'defended himself to his last breath, shouting again and again that he was betrayed, and crying 'Treason! Treason! Treason!': translation in Alison Hanham, *Richard III and his early historians 1485–1535* (Oxford 1975), p. 121. The desertions had apparently already begun before the battle among those accompanying

Sir Robert Brackenbury northwards: *The Great Chronicle of London*, ed. A.H. Thomas and I.D. Thornley (1938), p. 237.

12. As the Earl of Lincoln, erroneously proclaimed dead after the battle (*York Civic Records*, vol. I, ed. Angelo Raine, Yorks. Arch. Soc. Record Series vol. 98 (1938), p. 121), was present at the first parliament of Henry VII, there are doubts even about Richard's heir to the throne.

13. Scrope of Masham was with Richard at Nottingham on 1 August (*CCR 1476–83*, pp. 431–3); Shrewsbury was said to have been taken prisoner (*The Chronicle of Calais*, ed. J.G. Nichols, Camden Society, vol. 35 (1846), p. 1).

14. T.B. Pugh, 'The magnates, knights and gentry' in *Fifteenth-Century England, 1399–1509*, ed. S.B. Chrimes, C.D. Ross, R.A. Griffiths (Gloucester 1972), p. 114, notes that 'the king was attended by only ten lords'. He goes on: 'Less than a quarter of the English peerage was sufficiently committed to fight for King Richard and it is remarkable how little positive support he could inspire or compel after ruling England for more than two years.' For the ten we are referred to J.R. Lander, *Conflict and Stability in Fifteenth Century England* (London 1969), p. 99, footnote one. There the ten are listed: Norfolk, Surrey, Nottingham, Lovel, Ferrers, Dacre of Gillesland, Greystoke, Scrope of Bolton, Zouch and Northumberland. No source is given. Mr. Pugh, however, also refers us to W. Hutton, *The Battle of Bosworth Field*, ed. J.G. Nichols (1813), p. 209, and states that 'the list of peers said to have been present at Bosworth in B.M. Harleian MS 542, f. 34, is unreliable'. Hutton, p. 209 turns out to be BL Harleian MS 542 f.34, that is 'The Ballad of Bosworth Feilde'.

15. The *Cal. Papal Registers* evidence seems the most decisive we are going to get: from the horse's mouth with the horse likely to be at his most truthful. See K.B. McFarlane, *EHR* vol. 78 (1963), pp. 771–2.

16. The ten were Devon, Ferrers of Chartley, Lisle, Grey of Powis, Grey of Wilton, Hastings, Kent, Oxford, Shrewsbury, Strange: John Leland, *De rebus britannicis collectanea* (reprint 1970), vol. 4, pp. 210–13. Bedford, Clifford, Fitzwalter, Welles, and Northumberland might have been there. Clifford and Northumberland may have stayed at York, after they had turned back to defend it against rebel attack, and thus missed being at the actual battle: *York Civic Records*, vol. 2, ed. Angelo Raine, Yorks. Arch. Soc. Record Series vol. 103 (1941), pp. 22–3.

17. We have to bear in mind that the two Scropes (of Bolton and Masham), possibly with no great enthusiasm, had attacked the city of York on the rebels' behalf: *York Civic Records*, vol. 2, pp. 22–3.

18. Professor Ross, *Richard III* (London, 1981), p. 214, has pointed out one of the consequences of the speed with which battle was joined: 'the royalist army which surrounded the King at Bosworth on 22 August must very largely have arrived there on horseback'.

19. *HMC, Twelfth Report, Rutland Manuscripts*, vol. 1, p. 7.

20. *Paston Letters and Papers of the Fifteenth Century*, ed. Norman Davis, vol. 2 (1976), pp. 443–4.

21. 'Croyland Chronicle' in *Rerum Anglicarum Scriptores Veterum*, ed. W. Fulman (Oxford, 1684), pp. 573–4.

22.   *York Civic Records* vol. 1, pp. 118–119; cf Paul Murray Kendall, *Richard the Third* (London 1955), p. 493, note 12.

23.   In March 1481 it was agreed that a force of 120 soldiers, raised from the city and the Ainsty, should serve in the war against Scotland; the soldiers were still at York in September: *York Civic Records*, vol. 1, pp. 38–48.

24.   D.M. Palliser, 'Epidemics in Tudor York', *Northern History*, vol. 8 (1973), p. 61.

25.   'Inaugural Ceremonies of the Yorkist Kings and their Title to the Throne', *TRHS*, Fourth Series, vol. 30 (1948), p. 69.

26.   Charles Ross, *Richard III* (London, 1981), p. 224.

27.   Rosemary Horrox, note 70, p. xliii, *British Library Harleian Manuscript 443*, vol. 1. For the Charltons of Edmonton and South Mimms see J.S. Roskell, *The Commons and their Speakers in English Parliaments 1376–1523* (Manchester 1965), pp. 255–6 and further references there.

28.   J.S. Roskell, 'William Catesby, Counsellor to Richard III', *Bulletin of the John Rylands Library*, vol. 42 (1959), p. 170, and also Daniel Willliams, 'The hastily drawn up will of William Catesby, esquire, 25 August 1485', *Transactions of the Leicestershire Archaeological and Historical Society*, vol. 51 (1975–76), p. 43 *et seq*.

29.   In 1487 the time between the rebels' landing (at Furness on 4 June) and the decisive battle (at Stoke on 16 June) was shorter by three days than it was in 1485; but the rebels had been in Ireland (ready to cross) since 5 May, so that Henry VII had ample time to get his army together, and those summoned no excuse of shortage of time in which to get themselves to the king.

30.   *HMC, Rutland Manuscripts*, vol. 1, pp. 2–6. Whatever the defence he had offered for his failure to respond in 1471, it had been acceptable (or at any rate accepted) as his successful career thereafter testifies.

31.   For Howard's de Vere estates see BL Add. Charter 16559, his East Anglian Receiver's Account of 1483–4. For Richard's dealings with the Countess of Oxford see the references cited in C. Ross, *Edward IV* (London, 1974) p. 248 footnote 3, and G.E. Cockayne, *The Complete Peerage*, ed. V. Gibbs and others (1910–1959), vol. 10, p. 238, footnote; to these should be added BL Cotton MS Julius BXII, ff. 227–229, 315–317, and *Materials for a history of the reign of Henry VII*, ed. W. Campbell (Rolls Series 1873–77), vol. 1, pp. 270–1.

32.   Davis, vol. 2, No. 630 displays a close association between the twelfth earl and John Paston I; it seems to date from 1461. In the following year John was acting as a councillor of the dowager Countess Elizabeth: Davis II, no. 667. Then as the Dukes of Norfolk and Suffolk became the Pastons' opponents over the Fastolf inheritance, the 13th earl – in no position to become the third of their noble rivals (even if he had wanted to be) – became, when the time was ripe (in 1470–71), their influential ally. That brief interlude apart, the de Veres and the Pastons were 'outsiders' in East Anglian society in the 1460s and 1470s; theirs, therefore, was a natural alliance. They came in from the cold as a consequence of Henry Tudor's victory at Bosworth; thereafter their alliance was a triumphal progress.

33. Davis, vol. 2, No. 799.
34. The *Household Books of John Duke of Norfolk*. . . , ed. J. Payne Collier (Roxburghe Club, 1844) p. 480: 'The names of the men that my Lord hath graunted to the Kyng'. The list of names follows, pp. 480–492.
35. This list runs from pp. 488–490, but John Knight appears on p. 480 (with six men) and James Hobart (with 3 men 'and he hath promised my Lord to gete hym as many men as he can gete, to the nombre of [BLANK]') on p. 481.
36. It is stated, however, on p. 492.that Sir Harry Rosse, Thomas Hoo and Richard Lewknor have undertaken to 'get my Lordes grass of hys servantys and tenauntes, besyd all them a for namyt . . . owt of Sussex and Surey, well horssyt and harnest.' If these southern gentlemen were to be Howard's recruiting (and serving) officers for these parts, it is difficult to believe that they were active in 1485; only Thomas Hoo's career was even briefly interrupted by the verdict of Bosworth: he was off the commission of the peace for a year. For these men see J.C. Wedgwood, *History of Parliament 1439–1509, Biographies* (1936), p. 466 (Hoo), p. 540 (Lewknor), p. 726 (Rose).
37. It is worth noting that the poems on Bosworth ('The Ballad of Lady Bessy' and 'The Ballad of Bosworth Feilde') celebrate a treason done to a lord by his men. It is not a matter of good and bad lords; Ethelred was hardly a model lord and king; he too had usurped the throne in murderous circumstances. There is nothing like Bryhtnoth's:

> . . . there stands here 'mid his men not the meanest of Earls, pledged to fight in this land's defence, the land of Aethelred, my liege lord, its soil, its folk . . .
> [lines 51–4]

in the Bosworth poems. The equivalent around the year 1000 of their commemoration of Thomas lord Stanley would be a poem on the battle of Ashingdon with Eadric Streona as its hero.
38. See p. 12 note 2 above.
39. As James Hobart's career took even higher flight after Bosworth (he was appointed Attorney-General in 1486) we cannot conceive of him as being at the battle. He may have sent the men of course. For him (in brief) see my *John Hopton* (Cambridge 1981), pp. 186–192.
40. This also is not a new conclusion. The Croyland Chronicler commented, 'many, for the most part those northerners in whom King Richard had so trusted, took flight before it came to hand-to-hand fighting': quoted in Hanham, *Richard III and his early historians, 1483–1535*, p. 57.
41. Bodleian Library MS add. d. 113, folio 28, however, throws doubt even on Sir James Harrington's presence at Bosworth. In this bitter complaint of Richard Beaumont against the chicanery of the Stanleys, he states that Thomas earl of Derby 'causyd' Sir James to be attainted 'wher in for a treuth the seid Jamys was never ayeinst the Kyng in no feild'.
42. How far were the Harringtons especially, but Pilkington too, fighting their own battle at Bosworth against the Stanleys, and the Stanleys for that matter against

them? Here the local politics of Lancashire play an important part in a central drama. Moreover, as the Stanleys would certainly have had Sir Thomas Broughton attainted if they had been able to, the fact that in 1485 he was not, surely means he was not at Bosworth – even though he was excluded from the proclamation of pardon of 8 October 1485 (*York Civic Records* vol. 1, p. 126). The Stanleys had to wait until 1487 before they could get their hands on his north Lancashire estates.

43. 'But where the Earl of Northumberland stood, with a troop of a size and quality befitting his rank, no opposing force was visible, and no blows were exchanged in anger': the Croyland Chronicler quoted in Alison Hanham, *op. cit.*, p. 57. As he was imprisoned after the battle Henry may have been unsure what part he had taken (or, as it turned out, not taken) against him. For his imprisonment see M.A. Hicks, 'Dynastic Change and Northern Society: the Career of the Fourth Earl of Northumberland, 1470–89', *Northern History*, vol. 14 (1978), p. 92.

44. See p. 195 note 11 above.

45. D.A.L. Morgan, 'The King's Affinity in the Polity of Yorkist England', *TRHS*, Fifth series, vol. 23 (1973), p. 18. Their agreement appears not to have covered ecclesiastical patronage, for there was a contest between them when they backed different clients for the post of prior of Tynemouth; it was an unseemly struggle between unsuitable candidates and Richard's Nicholas Boston, a winner in 1478, was replaced by the earl's William Dyxwelle in 1480. Richard, however, got his man back in again after he had become king. It is an instructive story; see *Registra Johannis Whethamstede*, ed. H.T. Riley (Rolls Series 1873) vol. 2, pp. xxxv–xliii.

46. *Op. cit.*, p. 97.

47. One can perhaps imagine Richard's Middleham neighbour lord Scrope of Bolton joining in, although he was feed by the earl of Northumberland (Hicks, 'Dynastic Change', p. 89).

48. For this see A.J. Pollard, 'The tyranny of Richard III', *Journal of Medieval History* vol. 3 (1977), pp. 147–166. We await with increasing impatience the publication of Rosemary Horrox's 1977 Cambridge Ph.D. thesis, 'The Extent and Use of Crown Patronage under Richard III'.

49. The lone northerner was Sir Robert Middleton of Middleton Hall, Kirkby Lonsdale. I am omitting from 'the north' Lancashire, and I am conveneintly taking Sir Robert Brackenbury and Sir Richard Ratcliff to have become more than mere northerners by 1485: they were national figures.

50. All the northern magnates escaped attainder: Northumberland, Westmorland, the two Scropes, Greystoke, Dacre, Fitzhugh, and Lumley. Are we to assume that they argued themselves out of it during the critical discussions in parliament, or that they did not deserve it? If it was the arguing that did it, then it was Greystoke, Fitzhugh, Lumley and Scrope of Masham who made out the case; the others seem not to have been there.

51. Or that they fought but were not attainted. The act of attainder encountered opposition in parliament, which was only to be expected as the losers at Bosworth had fought for the king; thus, those eventually included in it may have

been selected with some thought, as in 1453. Yet if the northern affinity had fought at Bosworth in some numbers the lack of casualties is hard to explain.

52.   *The Great Chronicle of London*, ed. A.H. Thomas and I.D. Thornley (London 1938), p. 242.

53.   'Dynastic Change', p. 80.

54.   *Ibid.*, pp. 97–100. The quotation is from p. 100.

55.   They had never been otherwise. Is not the loyalty of man to lord chiefly a literary device, only active in reality when the lord is successful, that is when self-interest (or mutual interest) binds man and lord together – hence John of Gaunt's large retinue and William lord Hastings' important and effective one. Of course, life quite frequently imitates art and therefore there have been exceptions, idealists we might call them like some of Bryhtnoth's followers or Captain Oates. Yet even here we are obliged to ponder the pure poetry (or pure propaganda) of 'The Battle of Maldon' and the possibility of Captain Oates not knowing what he was doing, let alone where he was going when he went out of the tent; it was Captain Scott, Oates' loyal commander who then made Oates' death conform to an ideal (David Thomson, *Scott's Men* (1977), pp. 281–2.) We should also not overlook fame as an aspect of self-interest. To die according to the highest ideals of one's time preserved the 'self', as both 'The Battle of Maldon' and the story of Captain Oates so remarkably demonstrate. It is not in fact that life imitates art but that the two are and always have been inextricably confused, hence the Sagas, hence Scott's last expedition, hence (in its reflection of the fifteenth century's lack of such idealistic self-interest) 'The Ballad of Bosworth Feilde'.

56.   I have taken Cumbria because there the Earl of Northumberland's influence, despite his barony of Cockermouth, was weaker than anywhere else in the north. There Richard had a freer hand to recruit retainers than he had in Northumberland or in Yorkshire, the North Riding possibly excepted. Included in my Cumbria are Furness and Lonsdale which properly belong to Lancashire, but in all other respects belong to Richard's Cumbria.

57.   It is a very rough and extremely provisional count but here it is set out:

'Ricardian'	'anti-Ricardian'	'don't know'
Harrington	Musgrave	Wharton
Thornborough	Crackenthorpe	Thelkeld (Percy)
Huddleston	Eglesfield	Pennington (Percy)
Broughton	Salkeld	Lamplugh (Percy?)
Ratcliff	Tunstall	Legh
Redmain	Moresby	Blenkinsop
Hilton	Bellingham	Denton
Middleton	Lowther	Strickland
	Pickering	Curwen (Percy)
		Skelton (Percy)
		Heighmore (Percy)
		Beauley

For this rudimentary differentiation I have used no more than the works of
Hicks and Wedgwood (cited above), the commissions of the peace as they are
set out in the *Calendars of Patent Rolls*, and (very selectively) those *Calendars*
themselves (for grants, other commissions, and the like).

58. By Charles Ross, 'The Reign of Edward IV', *Fifteenth-century England 1399–
     1509*, ed. S.B. Chrimes, C.D. Ross, R.A. Griffiths (Gloucester 1972), p. 62.

59. The question of who gained most from the lord-retainer relationship and what it
     was that was to be gained, requires a fresh discussion, especially as recent work
     tends to assume, where it does not positively emphasize, first, a large degree of
     dependancy on the part of the retainer and, second, that this dependancy was
     exclusive. The second was seldom the case where the lord was noble and the
     retainer gentle – which at once reduced the dependancy to negligible propor-
     tions. Many gentlemen in the fifteenth century served two masters, few were
     dependant on one. A man like James Hobart served many lords at the same
     time: Mowbray and Howard as well as other gentlemen before 1485, many
     gentlemen, the earl of Oxford, and the towns of Norwich and Ipswich as well as
     the king after 1485 (*John Hopton*, pp. 186–190; Rosemary Horrox, 'Urban
     Patronage and Patrons in the Fifteenth Century', *Patronage, the Crown and the
     Provinces* ed. R.A. Griffiths (Gloucester 1981), p. 152). As Hobart was a
     talented lawyer perhaps he is, like other lawyers of the fifteenth century, a
     special case. Sir Humphrey Stafford of Grafton and Sir John Fastolf, however,
     were not lawyers and they were widely feed (K.B. McFarlane, 'The Wars of the
     Roses', *Proceedings of the British Academy*, vol. 50 (1964), p. 109; 'The
     investment of Sir John Fastolf's profits of war', *TRHS*, Fifth series, vol. 7
     (1957), p. 106 note 4). What had they to offer their lords in England c.1450? It is
     difficult to say. If they looked after their lords' interests in their locality, which it
     was hoped they would do (*The Stonor Letters and Papers*, ed. C.L. Kingsford,
     Camden Society, Third series, vol. 30 (1919), p.70), they would also be looking
     after their own and would be inclined to do so only when they were – there is a
     mutuality here which disguises what actually went on, that these clients pursued
     their own interests and advantages under colour of protecting or enchancing
     their patrons'. Thus, in this roundabout way, the patron was dependant on his
     clients –his interests had become theirs and he was in their pocket not *vice versa*.
     When Gervaise Clifton writes to William Wainfleet, bishop of Winchester,

> I trust to God to make you bigge ynough to trye with hym [Francis lord Lovel]
> within the shire with help of such other as ye shall easely haue the goode willes of,
> soo that my lorde Chaumbreleyn [William lord Hastings] take not the contrarie
> parte

it is evidently Gervaise Clifton's patron, William lord Hastings, who is about to
be 'used'. The letter is printed in full in McFarlane's lecture 'The Wars of the
Roses', cited above, p. 108. Where effective political power is concerned noble
lords had become by the mid-fifteenth century no more than socially prestigious
puppets, whose strings were worked by knights, esquires and gentlemen. This is

incontrovertibly revealed when the military aspect of retaining is considered. In spring 1471 Edward IV's return depended not on William lord Hastings but on William lord Hastings' retainers; they got both lord and king back into power. In August 1485 Richard III's own retainers did not care enough about him to keep him in power. Choice of courses (political and military) was open to retainers. Ultimately it was this freedom to choose on the part of the so-called led which renders the leaders of later fifteenth-century society so vulnerable, and which makes the politics of post–1450 England so much a maze for the historian, for they are determined not by half-a-dozen great men but by the hundreds of socially lesser ones. Trying to get to the heart of the maze by using the rigid retainer and the absolutely dependant affinity as short cuts only takes us into deadends.

60. 'The tyranny of Richard III', *Journal of Medieval History* vol. 3 (1977), pp. 147–165. There are some pertinent comments in Dermot Fenlon, 'Thomas More and Tyranny', *The Journal of Ecclesiastical History*, vol. 32 (1981), pp. 455–8. Where Richard's tyranny is concerned Sir Thomas Lewknor's petition for a pardon for his rebellion in October 1483 might also be considered (PRO C81/1531/48, for an accurate transcript of which I am indebted to David Morgan):

> Please it your most noble grace in consideracion of the princely pite which ye have shewed to your most sorowfull and repentaunt subgetts whoes names be marked with your owen gracious hand in the boke of excepcion delyvered to Maister Chaterton to graunt to all them whose names ensue your gracious lettres of pardon in forme following, Forasmuch as the saide bok canne be no sufficient warrant to make out theyr pardons advailable for theyr lyvis according to your blissed entent, And that this is the same forme nor more ne lesse that passed your grace at Notyngham to them that ye gaf your pardon to being thenne at Beaulieu, And that ther' is noon of thyes names but such as your grace appointed in the saide boke that shuld have your pardon.

The form of the pardon is then set out. The petition is initialled by Richard and was duly sent to the Chancellor, though there is no endorsement to that effect as on similar petition/warrants: C81/1531/14, 22 (Thomas Lovell, dated 24 November 1484 and, for his lands, dated 2 February 1485; but not granted? There was no enrollment and cf Wedgwood, p. 555); C81/1531/20 (Sir Roger Tocotes, 27 January 1485, granted same date, *CPR 1476–1485*, p. 507); C81/1531/27 (Sir William Berkeley of Beverstone, Glos., 10 March 1484, but not granted? There is no enrollment and cf Wedgwood pp. 69–70). Thomas Lewknor, nonetheless, got his pardon on 31 May 1484, *CPR 1476–1485*, p. 435. Like some other rebels however, he had had to enter into a bond on 24 May that he 'be true and of good bearing towards King Richard III': *CCR 1476–1485*, p. 365, cf Charles Ross, *Richard III*, p.113, footnote 24, and pp. 180–1. Sir William Berkeley forfeited his recognisance (presumably by flight to Brittany), and thus put Sir Edward Berkeley esquire, one of his sureties, in jeopardy: PRO C81/1392/17, 9 October 1484. Thomas Lewknor had been a particularly tough rebel; he held out in his castle of Bodiam until November: *CPR 1476–1485*, p. 370, cf. p. 535. For the important Edmund Chadderton, Treasurer of the King's Chamber at this time, who died 1499, see A.B. Emden, *A Biographical Register of the University of Oxford to 1500*, vol. 1 (Oxford 1981), p. 382; *Testamenta Eboracensia* IV, pp. 66–68, where the editor comments: 'It is a matter of surprise that he and Christopher Urswick were not raised to the bench'. Indeed, for Henry VII, in commending him to John Paston in August 1486, called him 'our trusty and wellbeloved clerke and counseilor': Davis, vol. 2, p. 447.

61. An explanation offered by Professor Ralph Griffiths in a talk given at the University of Keele on 8 December 1980. Buckingham's recently disclosed implication in the murder of the Princes before October would, if anything, support his late, almost impulsive commitment to 'the other side': R.F. Green, 'Historical Notes of a London Citizen, 1483–88', *EHR* vol. 96 (1981), pp. 585–590.

62. John Howard's response can be followed in his *Household Books*, pp. 468–479. From London on 7 October he dispatched a man into Kent 'for to speke with Schelle'; on 10 October he wrote to John Paston (Davis II, no. 799) and sent another man into Kent; the next day about 100 soldiers went off to Gravesend, and Thomas Thorp took £20 to Lord Cobham at Rochester. By 19 October, when about 150 men were paid for themselves and their horses for service which varied from five to thirty days, all was over. Thirteen guns had been taken along. Howard himself does not appear to have left London, which demonstrates how easily the rising was dealt with. Lord Cobham, on the other hand, was busy in Kent throughout October into November. He was entertained at Canterbury on 31 October, a contingent from that city was part of his mobile force, and it was Canterbury men who delivered the captured rebel Richard Hawte to him: Canterbury Chamberlains' Accounts 1483–4 (F.A. 7), folio X, at the Cathedral Library, Canterbury.

63. The Woodvill affinity and Edward IV's affinity were in March 1483 not distinct groups; after the king's death on 9 April they separated as William lord Hastings, the leader of Edward IV's affinity, and the Woodvills fell out over what form the minority government should take. After Hastings' murder they came together again (co-opting the 'old Lancastrians' as allies) against Hastings' (and probably the Princes') killer. The initiative undoubtedly lay with former knights and esquires of the body to Edward IV who led the various sectors of the rising: Sir Thomas Saintleger, Sir George Browne, Sir Giles Daubeney, Sir Walter Hungerford, Sir William Norris, John Harcourt. Sir George Browne's short note to John Paston, 'Hyt schal newyr cum howte for me' (Davis, vol. 2, no. 800), whether or not it dates to the time of the rebellion, was prophetic: he was executed in December 1483. Like his father, Sir George paid the full price for loyalty to his lord; in Sir Thomas's case, however, his lord Henry VI was still alive when he died for him; Sir George on the other hand is like the followers of Bryhtnoth who died for their dead lord. So, after all, we have found a fifteenth-century hero. For the unlucky

Brownes see Wedgwood, *op. cit.*, pp. 121–123. Their house at Tonford near Canterbury survives, trapped between railway lines and motorways and completely obscured by trees.

64. Dominic Mancini, *The Usurpation of Richard III*, ed. C.A.J. Armstrong (second edition, Oxford, 1969), p. 69; Thomas More, 'History of King Richard III' in *Richard the Third: the Great Debate*, ed. Paul Kendall (London, 1965), pp. 37–8; 'The Croyland Chronicle' in *Ingulph's Chronicle of Croyland*, ed. H.T. Riley (1854), p. 485.

65. Nor had there been any haste in the holding of Edward IV's funeral. Henry IV's was held at the same interval after his death, about ten days: Henry IV died 20 March; Henry V was back in London from taking the body to Canterbury on 2 April; the coronation was on 4 April; Edward IV died 9 April; the funeral was on 20 April; the coronation was set for 4 May. Less than half the nobility came to Edward IV's funeral: 19 out of 41 if we include the absent Duke of Gloucester in the total. Was this a poor or an average turnout? I have not followed that question up; it might be worth doing so, especially as the nobility are reckoned (see below p. 184) to have been disaffected at the time of Edward's death. Most of the absentees (16 out of 21) were at Richard's coronation.
Not at the funeral were Grey of Codnor, Lovel, Scrope of Bolton, Scrope of Masham, Zouch, Buckingham, and Northumberland. Howard was there, Suffolk surprisingly, was not. The College of Arms MS may not of course be exhaustive; it is printed in *Letters and Papers Illustrative of the Reigns of Richard III and Henry VII*, ed. J. Gairdner (Rolls Series 1861–3), vol. 1, pp. 3–10.

66. Mancini, *op. cit.*, note 44, p. 115.

67. Hastings' startled response to Richard informing him that he was the traitor to be arrested, 'What me my Lorde', in Thomas More's account captures his sense of shock: *The History of King Richard III*, ed. R.S. Sylvester (*Complete Works*, Yale Edition, vol. 2, 1963), p. 48.

68. Mancini, *op. cit.*, p. 85. As presumably Hastings was one of the Councillors who prevented this he ought to have had no illusions about the Protector's contempt for the laws of the land, yet any doubts he may have had about Richard's intentions at the time of the arrest of Rivers (Mancini, *op. cit.*, note 51, p. 116) seem to have disappeared during the following weeks.

69. Where at Kirby Muxloe and Bradgate, not a handful of miles apart, the two rivals were perhaps attempting to outbuild each other in the grand manner.

70. Henry duke of Buckingham, who had entered on his inheritance in 1473, had been 'relegated to political limbo'; this had been part of Edward IV's 'land policy': D.A.L. Morgan, *op. cit.*, p. 18; may it have also been part of that king's 'dynastic policy' as suggested by R.A. Griffiths in his Keele talk of 8 December 1980?

71. D.A.L. Morgan, *op. cit.*, p. 24 (but I wish there was a reference for this).

72. Quoted by Malcolm Vale, *Charles VII* (London 1974), p. 215.

73. See the remarks of Rosemary Horrox in her introduction to *BL Harleian MS 433*, vol. 1, p. xxii. And also (for men being aware of what was about to happen)

see Anne Crawford, 'The career of John Howard duke of Norfolk 1420–1485' (London University M.Phil. thesis 1975), pp. 199–200.

74.   Despite Professor Helmholz's elegant paper in this collection I continue to suspect that the illegitimacy of Edward's sons was a cloak of legality which most people observed as being of a style similar to that of the emperor's new clothes.

75.   For the most recent discussion of Richard's puritanism see Charles Ross, 'Rumour, Propaganda and Popular Opinion during the Wars of the Roses' in *Patronage, the Crown and the Provinces*, ed R.A. Griffiths (Gloucester 1981), pp. 27–28 and the references cited there, and the same writer's *Richard III*, p. 136 *et seq*, where Richard's open letter of 1484 to the bishops is quoted: '. . . our principal intent and fervent desire is to see virtue and cleaness of living to be advanced, increased and multiplied . . .'. In addition, we might note, because it suggests an attempted 'clean up' by the Protector, the proclamation issued in London probably in May 1483: 'For to eschewe the stynkyng and horrible Synne of Lechery . . . all suche Strumpettes and mysguyded and idill women . . . departe and withdrawe theym self and in no wise be so hardy to come ayen Resorte or abide within the said Citee or libertie . . .', *Calendar of Letter-Books . . . of the City of London*, ed. R.R. Sharpe, *Letter-Book L* (1912), p. 206. Prostitutes had been banned from the City itself since the late thirteenth century, but the inclusion of the Bankside brothel quarter in the Liberty of the bishops of Winchester at Southwark indicates that the City Fathers (or the Protector) were serious in their intention. For the fifteenth-century Southwark stews see J.B. Post, 'A Fifteenth-century customary of the Southwark stews', *Journal of the Society of Archivists*, vol. 5 (1977), pp. 418–428. For Jane Shore's divorce see N. Barker and R. Birley, 'Jane Shore', *Etoniana*, nos. 125, 126 (1972). For Richard's religion see Pamela Tudor-Craig, *Richard III* (catalogue of the exhibition at the National Portrait Gallery 1973), pp. 17, 23, 26–7, 96–7. Is it significant that Richard apparently never dowered his queen? See Anne Crawford, 'The King's Burden? – the Consequences of Royal Marriage in Fifteenth-century England' in *Patronage, the Crown and Provinces*, ed. R.A. Griffiths (Gloucester 1981), p. 47. And should we add to his bastard children (John and Katharine) the Richard Plantaganet buried at Eastwell in Kent on 22 December 1550? See Edward Hasted, *The History and Topographical Survey of the County of Kent* (Canterbury 1778–1799), vol. 3, p. 202.

76.   See his prayer, printed in Pamela Tudor-Craig, *op. cit.*, pp. 96–7.

77.   For the murder of innocents see the comments (with references) of C.A.J. Armstrong in his introduction to Dominic Mancini, *op. cit.*, pp. 20–21: '. . .the killing of children for reasons of State was regarded with aversion'. The muffled sense of outrage in the 'Croyland Chronicle' surely has its origin here. Like the beastly murder of Nicholas Radford in 1455 (most recently discussed by Martin Cherry, 'The struggle for power in mid-fifteenth-century Devonshire' in *Patronage, the Crown and the Provinces*, ed. Griffiths; 'The enormity of this crime horrified contemporary opinion', p. 136), the removal of the young king and his brother was untypical of fifteenth century *mores*.

78. Even if it may have crossed his mind when the Appellants confronted the young Richard with deposition at the Tower in December 1387: K.B. McFarlane, *Lancastrian Kings and Lollard Knights* (Oxford 1972), pp. 33–5.

79. The Princes bulk large in nearly contemporary explanations of Richard's fall. Thus an Italian in 1496: 'They [the English people] would treat him [Henry VII] as they did King Richard, whom they abandoned, taking the other side because he put to death his nephews, to whom the kingdom belonged', *Calendar of State Papers, Milan*, ed. A.B. Hinds (1912), p. 299. And cf Cotton Vitellius AXVI in C.L. Kingsford, *Chronicles of London* (Oxford 1905), p. 191, on the rebellion of October 1483, '. . .for anoon as the said Kyng Richard had put to deth the lord Chamberlyn and other Gentilmen . . . he also put to deth the ij childer of Kyng Edward, for whiche cawse he lost the hertes of the people.'

80. See above p. 000.

81. See, for instance, R.A. Griffiths, 'Local Rivalries and National Politics: the Percies, the Nevilles, and the Duke of Exeter, 1452–1455', *Speculum*, vol. 43 (1968), pp. 589–632.

82. For Boroughbridge, see J.R. Maddicott, *Thomas of Lancaster 1307–1322* (London 1970), chapter VIII; for Radcot Bridge, McFarlane, *Lancastrian Kings and Lollard Knights*, pp. 19–20.

83. R.H.C. Davis, 'What happened in Stephen's reign, 1135–1154', *History*, vol. 49 (1964), pp. 1–12, especially p. 10: 'Wherever we turn the politics of Stephen's reign seem to dissolve into family history.'

84. Edward I's responsibility for the dimension of the problem I am not competent to debate, nor am I the vexed question of that father's contribution to the character of his son. That is, like Edward IV's part in the moulding of the character of his 13 year old son (was he – to his uncle Richard at any rate – a 'Woodvill' prince?), debateable enough but difficult to resolve.

85. The two words are of course the same: Jenny Wormald, *Court, Kirk, and Community: Scotland 1470–1625* (London 1981), p. 30.

86. For Edward I, see K.B. McFarlane's discussion of this matter in his paper, 'Had Edward I a 'policy' towards the Earls?' *History*, vol. 50 (1965), pp. 145–159, esp. p. 158. The paper is reprinted in his *The Nobility of Later Medieval England* (1973), pp. 248–267, where the most relevant pages are pp. 265–66. For Edward IV see T.B. Pugh, 'The magnates, knights and gentry' in *Fifteenth Century England 1399–1509* (1972), where this view was first and most persuasively argued, pp. 109–112.

87. *The Nobility of Later Medieval England*, p. 157. The whole passage (pp. 156–158) should be read in conjunction with McFarlane's comments on the 'appanage policy' of English kings (*ibid.*, p. 72). His cautionary, 'please remember that Henry VII created (in 1494) a new cadet royal house of York in the person of his second son; only the death of Arthur undid the effects of that day's work', should particularly be borne in mind by those who condemn Edward IV for creating an appanage for his brother Richard in the North West.

88. Pugh, *op. cit.*, pp. 111–2.

89. *History*, vol. 50 (1965), p.158; *The Nobility of Later Medieval England*, p. 266.

90. 'The politics of the 1470s were the politics of land, and 1473–4 saw the shaping of a land policy which combined family endowment with a tidy–minded regionalism': D.A.L. Morgan, 'The Kings Affinity', p. 18. The two policies were not distinct, as this quotation shows.

91. D.A.L. Morgan, *op. cit.*, pp. 17–19. Edward's use of the household to 'run' the provinces (*ibid.*, pp. 19–21) is reminscent of later Anglo-Saxon kingship and the relationship between king, king's thegns, and the new provinces of the new England; see for instance, Sir Frank Stenton, *Anglo–Saxon England* (2nd. edn. Oxford 1947), p. 542.

92. Davis, 'What happened in Stephen's Reign, 1135–1154', pp. 1–12; R.H.C. Davis, *King Stephen* (London 1967); for an excellent study of one such family: W.E. Wightman, *The Lacy Family in England and Normandy, 1066–1194* (London 1966).

93. Henry Tudor, however, had a potential place, as the indenture between Margaret Beaufort and Thomas Stanley sealed in Edward's presence in June 1482 shows: see Michael Jones' important paper in this collection, p.000.

94. In Lincolnshire it was Sir Thomas Burgh who had stepped into Viscount Beaumont's (and Lord Welles') place: R.L. Storey, 'Lincolnshire and the Wars of the Roses', *Nottingham Medieval Studies*, vol. 14 (1970), pp. 64–82, esp. p. 71. Sir Thomas Burgh survived 1485 intact. It is striking – if nothing more – that although the Beaumont, Welles, and Roos attainders were reversed in 1485 it was only Welles (in the person of Henry Tudor's half-uncle) who got back lands and power. William viscount Beaumont 'lost his reason' in 1487; the Earl of Oxford had custody of his land and person, and after William's death in 1507, married his widow (*Complete Peerage*, vol. 2, pp. 63–4). Edmund lord Roos was found to be 'not of sufficient discretion to guide himself and his livlihood'; farm of his lands and custody of his person was granted to Sir Thomas Lovel; Edmund died 1508 (*Complete Peerage*, vol. 11, pp. 106–7).

95. Did Francis viscount Lovel offer them his support? He was another young nobleman who may have felt Lord Hastings to be overmighty in the midlands. Lovel had begun to 'throw his weight about' by the later 1470s; consequently he and Hastings were bumping into each other. This requires closer study; meanwhile, G.V. Belenger, 'Francis, viscount Lovel', University of Keele unpublished BA dissertation, 1980, chapter four; John Mills, 'The Foundation, Endowment and early administration of Magdalen College, Oxford', University of Oxford unpublished BLitt dissertation, 1977; and the agreement reached between Lovel and Hastings' widow Katherine on 5 May 1485 (John Nichols, *The History and Antiquities of the County of Leicester* (reprint 1971), vol. 3, part 2, p. 572, cf Dugdale's transcript, BL Harleian MS 3881, f. 24) are thought-provoking.

96. J.S. Roskell, 'The office and dignity of Protector of England, with special reference to its origins', *EHR*, vol. 68 (1953), p. 227.

97. Ed. J.G. Nichols (Roxburghe Club, 1860).

98. William's point is succinctly endorsed by a young man writing from Normandy

c. 1418: 'the time of worship for young men is now' (Sir John Pelham to his father: *A Medieval Post-Bag*, ed. Laetitia Lyell (London 1934), p. 273).

99. *Op. cit.*, pp. 77–8. Probably the loss of the English possessions in France gave William the advantage over the lords of 1449. They still put English affairs before the French war even at that date: A.R. Myers, 'A parliamentary debate of the mid-fifteenth century', *Bulletin of the John Rylands Library*, vol. 22 (1938), pp. 398–9, 403, and also R.A. Griffiths, 'The Winchester Session of the 1449 Parliament: A Further Comment', *The Huntington Library Quarterly*, vol. 42 (1979), pp. 186, 189 where William Booth, the bishop of Lichfield, stands out as the only speaker to have any imagination. Yet in 1425 Bishop Beaufort could write to the Duke of Bedford 'For your wisdom knows well that the prosperity of France stands in the welfare of England': Ralph A. Griffiths, *The Reign of King Henry VI*, p. 77. This inverting of priorities is probably one reason why the 'peace party' made such a botch of trying to end the war.

100. J.R. Lander, *Crown and Nobility, 1450–1509* (London 1976), p. 226: 'His enthusiasm for war by this time [1475], however, may well have been no more than an echo from a vanished past'.

101. *Literae Cantuariensis*, ed. J.B. Sheppard (Rolls Series), vol. 3 (1889), p. 282. The last sentence is most perceptive. If only Henry VI had made the war his primary concern all would have been different.

102. Having ended here in the morning, in the afternoon I came across Kipling's description of them, as 'these savage wars of peace', which, whatever his meaning, has a striking resonance here.

103. '. . .the question. .of what men do if there is *not* a war: what is worth doing, that is, and does not mark some kind of moral collapse.': Alexander Murray, *Reason and Society in the Middle Ages* (Oxford, 1978), p. 19.

104. Richard 'and several others' were said by Commynes to have been opposed to the peacemaking of Picquigny, though they afterwards reconciled themselves to the peace which was made there: *Memoirs*, ed. Michael Jones (London 1972), p. 259. Can Richard's thwarted military ambition be detected in his exclamation to Nicholas von Poppelau in May 1484 on hearing of an Hungarian victory over the Turks, 'I wish that my kingdom lay upon the confines of Turkey'?: Mancini, *op. cit.*, appendix, p. 137. I owe both question and reference to the good memory and kindness of Joan Cooksley. Other Englishmen dissatisfied with the unwarlike conclusion to the expedition of 1475 joined the army of Charles the Bold: *Calendar of State Papers and Manuscripts existing in the archives and collections of Milan*, vol. 1, ed. A.B. Hinds (1912), pp. 217, 218, 221. They swelled the ranks of Englishmen already in his service: I am grateful to Richard Walsh of Leeds for telling me of this – from Burgundian financial records and a Dutch chronicle.

105. *Op. cit.*, pp. 223, 238 and appendix E. Do the distinctions 'Country' and 'Court' mean very much? Lords Hastings and Howard were surely as much 'Country' as 'Court'; that indeed was their intended dual role. Should the queen's brother-in-law Edward Grey lord Lisle be designated 'Country', and does the bumpkin duke of Suffolk qualify for 'Court'? Perhaps 'Active' and 'Inactive' might be

more useful descriptions, except that it turns out to be mostly the 'Active' who go on the expedition!

106. See Ross, *Edward IV*, p. 221. Professor Ross is also unconvinced by Professor Lander's reluctant peers. Should we include as a noble participant John Blount esquire, for at the end of the year he would succeed his too young nephew Edward as lord Mountjoy? See *Complete Peerage*, vol. 9, p. 337, and for his service *Foedera*, ed. Thomas Rymer (1704–35), vol. 11, p. 845 (Tellers' Roll). Was Lord Clinton perhaps actively involved in the expedition, but at Calais, where he had been in the crisis years, 1469–1471? Presumably William viscount Bourchier (d. 1480) stayed at home.

107. *Crown and Nobility*, pp. 230–234.

108. *Op. cit.*, p. 221. Professor Lander's statement that 'Henry V badly misjudged his capacity to pay for a prolonged war' will have to be refuted another time.

109. Lander, *op. cit.*, p. 233.

110. *Lancastrian Kings and Lollard Knights*, p. 126.

111. '. . .a grant for which there was no precedent except the short-lived concession extorted by Richard II in 1398, and even that had not included tunnage and poundage.': Roskell, *The Commons and their Speakers in English Parliaments*, pp. 161–2.

112. *The Gulag Archipelago*, vol. 1 (Fontana edition 1974), p. 272.

113. *Conflict and Stability in Fifteenth-century England* (London 1969), pp. 103–114.

114. Cf. McFarlane, *The Noblility of later Medieval England*, p. 77: 'It is one of the ironies of history that it was those 'new monarchs' the Tudors who were so afraid to tax that they had once more to exploit the incidents of tenure. One might say 'how medieval of them!' had not the middle ages in fact been more modern'.

115. E.g. Edward's concern for his artillery, Cora L. Scofield, *The Life and Reign of Edward the Fourth* (London 1923), vol. 2, pp. 118–121.

116. 11000 combatants plus 2000 more sent to Brittany should be compared with the 8000 of 1415 and the 10000 of the 1417 army of conquest.

117. At least another 3000 soldiers were at sea in patrolling operations which extended from April to October and cost about £12000. The intelligent (and economical) use of seapower in this year deserves a paper to itself; it certainly can stand comparison with Henry V.

118. See, for example, John Albon's letter from Agincourt of 27 July to his master Thomas Palmer of Holt, Leics. (for whom see Wedgwood, *op. cit.*, pp. 658–9), which should be dated to 1475 not 1417 (as *HMC, Second Report*, appendix (Neville of Holt collection), p. 94, would have it). The confidence expressed in this that battle would soon be joined is akin to that of Thomas Stonor in his letter to his brother of a few days previously: *The Stonor Letters and Papers*, vol. 1, no. 153. The curious letter of Edward IV to Louis XI (copied into BL Add Ms 48031, f. 187) in the form of a Hunter's boast also suggests both commitment and confidence. Hunting terms and the badges of the English nobility are combined to answer Louis XI's 'mokke'. The White Lion, the Black Bull with gilt horns, the Boar, the Wolf, the Dragon, the White Bear, The

White Greyhound are among the beasts who must follow the chase; . . . 'and so shall we hunt through parts of France and there will I blow my horn and release my hounds. I trust to God and to our Lady that your mokke shall turn you to shame for ye wote of right I am master of the game'.

Appendix I: The Ballad of Bosworth Feilde

In the stanzas where the lords and knights are listed there are discrepancies between the two versions (the printed and Harleian 542).

  i   There are variations in the names themselves through faulty transmission. For example, the repeated and meaningless Lord Bartley of line 243 in the printed version is Lovel in Harleian 542; the repeated if more meaningful Audley (line 250) is Lord Ogle (Ougle). Lord Audley is unlikely to have been there in one person let alone two; Ogle might have been; Lovel was. The variations among the knights seem endless and are bewildering.

 ii   There are stanzas missing in one version which are present in another. For instance, two stanzas in the printed version (naming seven lords) are wanting in Harley 542. Four stanzas, two of them naming knights from the Midlands (Gervaise Clifton, Henry Pierpoint, John Babington, Humphrey Stafford among others), are lacking in Harley 542; on the other hand three stanzas in Harley 542 (with the names of the Yorkshire-men Sir Robert Plumpton, Sir William Gascoigne, Sir Thomas Markenfield and Sir John Pudsey among others) are not in the printed version. Perhaps these regional variations are significant.

iii   The order of the stanzas differs, though not significantly. Two stanzas of knights appear among the nobles in Harley 542; a stanza of the printed version has got broken up and dispersed among others in Harley 542. These transpositions no doubt are the result of faulty transmission.

In the later stanzas where the valiant dead are named, Richard's heroic standard-bearer is Sir Percival Thriball in the printed version, Sir Richard Percival in Harley 542.

    Possibly none of this goes beyond textual analysis. Yet, if the names can all be unravelled and made to fit identifiable Northern gentry of 1485, could we even then be sure (without corroborative evidence) that these men were at Bosworth with Richard? One other oddity might be noticed. How is it that in a poem written in the Stanley interest, no (or very few) Stanley retainers are mentioned, whereas Richard's followers are listed at length? If the latter is done for effect (such, you see, was the nature of the opposition which had to be overcome), as I believe it is (certainly so far as the noble name-dropping goes), the poet is being poetic not historical, and, however beguiling the question of his sources (general knowledge of the noblility of 1485 and of Richard's northern supporters; flawed oral tradition?), imaginative writers of his sort are not to be trusted to supply the routine information we are demanding of them.

Appendix 2

Poems		Coronation	1484 Parliament Summoned	Bosworth	Post Bosworth	1485 Parliament Summoned	1485 Parliament Present
BB only	Abergavenny	X	X			X	X
BB only	Arundel	X	X			X	X
	Audley lord treasurer 5 Dec 1484–14 July 1486	X	X	at Southampton? general pardon Nov. 85			
BB+542	Beauchamp	X	X			X	X
	Cobham	X	X			X	
	Dacre of the North	X	not sum till after 1500 though suc father May 1485 (born c. 1467)		lieutenant of West March May 1486		X
	De La Warre		X			X	
	Dinham		X			X	
	Dudley		X			X	X
BB [+542]	Ferrers of Chartley	X	X	K. and attainted.			
BB+542	Fitzhugh	X	X		granted Middle-ham etc. & com. of array Sept. 1485	X	
BB only	Grey of Codnor	X	X				
	Grey of Powis	X	X			X	
	Grey of Wilton	X	X			X	X
BB+542	Greystoke		X		com. of array Sept. 1485	X	X
	Hungerford (Hastings)		X				X

Poems		Coronation	1484 Parliament Summoned	Bosworth	Post Bosworth	1485 Parliament Summoned	1485 Parliament Present
BB+542	Huntingdon	X	X			X	
	Kent	X	X			X	
BB only	Lincoln	X	X		with King at Nottingham. proc. as dead.		X
[BB+542]	Lisle (Grey of Groby) viscount 28 June 83	X	X		constable of Kenilworth Sept. 1485.	X	
542 [+BB]	Lovel	X	X	pres. & attainted.		X	
BB [+542]	Lumley	X	father died April 1485		com. of array Sept. 1485	X	
BB only	Maltravers	X Capt. of Guines (wife at Coro)	X			X	
	Mountjoy		X	very ill 1484 & died 12 Oct. 1485.			
BB+542	Norfolk (Howard) duke 28 June 1483	X	X	K. and attainted.			
BB+542	Northumberland	X	X	pres. (inactive)			
BB+542	Nottingham (Berkeley) earl 28 June 1483	X	X			X	X
542 [+BB]	Ogle	X	X			X	
BB+542	Scrope of Bolton	X	X				
BB+542	Scrope of Masham	X	X	with King at Nottingham.	com. of array Sept. 1485	X	

Poems		Coronation	1484 Parliament Summoned	Bosworth	Post Bosworth	1485 Parliament Summoned	Present
BB+542	Shrewsbury born 1486			taken prisoner?			X
BB+542	Stanley	X	X	pres. (inactive).			
	Stourton	X	X			X	
BB+542	Strange (George Stanley)		X	with King at Nottingham. pres. (inactive).			
	Suffolk	X	X			X	X
BB+542	Surrey (Howard)	X	X	prisoner & attainted.			
BB only	Welles (Hastings)	X	X				
BB + 542	Westmorland		suc autumn 1484		bonds to Henry VII Dec. 1485.		
BB only	Wiltshire	X				X	X
BB only	Zouch	X	X	prisoner & attainted			

INDEX

Peers are indexed under their family name, cross referenced from title.
Royal peers are under title, sovereigns under personal name.